LEGAL KNOWLEDGE AND INFORMATION SYSTEMS

Frontiers in Artificial Intelligence and Applications

Series Editors: J. Breuker, R. López de Mántaras, M. Mohammadian, S. Ohsuga and W. Swartout

Volume 106

Recently published in this series

Vol. 105. Y. Kiyoki et al. (Eds.), Information Modelling and Knowledge Bases XV
Vol. 104. A. Abraham et al. (Eds.), Design and Application of Hybrid Intelligent Systems
Vol. 103. B. Tessem et al. (Eds.), Eighth Scandinavian Conference on Artificial Intelligence – SCAI'03
Vol. 102. C. Turchetti, Stochastic Models of Neural Networks
Vol. 101. G.L. Torres et al. (Eds.), Advances in Intelligent Systems and Robotics – LAPTEC'03
Vol. 100. I. Aguiló et al. (Eds.), Artificial Intelligence Research and Development
Vol. 99. D. Šuc, Machine Reconstruction of Human Control Strategies
Vol. 98. H. Fujita and P. Johannesson (Eds.), New Trends in Software Methodologies, Tools and Techniques – Proceedings of Lyee_W03: The Second International Workshop on Lyee Methodology
Vol. 97. H.U. Hoppe et al. (Eds.), Artificial Intelligence in Education – Shaping the Future of Learning through Intelligent Technologies
Vol. 96. S. Handschuh and S. Staab (Eds.), Annotation for the Semantic Web
Vol. 95. B. Omelayenko and M. Klein (Eds.), Knowledge Transformation for the Semantic Web
Vol. 94. H. Jaakkola et al. (Eds.), Information Modelling and Knowledge Bases XIV
Vol. 93. K. Wang, Intelligent Condition Monitoring and Diagnosis Systems – A Computational Intelligence Approach
Vol. 92. V. Kashyap and L. Shklar (Eds.), Real World Semantic Web Applications
Vol. 91. F. Azevedo, Constraint Solving over Multi-valued Logics – Application to Digital Circuits
Vol. 89. T. Bench-Capon et al. (Eds.), Legal Knowledge and Information Systems – JURIX 2002: The Fifteenth Annual Conference
Vol. 87. A. Abraham et al. (Eds.), Soft Computing Systems – Design, Management and Applications
Vol. 86. R.S.T. Lee and J.H.K. Liu, Invariant Object Recognition based on Elastic Graph Matching – Theory and Applications
Vol. 85. J.M. Abe and J.I. da Silva Filho (Eds.), Advances in Logic, Artificial Intelligence and Robotics – LAPTEC 2002
Vol. 84. H. Fujita and P. Johannesson (Eds.), New Trends in Software Methodologies, Tools and Techniques – Proceedings of Lyee_W02
Vol. 83. V. Loia (Ed.), Soft Computing Agents – A New Perspective for Dynamic Information Systems
Vol. 82. E. Damiani et al. (Eds.), Knowledge-Based Intelligent Information Engineering Systems and Allied Technologies – KES 2002
Vol. 81. J.A. Leite, Evolving Knowledge Bases – Specification and Semantics
Vol. 80. T. Welzer et al. (Eds.), Knowledge-based Software Engineering – Proceedings of the Fifth Joint Conference on Knowledge-based Software Engineering
Vol. 79. H. Motoda (Ed.), Active Mining – New Directions of Data Mining

ISSN 0922-6389
Frontiers in Artificial Intelligence and Applications

ISSN 1570-3886
Legal Knowledge and Information Systems

Legal Knowledge and Information Systems

JURIX 2003: The Sixteenth Annual Conference

Edited by

Danièle Bourcier

Université de Paris II, CERSA-CNRS, Paris, France

IOS Press

Amsterdam • Berlin • Oxford • Tokyo • Washington, DC

ISBN 1 58603 398 0
Library of Congress Control Number: 2003114787

Publisher
IOS Press
Nieuwe Hemweg 6B
1013 BG Amsterdam
The Netherlands
fax: +31 20 620 3419
e-mail: order@iospress.nl

Distributor in the UK and Ireland
IOS Press/Lavis Marketing
73 Lime Walk
Headington
Oxford OX3 7AD
England
fax: +44 1865 75 0079

Distributor in the USA and Canada
IOS Press, Inc.
5795-G Burke Centre Parkway
Burke, VA 22015
USA
fax: +1 703 323 3668
e-mail: iosbooks@iospress.com

PRINTED IN THE NETHERLANDS

Preface

Exploring the computer's potential in Law

In the Stanford Law Review, vol. 23, no. 1, November 1970, Buchanan and Headrick wrote a pioneering paper titled 'Some speculation about artificial intelligence and legal reasoning'. In this paper they argued that "the time has come for serious interdisciplinary work between lawyers and computer scientists to explore the computer's potential in Law".

Thirty three years later, the Sixteenth Annual Jurix Conference, held 11–12 December 2003 in Utrecht, has proved again that their expectation was plausible. The interdisciplinary community is growing and active: for JURIX 2003, we received more papers than ever before. We had to double the plenary sessions with a parallel one. A new session, gathering research in progress, has been organized and work is reported here as short papers (Galitsky, De Maat & Van Engers, Smith, Drashsler *et alii,* Andrade, Governatori & Rotolo). In several Workshops the innovative aspects of the field have been discussed and will become material for the next meetings. The process of research and development is becoming dynamic and integrated.

The range of topics addressed in this volume is broader than in previous JURIX volumes. All the main legal functions are covered: legal drafting (Boer *et alii,* Delgado), legal negotiating (Zeleznikow & Bellucci), legal decision making (Muntjewerff *et alii*), legal argumentation (Holmström-Hintikka). The traditional tools in AI have been greatly improved: expert systems interfaces become more user-friendly through procedure maps (Gray). Generally speaking, progress has been made in process design for various legal tasks: to evaluate infringement (Renaux), to implement e-governance models (Gordon, Van Heel & Van Engers). Legal retrieval systems have shifted to the web (Dongilli & Gamper) and the recurrent question of legal language has become crucial in the building of the semantic web: new intelligent agents such as digital rights management integrate intellectual property laws from various legal systems (Dulong de Rosnay) and need specific ontologies as a means for accurately capturing the sense of legal rules (Delgado *et alii*).

Theoretical aspects of Artificial Intelligence (AI) and law continue to be explored (Graça & Quaresma) and modelling is the new way of making legal theory. As was noted in the introduction of JURIX 94, legal theorists continue to renew their concerns in logical aspects of legal reasoning (Chorley & Bench Capon) and more and more AI and Law projects are interested in legal theory (Ashley & Brüninghaus). Ways for representing abduction — scarcely modelled in legal theory — are explored (Tuzet). Today both practitioners and theorists think that new AI models including dynamics and complexity could highlight the penumbra of legal knowledge and analyze emergence and evolution of reasoning and concepts. Judges expect neural machines to be able to justify their own reasoning better than they do (Borges *et alii*). Legislators hope that the intelligibility of laws will be improved with computer-aided legal drafting. Administrators encourage e-administration to develop interactive process between public customers and civil servants.

The role of the European Union should not be neglected in the development of AI and Law research. A lot of projects have been supported by European programs. For example, the policy of legal simplification is expected to be aided by AI and Law computer scientists (Boer *et alii*). But European policies — traditionally *legicentered* — are also concerned with using computers for their own legal needs (implementation, control and so on).

Research in AI & Law thus faces a new challenge not only in the Netherlands but also in the larger European community. We congratulate the JURIX association in inviting all other countries to share their enthusiasm and their skill in taking law and technology seriously to surpass economical barriers and political inequality. The conference provides opportunities for cross-cultural exchanges which enable each culture to benefit from the experiences and insights by the use of technology in other countries.

The Invited Speakers this year were: D.J. van Dijk, a well known member of the Dutch Council for the Judiciary ("Raad voor de Rechtspraak"). Giovanni Sartor, CIRSFID and Faculty of Law, University of Bologna, who, as a famous international researcher, also promotes AI and Law discipline in Italy. Willem Wagenaar, Dean, University College, who, as a NIAS researcher, was also a colleague of mine; a specialist in legal psychology, he wrote important works on the psychology of proof in Criminal Law.

Acknowledgments

The JURIX 2003 Conference organizers express their warm thanks to the Utrecht Faculty of Law for hosting the event.

We would also like to thank the French Centre National de la Recherche Scientifique (CNRS) and specially the Pluridisciplinary Network (RTP) on Law and Information Systems, created in February 2002, who sponsor the Conference and subsidized French researchers to join the meeting. I personally enjoyed preparing the Conference with my Dutch colleagues (Henry Prakken, Radboud Winkels and all the others) in Paris and Amsterdam.

The conference was organized in collaboration with the Leibniz Center for Law (University of Amsterdam) and SIKS, the Dutch research school for information and knowledge systems.

For this Conference, thirty-one submissions were received of which twenty-three were selected. The authors represented thirteen countries. The papers were reviewed by members of the Programme Committee:

Trevor Bench Capon (University of Liverpool)
Jon Bing (University of Oslo)
Paul Bourgine (CREA, Ecole polytechnique, Paris)
Danièle Bourcier (CERSA-CNRS, University of Paris II)
Didier Bourigault (Université de Toulouse)
Tom Gordon (Fraunhofer FOKUS, Berlin)
Patricia Hassett (Syracuse University)
Marie-Francine Moens (Katholieke Universiteit Leuven)
Anja Oskamp (Vrije Universiteit Amsterdam)
Henry Prakken (Utrecht University)
Christophe Roquilly (EDHEC, Lille)
Marek Sergot (Imperial College London)
Radboud Winkels (University of Amsterdam)

The Organising Committee comprised:

Tom van Engers (Universiteit van Amsterdam / Dutch Tax and Customs Office)
Tina van der Linden-Smith (Utrecht University)
Henry Prakken (Utrecht University)
Filipe Borges (Université de Paris II)
Rinke Hoekstra (Universiteit van Amsterdam)
Gerard Vreeswijk (Utrecht University)

We would also like to thank all external reviewers. The conference would not have been possible without the time and effort put in by these people and so thanks are due to them all.

Particular thanks to Filipe Borges who worked very diligently for the Programme Committee and had to change the date of his Dissertation defence.

Finally thanks are due to Rinke Hoekstra (University of Amsterdam) for struggling again with LaTeX and succeeding to get the final version of this book in good shape before the deadline.

Danièle Bourcier
Programme Chair

Contents

Preface vii

Antoinette J. Muntjewerff, Astrid Jordaans, Rinke Hoekstra and Ronald Leenes
Case Analysis and Storage Environment: CASE 1

Filipe Borges, Raoul Borges and Danièle Bourcier
Artificial Neural Networks and Legal Categorization 11

John Zeleznikow and Emilia Bellucci
Family_Winner: Integrating Game Theory and Heuristics to Provide Negotiation Support 21

Ghita Holmström-Hintikka
Agency in Legal Reasoning 31

Giovanni Tuzet
Legal Abductions 41

Pamela N. Gray and Xenogene Gray
A Map-Based Expert-Friendly Shell 51

Pierre Renaux
CATMInE – Computer Assisted Trade-Mark Infringement Evaluation 61

Evert van Heel and Tom M. van Engers
GoldminePower: Decisions in Governmental Process Design 71

Thomas F. Gordon
A Use Case Analysis of Legal Knowledge-Based Systems 81

Alexander Boer, Radboud Winkels, Rinke Hoekstra and Tom M. van Engers
Knowledge Management for Legislative Drafting in an International Setting 91

Juan José Iniesta Delgado
Substitution of Legal Statement and Identification of Law 101

Jaime Delgado, Isabel Gallego, Silvia Llorente and Roberto García
IPROnto: An Ontology for Digital Rights Management 111

Mélanie Dulong de Rosnay
Cognitive Interfaces for Legal Expressions Description – Application to Copyrighted Works, Online Sharing and Transactions 121

Paolo Dongilli and Johann Gamper
MIRIS Unleashed 131

Boris Galitsky
An Interactive Form for Customer Complaints: Matching the Cases 141

Emile de Maat and Tom M. van Engers
Mission Impossible? Automated Norm Analysis of Legal Texts 143

Clara Smith
On the Structure and Soundness of AI and Law Objects 145

Erich Schweighofer, Doris Liebwald and Mathias Drachsler
Electronic Notification of Block Exempted State Aid 147

Francisco C.P. Andrade
Intelligent Electronic Inter-Systemic Contracting – Issues on Contract Formation 149

Guido Governatori and Antonino Rotolo
A Computational Framework for Non-monotonic Agency, Institutionalised Power and Multi-Agent Systems 151

Kevin D. Ashley and Stefanie Brüninghaus
A Predictive Role for Intermediate Legal Concepts 153

Nuno Graça and Paulo Quaresma
How to Model Legal Reasoning Using Dynamic Logic Programming: A Preliminary Report 163

Alison Chorley and Trevor Bench-Capon
Reasoning with Legal Cases as Theory Construction: Some Experimental Results 173

Previous Publications by JURIX 183

Contact Information on JURIX 185

Author Index 187

Case Analysis and Storage Environment CASE

Antoinette J. Muntjewerff* Astrid Jordaans† Rinke Hoekstra* Ronald Leenes‡
*Faculty of Law, Universiteit van Amsterdam
Amsterdam, The Netherlands
{muntjewerff, hoekstra}@lri.jur.uva.nl
†Open Universiteit, Heerlen, The Netherlands
astrid.jordaans@ou.nl
‡Concept & Code, Deventer, The Netherlands
ronald.leenes@concept-en-code.nl

Abstract. It is essential for law students to learn about the applicable general rules of law. A major source of applicable rules within the Dutch legal system is the category of decisions by judges. Law students experience difficulties with reading and comprehending these decisions. CASE is proposed to support students in structuring and analysing decisions. CASE stands for Case Analysis and Storage Environment. CASE presents the student an environment in which she can practice with structuring and analysing a decision in order to determine in what way this decision adds to the body of applicable rules. The application can be used by law teachers to store decisions and to add key words and by law students to search, structure and analyze a decision.

1 Introduction

The law that applies in a legal system such as the Dutch legal system consists of general rules that are determined or acknowledged by authoritative bodies. The two most important authoritative bodies within the Dutch legal system are the legislator and the judge. While it is obvious the legislator determines rules that apply in general, this is more complicated with judges. A judge has to decide in individual cases, she has to construct a legal solution based on the facts of the case and the applicable legal rules. In the majority of cases that come before the court, a judge formulates a decision that applies only to the case at hand. These decisions do not add to the body of applicable rules in the legal system. However, in cases where a judge first has to construct an applicable rule, before being able to decide the case on the basis of this rule, we have a different type of decision.

The rule constructed by the judge to decide the case, may add to the body of applicable rules in the legal system. Legal practitioners and legal scientists need to have knowledge of the general rules that apply in the legal system. This involves both knowledge of the legislation and knowledge of the decisions by judges that function as general rules of law. Law students preparing themselves for the legal profession of course also need these kinds of knowledge. They have to acquire knowledge about the role of decisions by judges in the legal system, and they need to understand the two categories of decisions by judges. A student has to have knowledge about where to look for decisions of the second category, understand the structure of decisions and learn to determine what makes a decision relevant to the body of applicable rules in the legal system. Legal education primarily aims at acquiring insight in the legal sources, their history and background. This basic knowledge is of great importance;

Antoinette J. Muntjewerff, Astrid Jordaans, Rinke Hoekstra, and Ronald Leenes, 'Case Analysis and Storage Environment - CASE' in D. Bourcier (ed.), *Legal Knowledge and Information Systems. Jurix 2003: The Sixteenth Annual Conference.* Amsterdam: IOS Press, 2003, pp. 1-10.

legal problem solving is hardly possible without an understanding of the legal knowledge. To illustrate the use of this knowledge in practice, teachers work through decisions as examples. However, it is difficult, if not impossible, to learn by explanation or by imitation alone. A more effective way to obtain expertise (skill) is by actually performing the task, i.e. students should do the exercises, while the teacher provides feedback ontheir solutions. Not only feedback on the solution provided by students is important. For effective learning, also the solution process should be monitored and provided with feedback. Furthermore it is desirable for students to be able to ask for help at any time during the process. They should also be able to practice over and over again. An ideal situation would have a teacher available for every student, monitoring the student while practicing and providing support where and whenever necessary. However, this being not practically feasible, the second best option is to offer the student electronic support. Using a computer program as the instructional medium does have has a number of advantages. It may offer individualized instruction and practice combined with immediate support and feedback. It can have the capacity to adapt to the individual student's performance and, last but not least, may support the management of information.

CASE (Case Analysis and Storage Environment) is an environment where a law student can practice with finding decisions, with structuring its text and with analysing the decision in order to be able to determine in what way it adds to the body of applicable rules in the legal system. These functionalities are implemented in two integrated modules in CASE:

1. *The Assembler, a module to compile and store decisions.*
   In essence the Assembler is a database containing a selection of decisions used in legal education. The law student can do a search (key word and/ or full text) for a specific decision or a set of decisions. Decisions can be added to the database and key words can be indicated for each decision by the teacher. This module can be used separately or in combination with the PAT module.
2. *The Precedent Analysis Tool (PAT), a module to structure and analyse decisions.*
   In essence PAT is an instructional environment for learning to structure and analyse a decision to determine how it adds to the body of applicable rules in the legal system. PAT builds on the Assembler module. It presents the student the text of a selected decision together with a framework containing the main elements in a decision text (as, for instance, the different parties and their roles in the various stages of their procedures before the different courts). It allows the student to fill the framework with the relevant parts from the text of the decision. The activities of the student are monitored, and compared to a model where deviations are diagnosed to be able to present the student with a hint or a remediation.

CASE is developed using the principled and structured design approach as described in the HYPATIA project [1, 2]. A short description of this approach is followed by an analysis of the learning task, the difficulties law students experience and the remedies proposed on the basis of both the task analysis and the stated difficulties. This is followed by a description of architecture, functionality, platform and implementation of CASE and a description of a session with CASE and future work.

2 Principled and Structured Design Approach

The HYPATIA project [1, 2] aims at designing and developing new additional electronic materialsfor law students to learn the law. Law students experience difficulties in acquiring legal knowledge and in using this knowledge. These problems are acknowledged by law teachers. However, there is no material available to help students to overcome these difficulties. HYPATIA aims to fill this gap. HYPATHIA develops electronic tools because they can offer individualized instruction and practice by adapting to the individual student's performance combined with immediate support and feedback. They can also support the management of information and present different representations and visualisations of legal knowledge and legal tasks. The principled and structured design approach guides the development process in such a way that difficulties and mistakes encountered during the design process may be accounted for. The design proces involves three interrelated research streams: basic research, applied research and integration research. Basic research is concerned with developing well-founded models of legal knowledge and skills to be learned by law students, examining the difficulties they have with acquiring legal knowledge and legal skills and finding remedies to enhance effective and efficient learning of the required knowledge and skills. In the applied research part, these findings are used to construct computer supported models of legal knowledge and legal reasoning to diagnose and remedy the specific difficulties of law students in learning the law. Instructional design decisions are made on the basis of a global theory on learning and instruction. In this way the design process will result in a coherent and consistent instructional model. It finally indicates that electronic materials are evaluated extensively (developmental testing and field testing).The integration research part is concerned with the construction of an infrastructure for learning object repositories The HYPATIA projected is divided into specific research programs. The design approach was founded and used successfully in the construction of an instructional environment for learning to solve legal cases: PROSA [3, 4, 5].

The approach taken in PROSA is reusable for a variety of applications for learning the law. The legal case solving research within HYPATIA has been realized and reported in detail [3, 4, 5][1].

3 Analysis

What is structuring and analyzing a decision? In order to to answer this question and to design an environment to support law students in finding, reading, structuring and analyzing decisions to indicate and understand the legal meaning of a decision, it is necessary to analyse the task. The HYPATIA design approach starts with (re)constructing explicit models of legal knowledge and legal reasoning. In this (re) construction process, two components are distinguished. (1) A theoretical component of exploration, conceptualization and specification of legal knowledge and legal reasoning resulting in explicit models of legal knowledge and legal reasoning. Two perspectives are taken within this approach: a legal perspective and a knowledge engineering perspective. From the legal perspective different legal sources, being legal empirical research, legal educational practice, legal dogmatic and legal theoretical research, are examined to specify the required models. The knowledge engineering perspective is used to constructmodels at a high level of explicitness as they have to be executed by a computer (see, for example, [6, 7, 8]). This explicitness of models is exactly what is needed in instruction. (2) An empirical component where empirical studies are carried out to acquire insight in the way legal practitioners and legal scientists handle legal knowledge in general and in carrying out specific legal tasks. In this case, law students are studied to see how they handle and use legal knowledge to perform a specific legal task and what difficulties they experience. The legal sources that were examined to model the task of reading and comprehending decisions all describe a series of steps to be taken by the student when reading a decision to determine the legal significance [9, 10, 11, 12, 13, 14, 15, 16, 17].

However, merely instructing a method does not work for novices (see for details [3]).

[1] See for a demonstration of PROSA http://www.lri.jur.uva.nl/ munt/manualprosa.html and http://www.lri.jur.uva.nl/ munt/prosa.html.

This is partly due to the fact that instructing a method is a problem in itself, as it is difficult to communicate a method, because this requires the translation of actions into words. A method is in fact empty; explaining content is much more "substantial" and therefore easier. The somewhat paradoxical situation is that novices have to learn to determine the legal meaning by determining the legal meaning (see also [3]). Law students especially have difficulties with determining what the decision adds to the body of applicable rules in the legal system. Based on findings in research in legal problem solving (e.g. [3]) it is stated that the difficulties are first of all caused by insufficient mastery of, or insight in, the subject matter. Secondly, especially for novices, methods, often as a side effect, emerge from (novice) problem solving, instead of being the driving force. The subject matter appears to be the major source for finding or trying (a) solution (steps). On closer inspection, a decision is a legal solution for a specific problem situation constructed on the basis of abstract legal rules. Structuring and analysing a decision is in fact the task of reconstructing the problem situation (consisting of a reconstruction of both the facts and the legal question), tracing the abstract legal rules that were applied and specifying the legal solution consisting of the argument structure and the conclusion.

Reading and understanding a decision is not a trivial activity. Observations with first year law students reading decisions showed that they experience difficulties with seeing through the composition of the decision, with reconstructing the argument structure and with determining the legal significance of the decision.

These difficulties are first of all caused by the fact that a decision is an incomplete reproduction of what happened. Next to that the text of the decision contains many references, both explicit and implicit, to regulations, other decisions and concepts. The fact that a decision has a stratified structure which is also not supported by recognizable clues or elements in the text does not help either. All of this means that the student has to reconstruct the process and the product which involves keeping track of intermediate results. To support the student in performing these tasks, the following remedies are proposed. Present the student a structure to help her to reconstruct the decision, support the management of information and engage the student in structuring and analysing the decision by having her actually carry out these tasks. This is realised by presenting the student with both the full text of the decision and a framework which visualises the elements in a decision necessary to reconstruct the decision in order to determine the legal significance of the decision (see Fig. 1).

There are no applications available that support law students in structuring and analysing a decision suiting the Continental legal system. For the Anglo-American legal system, the CATO application is available [18]. In CATO the student is trained to construct arguments with cases.

4 Architecture and Modular Design

The aim of the CASE project is to realize an environment in which law students are supported in structuring and analyzing a decision. This means that both the decision at hand has to be presented to the student, as well as the framework for analysis. The student must be able to select text fragments from the decision and paste these within the correct cell in the relevant table in the framework. Since finding cases is also part of the training of law students search facilities have to be available in the environment. The functionality of searching for a decision is implemented in the module called 'Assembler'. The functionality of structuring and analysing a decision is implemented in the module called 'PAT'. Other basic requirements are maintenance and re-use. It should be possible to make changes to the system and its content without much costs and efforts. Errors in system and content should be easily traceable and

Structuring the decision

name

court	place	date	source (publication source, year, number)
area of law	private law		
	public law	criminal law	
		administrative law	
		constitutional law	
		international law	

Parties

instance	initiator	opponent
first instance		
appeal		
cassation		

Facts

instance	indisputable facts	disputable facts
first instance		
appeal		
cassation		

Claim

instance	claim/request
first instance	
appeal	
cassation	

Question

instance	factual	qualification	legal
first instance			
appeal			
cassation			

Legal ground

instance	legislation	decisions
first instance		
appeal		
cassation		

Dictum

instance	dictum
first instance	
appeal	
cassation	

Reconstructing the legal conclusion

legal rules	reconstruct legal solution	facts
	conclusion	
	argument structure	
	legal question	

Figure 1: Framework

correctable. It must be possible to add and delete content without causing problems elsewhere in the system. Transparency of the architecture and tools are therefore design goals, as it may facilitate maintenance. The system has functions for adding decisions, adding key words to decisions and preparing decisions for use in PAT. System functionalities are attributed to a user on the basis of her status: administrator, editor, teacher or student. The CASE architecture is depicted in Fig. 2. The Assembler module holds the decisions and allows for search and retrieval of cases and allows teachers to prepare cases for use in the PAT module. Students can use the Assembler to locate cases on the basis of key words and/or full text search to find specific decisions. When the student wants to structure and analyse a decision she can select one of the reported decisions. This decision and the analysing framwork are then made available to the student in PAT. The student can start structuring the decision by selecting text fragments in the decision and pasting these in the correct part of the frame.

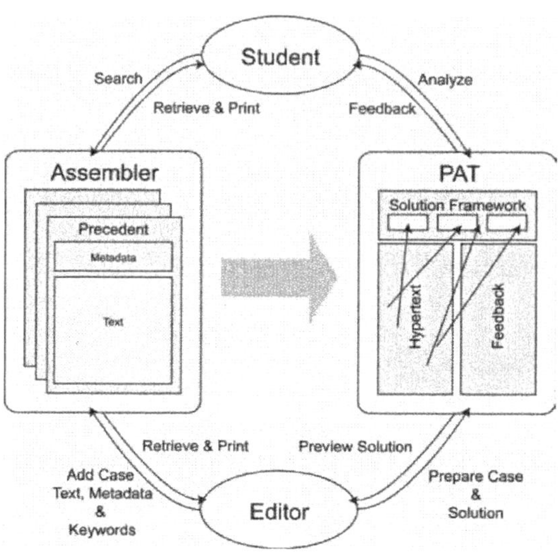

Figure 2: CASE Architecture

5 Platform and Implementation

CASE is implemented using a web-based server-side application model[2]. The user interacts with the system using a standard web browser, such as Netscape Navigator, Apple Safari or MS Internet Explorer. The Casetool application is developed using Open Source Software, MySQL (4.0.14) and PHP (4.3.2) and JavaScript. The MySQL database backend contains a number of tables, the most prominent ones being a text fragment table, a solution table and a table storing the student's activities. Casetool's primary component is the server-side application implemented in PHP (4.3.2). This application handles form processing, storage and retrieval of information from the various tables in the database and generating the HTML pages that are output to the user. A small number of simple functions are implemented using client-side JavaScripts. Casetool offers extensive support for administrative-, editing-, browsing-, tracking- and educational tasks. Using the same portal, administrators can add, remove and change users and cases; editors can add keywords to cases and prepare the solution framework of a case for use in PAT; teachers can use the interface to track the results of students, previewing the solution framework and for browsing and searching the database; and students can browse and search the database, and test their analysis skills using PAT.

The search engine allows for both Boolean keyword- and free text search in combination with metadata fields such as: date, name, court etc. The principal concept in CASE is that a precedent can be seen as an ordered set of text fragments, each of which can be labelled according to their place in the solution template. The student can select a text fragment and place in a specific position within the solution framework. Text fragments can be as short as a single sentence, but more often, they are as long as a paragraph. The text fragments are stored in a database along with metadata such as a reference to their position in the solution. Although a text fragment as described is the basic building block, these fragments can have one or more sub-fragments (such as single words) which can also be selected by the student. For instance, the text fragment

> "Op het beroep van Ronald G, geboren te Amsterdam op 6 aug. 1954, wonende te Amsterdam, req. van cassatie tegen een bij verstek gewezen arrest van het Hof te Amsterdam van 12 dec. 1977, waarbij in hoger beroep een vonnis van de Rb.",

contains the sub-fragment 'Ronald G', the accused. In some cases the student needs to select the whole sentence, and in others only the sub fragment. The solution framework consists of a number of tables, such as parties, facts, claim and the argument structure before the Supreme Court (see Fig. 1). Each table is two dimensional and contains a small number of cells, e.g. facts as presented by the initiator, and facts presented by the opponent. Each cell in the solution, therefore, can be designated by three coordinates: table, row and column. These coordinates are used to mark the proper location of text fragments within the solution framework. They allow the student's solution to be tested against the solution defined by the teacher; the cell in which the student places the fragment has to match the metadata reference of the text fragment. In the case of an incorrect placement of a fragment, its position relative to the correct place is also known. This allows for standardised responses to common errors. For instance, when a student puts the initiator's name in the opponent's cell, the following response can be generated on the basis of this mixing up of the parties in the dispute: "This indeed is one of the parties in the dispute, but unfortunately it is not the opponent.". To get a basic idea of the functionality of the system we now describe a session with CASE.

[2] http://www.casetool.nl

6 A session with CASE

As mentioned above, CASE distinguishes four types of user: administrators, editors, teachers and students. User rights are distributed in an incremental fashion in CASE, this means that a teacher has access to both student- and teaching facilities; an editor has access to editing-, teaching- and student facilities; and the administrator user has rights to do everything the other users can, plus adding, removing and changing users, and removing cases from the database. This section describes a typical process from preparation to analysis of a case.

The Editor After login, the editor is presented with a menu containing multiple options: editor's menu, teacher's menu, Assembler, PAT, change password and logout. Since she recently came upon a decision relevant for law students, she decides to add it to the CASE database. The editor's menu gives access to the add decision screen.

Here she fills in a few facts about the decision (name, publication date, court etc.) and with copy- paste actions, she adds the text of the decision to the database. Next, she visits the metadata editor (see Fig. 3).

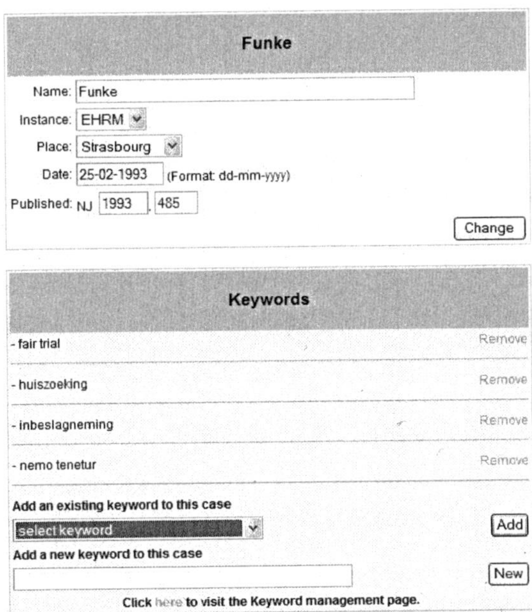

Figure 3: Metadata Editor

The metadata editor interface is used to add or change metadata of a decision and, more importantly, to add new keywords, or remove existing ones. After completing this procedure, the decision can be searched for using the search interface.

The next step is the preparation of the decision for use in PAT. The PAT Prepare tool offers an interface that mimics the regular PAT interface: the editor needs to place pieces of text in the correct position within the solution framework (see Fig. 4).

Where the regular PAT interface checks whether the correct text is in the correct position by consulting the database, the PAT prepare tool writes the action of the editor to the database. The editor in a sense teaches PAT the solution of the case at hand. Note that the editor does not have to add feedback to the database. Feedback is provided to the student in a case-independent way. When the teacher only wants part of the text fragment to be part of the

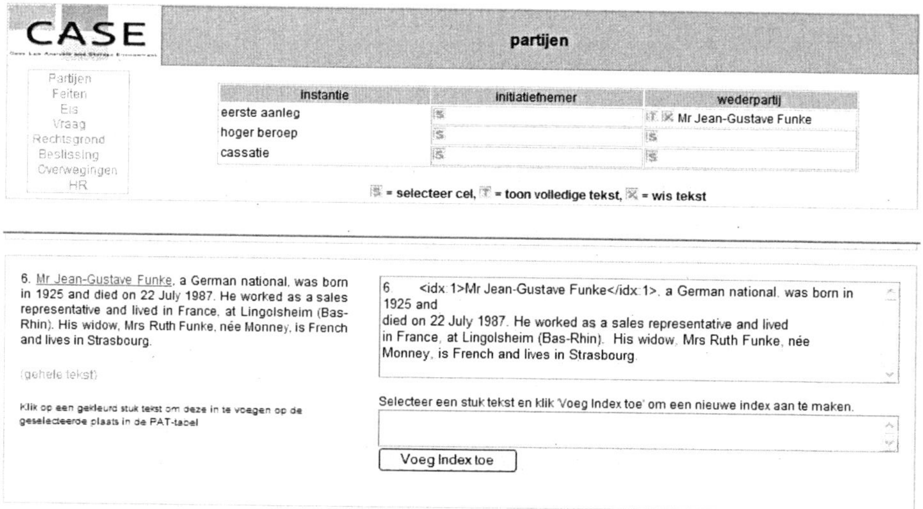

Figure 4: PAT Prepare Tool

solution, the editor can simply mark these smaller parts. This results in a text fragment with color coded sub fragments that can be placed in the solution table (e.g. Mr Jean-Gustave Funke in figure 4.).

After the editor has finished the above steps, the decision is ready for use by both teachers and students.

The Teacher The teacher is not allowed to change the information or the solution framework of a decision. However, he can add students to the CASE user database, and preview the correct PAT answers (the prepared solution framework) for each decision. More importantly, the teacher has access to a student tracking facility to analyze student behavior.

This way the teacher can determine whether a student came to his or her end-result by simply trying every option, or by purposefully placing fragments in the solution framework.

The Student Students can search the decision database using the Assembler search interface (see Fig. 5). This interface allows for metadata search - i.e. on publication date, publication place, court type, court location - but also supports Boolean keyword search and Boolean full text search. The student can also browse through all decisions in the database. The search result page offers support for associative search because key words and other attributes of the cases found are shown. The student can click on any of these to start a search on this attribute. Thus, for example, searching on all decisions with the same keyword of one of the decisions that were found by the original search is done by simply clicking on that keyword in the results page. From the same page, the student can print a decision or open it in PAT.

The PAT interface, shown in Fig. 6, is divided into three frames. The left frame shows all text fragments of the decision at hand. The top right frame contains the tables of the solution framework. The bottom right frame provides feedback to the student's actions. A text fragment is placed in a cell of the solution table by first selecting the cell, and then selecting the fragment to fill this cell. Once placed, the application will check the combination of cell and fragment and provide a feedback message from the database in the feedback frame. Text fragments can be removed from a cell by clicking the 'x'-button in the table. Once the student has placed all correct fragments in a specific table, she is notified of this through the feedback frame.

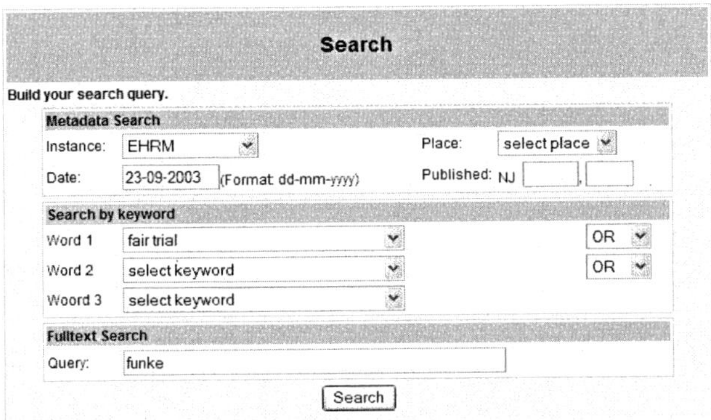

Figure 5: Search the Database

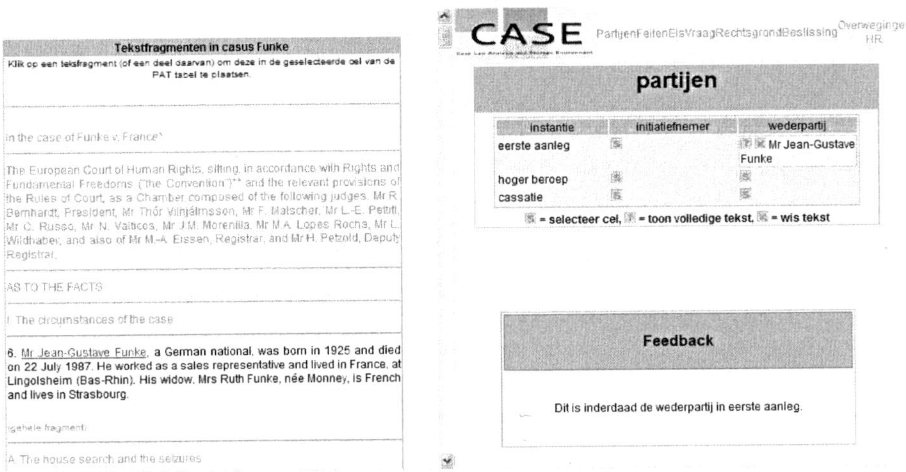

Figure 6: Structuring and analysing a decision

7 Summary and Future Work

Learning the law involves reading, structuring and analyzing decisions to be able to indicate the legal significance of the decision. Law students experience difficulties with tasks, especially with determining what the decision adds to the body of applicable rules in the legal system. Within the current curriculum there is not enough time to read and analyze decisions in the presence of a teacher who may provide immediate feedback. Law students are also not presented with models that may guide them in the process of reading and analyzing decisions. In learning the law it is essential to know how to structure and analyze a decision. CASE was designed to present the law student with an instructional environment in which she is able to analyze a decision in such a way that the structure is made explicit and the legal meaning can be extracted. CASE has been implemented as a web-based server-side application model.

It is implemented using open source software. The Casetool is easy to maintain and re-use and can be made available in different languages. Future work involves testing the effectiveness of Casetool. The claim that law students are supported by Casetool in structuring and analysing a decision in such a way that they are able to grasp the legal significance of the decision should be tested. The claim that it is easy to add a decision, to add key words and to prepare a decision for use in PAT should also be tested.

Acknowledgements

The CASE project is partially funded by the Association of Universities in the Netherlands (VSNU) within the project RechtenOnLine.

References

[1] Muntjewerff, A.J. (2002). HYPATIA research program. Models of Legal Knowledge and Legal Reasoning in Electronic Materials for Learning the Law. Amsterdam: University of Amsterdam, ISBN 90-806969-1-9.

[2] Muntjewerff, A.J. (2002). Principled and Structured Design of Electronic Materials for Learning the Law in T.J.M. Bench-Capon, A.Daskalopulu and R.G.F. Winkels (eds.), Legal Knowledge and Information Systems. Jurix 2002: The Fifteenth Annual Conference. Amsterdam: IOS Press, 2002, pp. 133-142.

[3] Muntjewerff, A.J. (2000). An Instructional Environment for Learning to Solve Legal Cases. PROSA. Amsterdam: University of Amsterdam.

[4] Muntjewerff, A.J. & J. Groothuismink (1999b). Supporting the Learning of Legal Case Solving using a Computer Program as the Instructional Environment. In Proceedings CATE'99 Computers and Advanced Technology in Education. Philadelphia, USA: IASTED.

[5] Muntjewerff, A.J. (2002). Evaluating the Instructional Environment for Learning to Solve Legal Cases PROSA. In Gustavo A. Santana Torrellas ans Vladimir Uskov (eds.). Proceedings of the IASTED International Conference Computers and Advanced Technology in Education. Anaheim Calgary Zurich: ACTA Press: , pp. 374 - 379.

[6] Haan, N. den & Sartor, G. (1999). Editorial: Model-based Legal Knowledge Engineering. In Gaines, B.R. (Ed.). International Journal of Human-Computer Studies. Special Issue Model-based Legal Knowledge Engineering. Academic Press, pp. 1037 - 1042.

[7] Breuker, J.A. & Van de Velde, W. (1994). CommonKADS library for expertise modeling. Reusable problem solving components. Amsterdam: IOS Press.

[8] Valente, A. (1995). Legal Knowledge Engineering. Amsterdam: IOS Press.

[9] Bos, A.M. (2003). Jurisprudentieleidraad. In Encyclopedie der Rechtsgeleerdheid Vaardigheden. Amsterdam: Universiteit van Amsterdam.

[10] Eemeren, van F.H., E.T. Feteris, R. Grootendorst, T. van Haaften, W. den Harder, H. Kloosterhuis & J. Plug (1996). Argumenteren voor juristen. Oefenboek. Grondingen: Wolters Noordhoff.

[11] Franken, H. e.a. (1991). Practicum Methoden en Technieken II. Casusoplossen. Bundel ter dienste van het Practicum Methoden en Technieken van de faculteit der rechtsgeleerdheid van de Rijksuniversiteit te Leiden. Arnhem: Gouda Quint.

[12] Henket, M. & P. van den Hoven (1999). Juridische Vaardigheden in argumentatief verband. Groningen: Wolters Noordhoff.

[13] Jansen, L. (1999). Nieuwe introductie in het recht. Utrecht: LEMMA.

[14] Scholten, P. (1974). Algemeen Deel. Zwolle: W.E.J. Tjeenk Willink.

[15] Soeteman, A. & A.J. Wolthuis (2003). Syllabus Juridische argumentatie 2003. Amsterdam: VU.

[16] Stolwijk, S.A.M. & M. Bosch (2002). Het bestuderen van arresten in strafzaken. In Arresten strafrecht/strafprocesrecht met annotaties ten behoeve van het onderwijs verzameld. Deventer: Kluwer.

[17] Werkgroep Vaardigheden-onderwijs Rechten (1990). Syllabus Vaardigheden I. Amsterdam: UvA.

[18] Aleven, V. (1997). Teaching Case-Based Argumentation Through a Model and Examples. Pittsburgh: University of Pittsburg.

Artificial Neural Networks and Legal Categorization

Filipe Borges Raoul Borges Danièle Bourcier
*Université de Paris II, CERSA-CNRS**
Paris, France
{fa_borges,paercebal}@hotmail.com, bourcier@msh-paris.fr

Abstract. This paper describes an experiment which consists in teaching a connexionnist model a legal dispute. The aim is to analyze the mode of representation of the dispute realized by the model, and to compare it with the representation elaborated by judges specialized in this kind of dispute. Comparison shows that the representation of the computer and that of the jurist are very similar, which makes relevant the use of these models and methods in the analysis of legal reasoning, and possibly in the optimization of its processing. The method described here also contributes to open a little more the "black box" that characterized the artificial neural networks.

1 Introduction

The main capacity of neural networks is to classify. However, the process of classification made by an artificial neural network is complex, and it *a priori* seemed difficult to explain their reasoning. It was the reason why artificial neural networks were often considered as irrelevant for legal domain [4]. Connectionist models have however been used for example to infer symbolic information [2], to study open structure issues [1], to analyse legal thesauri [5][6], or to enhance rule-based reasoning system [7]. But none of them aimed at explanation of the representation of a legal problem developed by artificial neural networks.

We will show that these models, such as the perceptron, cannot be considered only as a "black box", and that it is possible to study their *topography* and to decompose their functioning. In a previous experiment this approach allowed to obtain satisfying results, and to develop an algorithm of justification sufficiently precise to be used by jurists (PGA algorithm) [3].

In this paper our objective is to continue the study of the topography of a multilayer perceptron with backpropagation algorithm in order to better understand the question of connexionnist classification. We will see how hidden neurons can *specialize* themselves in order to match with legal sub-problems, and if this specialization allow us to better understand the *cognitive problem* of the human legal classification (detection, creation, optimization of the legal categories).

2 Hypothesis

In order to build and especially to understand a base of rules or cases a knowledge engineer has to integrate a certain part of the modeled expertise. However, as he is not able to remember the whole base which he is working on, he rationalizes naturally the information by

[1]A part of the work has been awarded twice in 2003 : by Electrophées (French Ministry of State modernization) and by a newspaper *Le Monde Informatique*.

Filipe Borges, Raoul Borges, and Danièle Bourcier, 'Artificial Neural Networks and Legal Categorization' in D. Bourcier (ed.), *Legal Knowledge and Information Systems. Jurix 2003: The Sixteenth Annual Conference*. Amsterdam: IOS Press, 2003, pp. 11-20.

creating categories or meta-rules. He tries to structure the problem before entering the phase of modelization. The same could be said of a neural network, but its mode of classification seems too complex and scattered to be exploitable, or, even, to be compared with that of the knowledge engineer.

However, in a previous experiment during which a perceptron was meant to model some parts of the French criminal code[1], a quick observation of the activity of the hidden neurons showed that they developed certain 'tendencies', or preferences, in their way of processing data. We were able to identify a neuron focusing particularly on 'murders', another on 'sexual crimes', and others were stoical or hyperactive. In spite of this type of specialization of the hidden neurons, the global solutions of the neural network were completely relevant. The development of some specializations of the hidden neurons seemed to show that the representation of a dispute in a neural network can be clarified.

The hypothesis is that it is possible, under certain conditions and by an adequate analysis of the topography of the artificial neural network, to determine the mode of representation of a dispute and to compare it with that of a knowledge engineer, or of a jurist, who would have worked on this dispute.

3 Experiment and Observation of the Results

As the connection weight of each neuron constitutes the source of the representation constructed by a neural network, and as each hidden neuron is supposed to represent a category, the method consists in analyzing the weight of every connection connecting the entries to the hidden neurons, to better understand the representation of a legal problem developed by a machine.

In order to confirm this hypothesis we made an experiment during which an artificial neural network was trained on the dispute of the applicability of the non-competition clauses domain. Let us recall that this dispute can be decomposed into 14 binary criteria used by the magistrate to decide if the clause of non-competition is applicable or not : (1) the clause is stated by contract ; (2) the clause is stated by a collective agreement ; (3) the employee has been informed of the existence of the clause ; (4) the employee has had access to strategic information ; (5) the duration of the clause is excessive ; (6) the area of the clause is excessive ; (7) the list of forbidden companies is excessive ; (8) the list of the forbidden activities is excessive ; (9) a financial counterpart is stated by contract ; (10) a financial counterpart is stated by a collective agreement ; (11) the financial counterpart has been paid ; (12) the employee demands the cancellation of the clause ; (13) the cancellation of the clause is stated by contract or by collective agreement ; (14) the clause is cancelled by the employer.

Four conditions must be gathered for the clause to be applicable : (1) the employee must be informed of its existence (by contract or by a collective agreement, which must be given to the employee at least the first day of work) ; (2) the clause must protect the interests of the employer without being excessive ; (3) the clause must not be cancelled by the employee (s/he can cancel it if a financial counterpart has not been paid) ; (4) the clause must not be cancelled by the employer (s/he can cancel it if such procedure is stated by contract or collective agreement). If one of these 4 conditions is not confirmed, the clause is inapplicable.

To model this dispute we used a multilayer perceptron with back propagation algorithm. It contains 14 binary entries, one hidden layer containing 3 hidden neurons and one output neuron. As the capacities of generalization are not tested, the learning base included the totality of possible iterations : 16 384 cases.

[1]Borges, F : *Théorie et modélisation du sentiment de justice*, mémoire de DEA., dir. Bourcier D., Centre de Théorie du droit, Université Paris-10, Nanterre, 1998

After 340,000 iterations and an average rate of error inferior to 1 %, we analyzed the importance given by each hidden neuron to each entry, to determine if certain hidden neurons are *specialized* in the processing of certain criteria of the dispute.

3.1 Specialization of the Hidden Neurons

The following picture shows the importance given by each hidden neuron to each entry. The absolute values of the connections weights are reported on the picture. The X axis corresponds to the entries (all the criteria of this type of case), the Y axis corresponds to the absolute value of the connections weights[2].

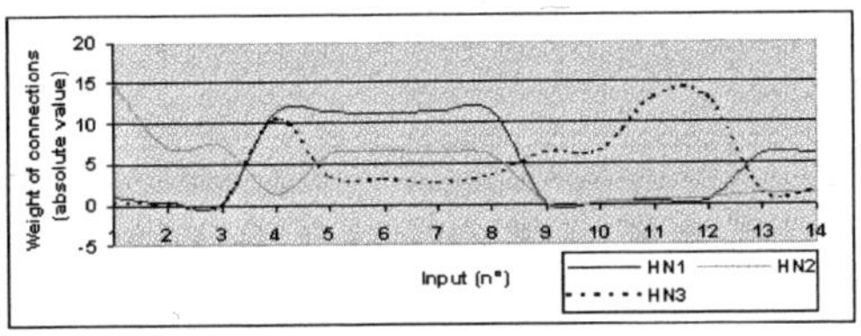

Figure 1: Weights of connections - Perceptron 1

We can notice that entries 1 to 3 have more importance for hidden neuron 2 (HN2) than for hidden neurons 1 (HN1) and 3 (HN3). Entries 4 to 8 are handled in priority by hidden neurons 1 and 2 (and by hidden neuron 3 but to a smaller extent). Entries 9 to 12 are handled by hidden neuron 3. Finally, entries 13 and 14 are processed by hidden neuron 1.

From the point of view of the hidden layer, it seems that every hidden neuron is specialized in certain entries.

- Hidden neuron 1 has specialized in entries 4 to 8 then 13 and 14.
- Hidden neuron 2 has specialized in entries 1 to 3 then 5 to 8.
- Hidden neuron 3 has specialized in entries 4 and 9 to 12.

So, we can distinguish 4 to 5 groups of specialization : (1) neurons 1 to 3 ; (2) neuron 4 (if we exclude it from the next category because of the importance this criterion represents for hidden neuron 3) ; (3) neurons 5 to 8 ; (4) neurons 9 to 12 ; (5) and neurons 13 to 14.

Specialization appears more sharply in the following picture, which indicates for each entry criterion the importance granted by each hidden neuron :

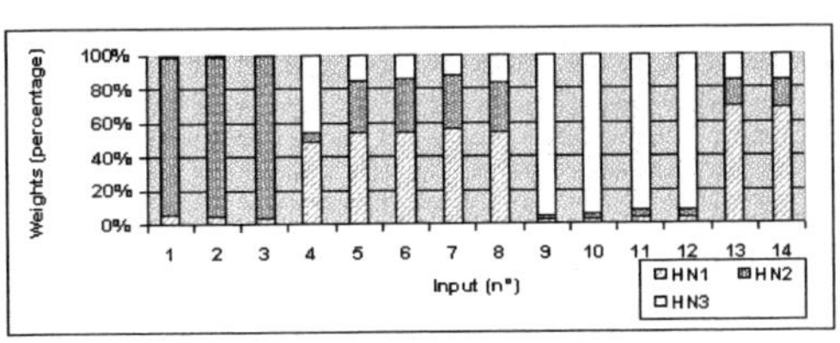

Figure 2: Specialization of the hidden neurons – Perceptron 1

In this picture we can see how every entry has been handled in priority by one hidden neuron (except for the fourth criterion which is handled by two hidden neurons).

[2]The weights of the connections connecting the hidden neurons to the output neuron can be considered as equivalent (values going from 20 to 22). As these weights become quickly equivalent during the learning of the dispute, their effect can be neglected.

3.2 Similarities of the Artificial and Legal Categories

The most surprising observation is not that the artificial neural network develops a specialization of its hidden neurons, but that the *groups of interests* of the hidden neurons present an interesting similarity with the categories developed by the judges[3].

The following picture shows, on one hand, the division of the problem realized by the neural network and, on the other hand, the division realized by the jurisprudence. We notice that the representation of the problem developed by the model corresponds precisely to the representation developed by the jurists.

Entry (n °)	Name of the corresponding criterion	Hidden neuron (n °)	Categories elaborated by the jurisprudence
1	The clause is stated by contract		
2	The clause is stated by a collective agreement	2	Existence of the clause
3	Employee informed of the existence of the clause		
4	Employee has had access to strategic information	1 & 3	Protection of justifiable interests of the company
5	The duration of the clause is excessive		
6	The area covered by the clause is excessive		
7	The list of forbidden companies is excessive	1	Principle of 'freedom of work'
8	The list of the forbidden activities is excessive		
9	A financial counterpart is stated by contract		
10	A financial counterpart is stated by a collective agreement	3	Financial counterpart
11	The financial counterpart has been paid		
12	The employee demands the cancellation of the clause		
13	The cancellation of the clause is stated by contract or by collective agreement	1	Cancellation of the clause by the employer
14	The clause is cancelled by the employer		

Thus, concerning the perceptron described above, we can say that :

- Hidden neuron 1 became specialized in the problems of protection of the justifiable interests of the company, the respect of the freedom of work and the cancellation of the clause.
- Hidden neuron 2 became specialized in the question of the existence of the clause.
- Hidden neuron 3 became specialized in the problems of protection of the justifiable interests of the company and the payment of the financial counterpart.

Only the question of the protection of the justifiable interests of the company is the object of a distribution balanced between 2 hidden neurons.

This kind of classification can seem completely natural, but when we know that artificial neural networks scatter their 'expertise' on their structure, there was no reason for the hidden

[3]The French Supreme Court (Cour de Cassation) stated in a series of decisions (July 10, 2002) the conditions of applicability of a clause of non-competition. These conditions are cumulative: protection of the justifiable interests of the company, limitation of the clause in time and space, consideration of the specificities of the activity of employee, obligation to pay a financial counterpart. The magistrates, who participated in the construction of the knowledge base used here, were more precise by adding the problems of existence of the clause and the cancellation of the clause by the employer.

neurons to develop clear categories and to show this kind of cooperative behaviour. Because of the dispersal of the information, we could think that every hidden neuron would participate in the resolution of the problem, but not that these categories would appear on the network structure.

To verify that this phenomenon of categorization was not unpredictable, the same experiment was repeated. All the parameters remained identical with the exception of initial weights of the connections. Results are corresponding. Although the weights are not perfectly identical and although the various hidden neurons can appropriate differently the same categories, we observe systematically a strong phenomenon of categorization.

3.3 Increase of the Number of Hidden Neurons and Evolution of the Phenomenon of Categorization

To push this experiment further, and to continue to observe the mode of representation of a legal dispute by a perceptron, we changed the experiment by incrementing the number of hidden neurons. Furthermore, the same entries were distributed differently on the first layer of the neural network.

Initially (300 iterations), categories are not differentiated. All the hidden neurons deal with all input neurons. Then (20,000 iterations), gradually, all hidden neurons attribute themselves some tasks. Finally (from 200,000 to 340,000 iterations), the legal categories we were expecting do appear.

- Distribution at 340,000 iterations :

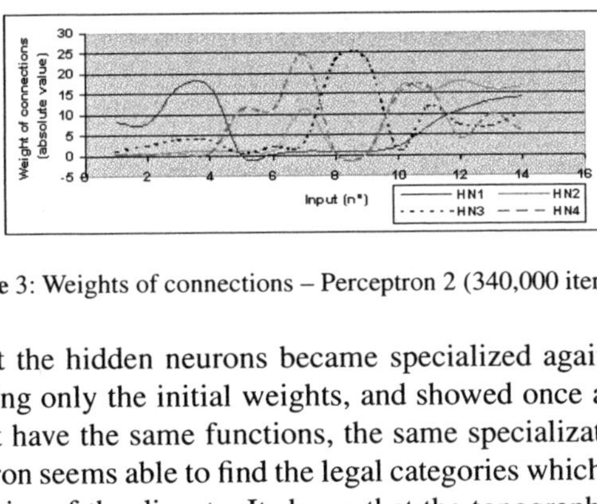

Figure 3: Weights of connections – Perceptron 2 (340,000 iterations)

We can notice that the hidden neurons became specialized again. The experiment was also repeated, modifying only the initial weights, and showed once again that, although the hidden neurons do not have the same functions, the same specializations are systematically found. So, the perceptron seems able to find the legal categories which were elaborated by the expert during his practice of the dispute. It shows that the topography of an artificial neural network, although 'complex', is not as dark and unorganized as we can suppose when we look at the list of weights. In fact, the distribution of weights can be very structured.

Furthermore, we notice that the most determining criteria in the dispute tend to be managed by several hidden neurons, as it is the case for the entries 10 to 14. It seems that the hidden neurons combine their efforts when it is necessary to give more weight to the most important criteria, although a hidden neuron can remain dominating.

Specialization appears more sharply in the following picture :

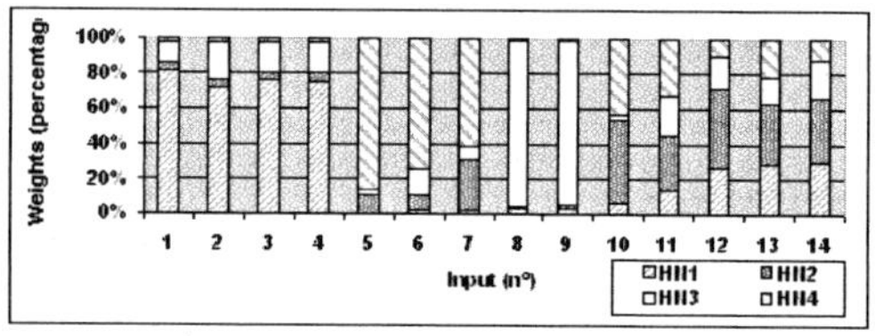

Figure 4: Specialization of the hidden neurons – Perceptron 2

The structuration of the legal problem by the neural network is very close to the representation built by the judge to resolve this problem[4].

Entry (n °)	Name of the corresponding criterion	Hidden neuron (n °)	Categories elaborated by the jurisprudence
1	A financial counterpart is stated by contract	1	Financial counterpart
2	A financial counterpart is stated by a collective agreement		
3	The financial counterpart has been paid		
4	Employee demands the cancellation of the clause		
5	The clause is stated by a collective agreement	4	Existence of the clause
6	Employee informed of the existence of the clause		
7	The clause is stated by contract		
8	The cancellation of the clause is stated by contract or by collective agreement	3	Cancellation of the clause by the employer
9	The clause is cancelled by the employer		
10	The duration of the clause is excessive	2	Principle of 'freedom of work'
11	The area covered by the clause is excessive		
12	The list of forbidden companies is excessive		
13	The list of the forbidden activities is excessive		
14	Employee has had access to strategic information	2	Protection of justifiable interests of the company

The main contribution of the supplementary hidden neuron is a better *distribution of the criteria* in the mode of structuration of the problem. For example , we note that the category 'Protection of the justifiable interests of the company ' is managed by a single hidden neuron, while it was shared between two different hidden neurons in a perceptron counting only 3 neurons in its hidden layer.

3.4 Application of the Method to Other Types of Disputes

This method was applied to two other disputes to verify that categorization was not due to the particular problem of the applicability of the clauses of non-competition.

The first dispute concerns the legal problem of determining if an employee is dismissed during or after his probationary period (which has very different consequences). The protocol of experiment is identical, and, in terms of categorization, although less clear, results remain similar :

[4]The weights of the connections connecting the hidden neurons to the output neuron can be considered as equivalent (values still going from 8 to 10). As these weights becomes quickly equivalent during the learning of the dispute, their effect can be neglected.

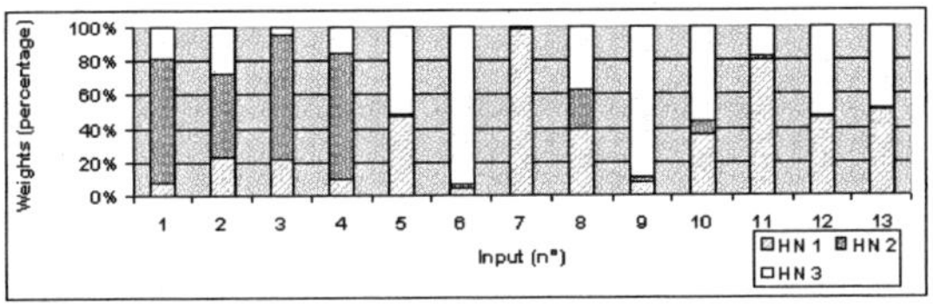

Figure 5: Specialization of the hidden neurons – Perceptron 3

We notice that hidden neuron 1 has specialized in entries 7 and 11, that hidden neuron 2 has privileged neurons 1 to 4, and that hidden neuron 3 has kept entries 6 and 9. Entries 5, 10, 11 and 12 are shared between hidden neurons 1 and 3, and entry 8 is handled by the 3 hidden neurons.

Categorization is not as sharp in this dispute as it is in the problem of the clause of non-competition. However, after analysis of this dispute, we notice that the first four entry criteria correspond exactly to the legal sub-question relative to the existence of a probationary period. It shows that the second hidden neuron found a legal category used by the jurisprudence. We can explain the lack of sharpness which affects the categorization of the other criteria by the fact that the other sub-questions (renewal of the probationary period, announcement of the renewal), are more bound together; what makes the division developed by the perceptron more delicate.

The second type of dispute concerns the problem of the determination of the amount of money which must be attributed to the victim of an aesthetic damage. This dispute combines several fuzzy elements in a rather complex way, which differentiates it from more simple disputes, like the applicability of a clause of non-competition or the analysis of the probationary period. As the values of most entries are continuous, the learning base was constituted by a more limited number of cases (270). The results of this experiment only show a very limited phenomenon of categorization after 3,000,000 iterations.

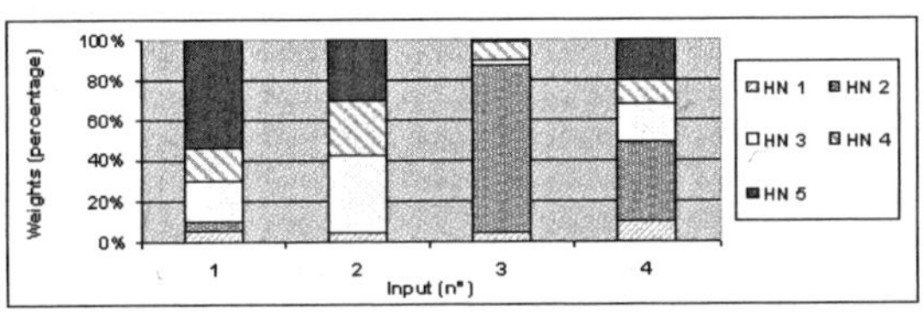

Figure 6: Specialization of the hidden neurons – Perceptron 4

Only hidden neuron 2 has particularly specialized in entry 3 (which is also the only binary entry, which concerns the gender of the victim : male or female), unlike of criteria 1 and 2. The other hidden neurons do not seem to have specialized.

The limited specialization can be explained by the complexity of the dispute, or by the fact that the activity of every entry is either very similar or very different. In both cases, it does not allow to further structure the problem. Moreover it was not possible for the expert to identify categories in this particular dispute.

By analyzing the criteria, we observe that all entries have a similar behaviour : they strongly interfere with each other, which could constitute an obstacle in categorization (only one criterion possessed a peculiarity with regard to the others - its binary character - and a hidden neuron was able to specialize in it). On the contrary, in the previous disputes, the combination of certain criteria created no information and had no effect in the returned decision. That allowed the perceptron to separate entries and to classify them in various categories.

So, we can suppose that, even in a complex dispute, analyzing the weights of connections in a perceptron can help starting a work of categorization.

4 Interpretation of Results

4.1 Optimization of the Representation of a Dispute

So, the method consists in modeling the resolution of a legal problem, by means of an artificial neural network, and to 'overlearn' it until the modifications of the weight of connections are marginal. At this stage we are susceptible to observe a specialization of the hidden neurons on some entry criteria. Differences between the weights of connections for every criterion allow to identify the nature of specializations, and then to distinguish categories by regrouping the various types of specialization.

Finally these categories are susceptible to correspond to recognized legal categories.

Because of the variation of the number of hidden neurons this method enables us to investigate various types of representation of the same legal problem.

It also allows us to determine the minimal number of categories necessary for the resolution of the same dispute. Thus, it was not possible to teach a perceptron the problem of the applicability of a clause of non-competition containing less than 3 hidden neurons. This observation suggests that the division in 3 categories constitutes the minimal representation allowing us to solve this problem. This automated representation, even optimal for the model, remains too complex to be used as such. That is why it is not certain that the jurist can find a direct interest in it, except that s/he realizes that the representation in 4 or 5 categories he has been using is not the minimal - although it is optimal from the point of view of its cognitive capacities - representation. This observation shows that it would be possible to use artificial neural networks to help us criticize our human representations of legal problems.

4.2 Capacity of Abstraction

If we consider that a category constitutes an abstraction of perceived information, then the fact that an artificial neural network is able to build categories from information provided by its environment, seems to demonstrate that computers are capable of abstraction, which is a logico-mathematical process. This capacity of abstraction is interesting for the jurist because the categories found in this experiment match the categories used by the French judges. Moreover, the automatic identification of the categories by a perceptron modeling a legal problem literally constitutes a stage of the automatic qualification of facts. For example it could enrich the connectionist algorithm of justification (PGA algorithm) [3], by clarifying how the decision was shaped "inside" the model, which would add to the analysis of the entry criteria influence on the decision, envisaged first.

It could be interesting to make this type of experiment on a neural network containing several hidden layers, to check if each hidden layer can represent a level of abstraction. Eventually, other modes of representation of a legal dispute could emerge by modifying the number of hidden layers.

4.3 Limits: the Problem of Generalisation

We systematically taught the network of artificial neurons <u>all</u> the possible iterations, to limit the number of variable elements in the protocol. It would be useful to verify that this phenomenon of categorization does not depend on this element, because it would be an extremely strong constraint. It is not possible to teach all the exercises to a neural network containing several dozens of entries, and even less when their value is continuous, especially so as this method reduces the main interest of the artificial neural networks, i.e. their generalization capacity.

Furthermore, to reach these results, we had to "overtrain" the perceptron; what is not recommended for a normal use. 35,000 iterations are sufficient for the model to learn the dispute of the applicability of the clauses of non-competition. But, the process of categorization, if it begins as soon as the first iterations, is very visible by this method only beyond 300,000 iterations. This "overtraining" limits the generalization capacities of the artificial neural network.

Very concretely, observing the evolution of the weight of connections showed a kind of atrophy of connections considered useless by the model. In fact, the perceptron undergoing an "overtraining", has literally "learnt by heart" the exercises of its learning base, and optimized its structure to improve its performances. On one hand, this optimization corresponded to the observed process of categorization, and on the other hand, in a decrease of the connections weight connecting the entry criteria to the hidden neurons which were not handling their category. So we can speak of the *atrophy* of useless connections. This process of atrophy makes the structure of the perceptron comparable with that of a tree of neural networks and even more with that of a decisional tree ; the difference is that in the case of a tree of neural networks connections are suppressed manually, according to the necessities of the user, while in the case of overtraining, the suppression is piloted by the neural network itself. The problem is that this overtraining process is known to ruin the performances of the model in terms of generalization, and it explains why this method is rarely used.

The perceptron generalization capacity was not tested in the previous experiments. It explains that we had to carry on the learning phase beyond what was necessary. But, in the evaluation phase, it would be interesting to develop a method of identification of the legal categories which does not require an overtraining of the dispute.

5 Conclusion

The results of this experiment are interesting for the jurist in many aspects.

First, they show that it is possible to use connexionnist models to investigate various representations of a legal problem, because, according to the structure of these models, it could be possible to obtain various representations of the same problem. The automatization of the process of categorization of a legal problem allows us to discover new configurations and therefore to build a useful representation of a vague legal problem. We have, here, an example of feedback of an experiment of modeling in legal knowledge.

Then, this method can help to control the learning process of neural networks for two reasons. On one hand the "artificial representation" of the modeled legal problems becomes *dynamically* accessible to the user, which helps him/her to understand his/her own representation by a mirror effect. It is actually a matter of opening the "black box" *while it is functioning*. On the other hand, by indicating which hidden neurons are the least used with the network of neurons, this method of detection of categories allows us to optimize the internal structure of these models by the suppression of the unused hidden neurons. It would enable us to reach an optimal structure quicker. As there is currently no method applicable to artificial neural networks, allowing to determine their optimal structure according to problems to learn, it could be useful tool.

Acknowledgements

The authors are grateful to the *'Pluridisciplinary Network (RTP) on Law and Information Systems'* – Centre National de la Recherche Scientifique, F – for the support to this research field : http://www.cnrs.fr/STIC/actions/rtp/rtp_thematiques.htm

References

[1] Bench-Capon, T.J.M. : *Neural networks and open texture*, in *Proceedings of the* 4th *International Conference on Artificial Intelligence and Law*, pp. 292-297, Amsterdam : ACM Press, 1993.

[2] Bochereau L., Bourcier D., Bourgine P. : *Extracting legal knowledge by means of a multilayer neural networks : application to municipal jurisprudence*, in *Proceedings of the Third International Conference on artificial intelligence and law*. Oxford, June 25-28, 1991. New York : ACM Press [99], pp. 288-296.

[3] Borges, F., Borges, R., Bourcier, D. 'A connectionist model to justify the legal reasoning of the judge', in Bench-Capon, T.J.M., Daskalopulu, A., Winkels, R.G.F. (eds), *Legal Knowledge and information systems. Jurix 2002 : The fifteenth annual conference*, Amsterdam : IOS Press, 2002, pp. 113-122.

[4] Hunter, D (1994) : *Looking for law in all the wrong places : Legal theory and legal neural networks*, in Prakken, H., Muntjewerff, A.J. Soeteman, A. and Winkels, R. (eds) *Legal knowledge based systems : The relation with legal theory*, pp. 55-64, Lelystad: Koninklijke Vermande.

[5] Schweighofer, E. : *Knowledge Acquisition in Concept and Document Spaces by Using Self-organizing Neural Networks* (mit D. Merkl und W. Winiwarter), in *International Joint Conference on Artificial Intelligence and Law - IJCAI'95*, Proc. Workshop on New Approaches to Learning for Natural Language Processing, 9-16, 1995.

[6] Schweighofer, E. : *Analysis of Legal Thesauri Based on Self-organising Feature Maps* (mit D. Merkl und W. Winiwarter), in *Proc. Fourth International Conference on Artificial Neural Networks*, Cambridge, 1995.

[7] Stranieri, A., Zeleznikow, J., Gawler, M., Lewis, B. : *A hybrid rule - neural approach for the automation of legal reasoning in the discretionary domain of family law in Australia*, in Artificial Intelligence and Law, Kluwer Academic Publishers, September 1999, pp. 153-183.

Family_Winner: Integrating Game Theory and Heuristics to Provide Negotiation Support

John Zeleznikow* Emilia Bellucci†
*School of Information Systems, Victoria University
P.O Box 14428, Melbourne City, Victoria, Australia 8001
john.zeleznikow@vu.edu.au
†Department of Computer Science, La Trobe University
Bundoora, Victoria Australia, 3086
bellucci@cs.latrobe.edu.au

Abstract. Negotiation, is in general very context sensitive. Since our research laboratory has successfully developed decision support systems in Australian Family Law, we have used our domain expertise to construct a variety of Family Law negotiation support systems.

Family_Winner uses a variety of artificial intelligence and game theoretic techniques to advise upon structuring the mediation process and advising disputants upon possible trade-offs. Heuristic utility functions were developed from cases supplied to us by he Australian Institute of Family Studies. Family_Winner operates best when it is possible to allocate points to issues, and creative decision-making is not required.

Whilst conducting an evaluation of the Family_Winner system, we observed that Family_Winner, in focusing upon providing advice with regard to bargaining, had neglected considering issues of justice. In a domain such as Family Law, issues of justice are of paramount concern. This indicates that use of negotiation support systems should be limited to domains in which principles of equity do not conflict with user satisfaction.

When Family_Winner was used in a variety of other negotiation domains (international disputes, enterprise bargaining and company mergers) the advice offered strongly resembled the eventual negotiated outcome.

1 Introduction

[17] states *'The principal institution of the law is not trial; it is settlement out of court'*. Nevertheless, judicial decision-making has a major influence on the outcome of negotiated settlements, because judicial decisions serve as the very basis from which negotiations commence [24].

Litigation can be damaging to both parties in a dispute. It is a zero-sum game; in that what one party wins the other loses.[1] Mediation can strive to reduce hostility between the parties, to fashion an agreement about tasks each party is willing to assume and to reach agreement on methods for ensuring certain tasks have been carried out. It can lead to a win-win result.[2]

[1] It is actually worse than a zero-sum game and indeed can often lead to a lose-lose result. This is because of the large legal fees arising from litigation.

[2] For example if both parties value the list of items in dispute, it is not uncommon (as long as they do not value the items in an identical manner) for each party to receive 70% of their requested points.

John Zeleznikow and Emilia Bellucci, 'Family_Winner: Integrating Game Theory and Heuristics to Provide Negotiation Support' in D. Bourcier (ed.), *Legal Knowledge and Information Systems. Jurix 2003: The Sixteenth Annual Conference*, Amsterdam: IOS Press, 2003, pp. 21-30.

The Harvard Negotiation Project [9] introduced the concept of principled negotiation, which advocates separating the problem from the people. Fundamental to the concept of principled negotiation is the notion of *Know your best alternative to a negotiated agreement (BATNA)* - the reason you negotiate with someone is to produce better results than would otherwise occur. If you are unaware of what results you could obtain if the negotiations are unsuccessful, you run the risk of: (1) Entering into an agreement that you would be better off rejecting; OR (2) Rejecting an agreement you would be better off entering into.

[20] notes that in developing real world negotiation support systems one must assume bounded rationality and the presence of incomplete information. [18] observed bounded rationality in laboratory experiments on bargaining. Our model of legal negotiation assumes that all actors behave rationally, in their own economic best interests.

[1] investigates how dispute-mediators handle impasse in the negotiation of divorce decrees. Rather than examine the disputants' arguments, he examines the discussion procedures mediators use to craft the disputant's argumentation into a tool to solve conflict.

Some recent work on negotiation concerns the area of discourse and argumentation theory. [23] defines six main types of dialogues, of which negotiation is one: persuasion dialogue, negotiation, inquiry, deliberation, information seeking and eristic dialogue. Whilst we are aware of the importance of discourse and deliberation systems (especially for the domains of e-democracy and e-government), our aim is to provide negotiation decision support rather than model a negotiation discourse. Of significance to our research is the work of [11]. They develop an automated agent that can negotiate effectively with humans. The model used in constructing the agent is based on the formal analysis of their scenario, using game theoretic methods and heuristics for bargaining. [8] discuss trade-offs made by agents during automated negotiations.

In this paper we discuss various approaches we have developed for building negotiation support systems. We confine ourselves to discussing two-party disputes. Since negotiation is domain dependent, we begin by a discussion of negotiation in Australian Family Law. Next we consider two early Family Law Systems we developed – DEUS and Split-Up. DEUS is a template-based system that helps mediators understand the extent of the issues in dispute. Split_Up is a knowledge-based system that advises upon BATNAs.

Family_Winner extends the game-theoretic principles developed by [7] through the use of trade-off rules and maps to proffer advice upon structuring a mediation and reaching an equitable outcome. Because we hope that the techniques we have developed in Australian Family Law can be generalized to other domains, we conducted two evaluations of the Family_Winner system:

(a) Having family law domain experts analyse the operation of Family_Winner;

(b) Using the Family_Winner system to advise upon non family law cases and then comparing the outcome derived by Family_Winner to the eventual negotiated outcome.

As a result of our research in a), we have noticed that a fundamental conflict can arise when building negotiation support systems in legal domains – is our system concerned with supporting mediation or providing justice? When issues of justice influence the outcome of the mediation process, bargaining theory as developed in Family_Winner has its limitations. We illustrate this issue with examples from the domain of Australian Family Law.

We conclude by discussing how research on negotiation support systems is now focusing upon On Line Dispute Resolution. Examples of current research include the UK building industry and plea bargaining about sentencing in Australia.

2 Negotiation Support Systems in Australian Family Law

2.1 Negotiation in Australian Family Law

Negotiation support systems are, in general, very context sensitive. We chose as our domain to be modeled Australian family disputes. Family Law [12] varies from other legal domains in that in general:

1. There are no winners or losers - save for exceptional circumstances, following a divorce both parents receive a portion of the property and have defined access to any children.
2. Parties to a family law case often need to communicate after the litigation has concluded. Hence the Family Court of Australia encourages negotiation rather than litigation.

The overriding principle in Australian Family Law is *the consideration of the paramount interests of the children*. Many men's rights groups have claimed Australian Family Law is feminist. Whilst there is no basis for such claims in any legislation, the incontrovertible fact is that following divorce, the place of primary residence for most children is with their mother. Given this fact, and that the Family Court of Australia is obliged to place the interests of children first, it is inevitable that primary caregiver mothers will receive a greater share of marital property than would other women. This is particularly the case in marriages that have minimal financial resources. These principles are significant in developing BATNAs for Australian Family Law Property distribution. They heavily influence bargaining strategies in Family Law mediation.

2.2 Template and Knowledge Based Negotiation Support Systems

Our first attempt at building negotiation support systems was to build a template-based system, DEUS [25]. In building DEUS, we developed a model of family law property negotiation, which relies upon building a goal for each of the litigants, with the goals being supported by their beliefs. The model calculates the agreement and disagreement between the litigants' goals at any given time. The agreement and disagreement are only in relation to the goals and hence do not resolve the negotiation. In order to reach a negotiated settlement, it is essential to reduce the difference between the goals to nil.

DEUS helps mediators understand what issues are in dispute and the extent of the dispute over these issues. Whilst DEUS does not perform belief revision nor indeed does not have any intelligent functions, it is very useful in informing disputants as to their level of disagreement. DEUS is not concerned with the principles of justice. Its goal is to indicate the range and significance of issues in dispute.

Split-Up [19] is a hybrid rule-based/neural network systems that advises upon property distribution following divorce in Australia. A separate system of justification, using Toulmin Argument Structures [22] is provided. Whilst Split-Up is not a negotiation support system, it can be used to determine one's BATNA for a negotiation and hence provides an important starting point for negotiations. Split-Up first shows both litigants what they would be expected to be awarded by a court if their relative claims were accepted. It gives them relevant advice as to what would happen if some or all of their claims were rejected. Users are then able to have dialogues with the system to explore hypothetical situations to establish clear ideas about the strengths and weaknesses of their claims.

Suppose the disputants' goals are entered into the system to determine the asset distributions for both parties. For the example taken from [6], the Split-Up system provided the following answers as to the percentages of the marital assets received by each party:

	W's%	H's %
Given one accepts W's beliefs	65	35
Given one accepts H's beliefs	42	58
Given one accepts H's beliefs but gives W custody of the children	60	40

Clearly custody of the children is very significant in determining the husband's property distribution. If he were unlikely to win custody of the children, the husband would be well advised to accept 40% of the common pool (otherwise he would also risk paying large legal fees and having on-going conflict).

2.3 Game Theory Based Approaches for Developing Negotiation Support Systems

[13] developed a generic framework for classifying and viewing automated negotiations. It incorporates:

1. Game theory
2. Heuristics
3. Argumentation based approaches.

We have used all three techniques in building negotiation support systems. Family_Negotiator [4] is a hybrid rule-based and case-based system which attempts to model Australian family law.

Game theoretic techniques and decision theory were the basis for the AdjustedWinner algorithm [5], which implemented the procedure of [7]. AdjustedWinner is a point allocation procedure that distributes items or issues to people on the premise of whoever values the item or issue more. The two players are required to distribute 100 points across the range of issues in dispute. The Adjusted Winner paradigm is a fair and equitable procedure. At the end of allocation of assets, each party accrues the same number of points, in a manner similar to that of the Nash equilibrium [15]. It often leads to a win-win situation. Although the system suggests a suitable allocation of items or issues, it is up to the human mediators to finalise the agreement acceptable to both parties.

Arising from our work on the AdjustedWinner algorithm, we noted that

1. The more issues and sub-issues in dispute, the easier it is to form trade-offs and hence reach a negotiated agreement;
2. We should choose as the first issue to resolve the issue on which the disputants are furthest apart - one wants it greatly, the other considerably less so.

Instead of using points as in AdjustedWinner, we decided to use influence diagrams in Family_Winner. We then reformulate the influence diagrams with the aim of both disputants eventually reaching equality in their utilities – the points they give to each issue and sub-issue.

Family_Winner [6] uses both game theory and heuristics. It supports the process of negotiation by introducing importance values to indicate the degree to which each party desires to be awarded the issue being considered. The system uses this information to form trade-off rules.

As an allocation enables trade-offs to be executed, the details of an allocation will have some input into the resulting changes. It was necessary to obtain some negotiation specific data to provide an insight into what change, and what amount of change was expected as a result of trade-off execution. 650 negotiated and litigated cases, provided by the Australian Institute of Family Studies, were analysed. It was hence discovered the shift in most issues appeared to be similar in number. We analysed the data and set numbers to each issue and position pair, and developed trade-off rules.

The trade-off rules are used to allocate issues according to the logrolling strategy. The system makes this analysis by transforming user input into trade-off values, used directly on trade-off maps, which show the effect of an issue's allocation on all unallocated issues.

To use Family_Winner, we must assume:

1. The dispute can be modeled using Principled Negotiation,
2. That weights can be assigned to each of the issues in dispute; and
3. that sufficient issues are in contention to allow each side to be compensated for losing an issue.

Users of the Family_Winner system enter information such as the issues in dispute, indications of each issue's importance to the respective parties and how the issues relate to each other. An analysis of the information is compiled, which is then translated into graphical trade-off maps. The maps illustrate the relevant issues, their importance to each party and trade-off capabilities of each issue. The system takes into account the dynamics of negotiation by representing the relations that exist between issues. Maps are developed by the system to show the disputant's preferences and relation strengths between the issues. It is from these maps that trade-offs and compromises can be enacted, resulting in changes to the initial values placed on issues.

The user is asked if the issues can be resolved in its current form. If this is the case, the system then proceeds to allocate the issue as desired by the parties. Otherwise, the user is asked to decompose an issue chosen by the system as the least contentious. Essentially the issue on which there is the least disagreement (one party requires it greatly whilst the other party expresses little interest in the issue) is chosen to be the issue first considered. Users are asked to enter sub-issues. As issues are decomposed, they are stored in a decomposition hierarchy, with all links intact. This structure has been utilised because we recognise there may be sub-issues within issues on which agreement can be attained. It is important to note that the greater the number of issues in dispute, the easier it may be to allocate issues, as the possibility of trade-offs increases. This may seem counter intuitive, but if only one issue needs to be resolved, then suggesting trade-offs is not possible.

This process of decomposition continues through the one issue, until the users decide the current level is the lowest decomposition possible. At this point, the system calculates which issue to allocate to each party, then removes this issue from the each of the party's respective trade-off maps, and makes appropriate numerical adjustments to remaining issues linked to the issue just allocated. The resulting trade-off maps are displayed to the users, so they can see what trade-offs are made in the allocation of issues. When all issues are allocated at the one level, then decomposition of issues continues, re-commencing from the top level in a sequential manner.

The algorithms implemented in the system support the process of negotiation by introducing importance values to indicate the degree to which each party desires to be awarded each issue. It is assumed that the importance value of an issue is directly related to how much the disputant wants the issue to be awarded to her. The system uses this information to form trade-off rules.

3 Evaluating Family_Winner

3.1 Law and Negotiation

On Tuesday December 3 2003, we met with a number of family law solicitors at Victoria Legal Aid (VLA) to evaluate the performance of the Family_Winner system. We used the Context, Criteria, Contingency evaluation framework of [10]. Whilst the solicitors were very impressed with how Family_Winner suggested trade-offs and compromises, they had one major concern – that Family_Winner in focusing upon mediation had ignored issues of justice.

[2] has illustrated that women tend to be more reluctant than men to continue conflict and are more likely to wave their legal rights in a mediation session. If their major goal is to be the primary care giver for their children, they may reach a negotiated settlement, which whilst acceptable to them is patently unjust. The wife may for example, give the husband the bulk of the property, in return for her being granted the primary care of the children. Whilst such an arrangement may meet the goals of both parents, it does not meet the paramount interests of the children, who will be deprived of subsequent financial resources. Family Law is one domain where mediation conflicts with notions of justice. In such domains, the use of negotiation support systems that attempt to equally satisfy both parties is limited.

Similarly, suppose two parents both want primary residence of their children, to the exclusion of any other matters or indeed, the interests of the children. Although a compromise, acceptable to both parents, might be to have the children move households every night, no judge would sanction such a course of action, since it would be detrimental to the welfare of the children.

The judge (who is the final arbiter on what constitutes the paramount interests of the children) can over-ride an agreement negotiated by the parents. Indeed, since legal professionals are aware that judges are unlikely to approve a settlement where children move house every night, they would caution their clients against even proposing such a solution.

Hence, bargaining theory has its limitation in providing decision support for family law negotiation. However, we have noticed that various negotiation domains are far more suitable than family law, for modeling using integrated game theory and knowledge based systems to advise upon trade-offs. Thus, we decided to evaluate the use of Family_Winner in other negotiation domains.

3.2 Using Family_Winner in a Variety of Negotiation Domains

Given our research on compensation strategies for developing negotiation support systems, and the VLA evaluation of the Family_Winner system, we realised that we need to be careful in choosing negotiation domains that are amenable to the use of our systems. Further, we need to be careful that principles of justice do not conflict with the advice provided by our negotiation support systems.

Since Family_Winner has been designed with a view to being utilised in many negotiation domains, there are no domain-specific requirements that prospective cases need to exhibit. In [3] we discuss how Family_Winner has been used in a variety of negotiation domains. These examples include:

1. Family Law – This example taken from [7] concerns the real-life case of *Jolis v Jolis* which commenced in the state of New York on October 30 1981. New York assumes a default distribution of property on an equal basis, quite unlike Australian Family Law. The dispute was solely about property and included New York and Paris apartments, a farm, cash, securities a profit-sharing plan and life insurance.

The recommendations made by Family_Winner were identical to those made by the judge (admittedly this was a judicial rather than a negotiated settlement).

2. Family Law is a less suitable domain for building Negotiation Support Systems than is Enterprise Bargaining. We considered the Enterprise Bargaining Agreements of VLA for the period 2000-3. Issues in dispute were pay, the use of technology, flexitime, overtime, pre-natal leave, childcare, working from home and performance management.

   The solution generated by Family_Winner was very similar to that eventually concluded by VLA and its employees.

Both negotiations 1) and 2) involved the sharing of a pie. As it was possible to allocate points to issues, and creative decision-making was not required, the solutions suggested by Family_Winner were similar to the eventual settlements.

The next two examples come from the domain of International disputes: an analysis of the Panama Canal treaty of 1974 [16] and a negotiation held with terrorists [9].

3. The Panama Canal treaty involved a lengthy series of negotiations between the United States of America and the Panamanian Government. Issues in dispute were considerable: defence rights, use rights, land and water, expansion rights, duration and compensation. The negotiations continued from early in the twentieth century until 1974. A treaty was concluded in 1974. [Raiffa 1982] listed and assigned points to the issues in contention. He explained that the negotiations failed to resolve all the issues.

   Family_Winner's advice varied considerably from the settlement obtained from negotiations held between the parties. As Family_Winner only has the ability to allocate issues to one of the parties, a comparison based upon creative settlements is not possible. Also, there needs to be a better understanding of exactly what issues are in contention, and how these issue definitions can be translated into issues ready for allocation by Family_Winner. The Panama Canal treaty was particularly difficult to resolve, since the disputants changed their goals during the dispute. Unfortunately, Family_Winner has no temporal aspects.

4. The terrorist negotiation example showed that even critical situations could benefit from the use of an automated negotiation system. The example involved the 1988 hijacking of Kuwait Airlines flight 422. The hijackers were protesting the conviction of Shiites for committing acts of terrorism. The Cypriot and Algerian governments negotiated with the hijackers, allowing the plane to land on their territory, and providing the hijackers with deliveries of food and access to the media.

   Family_Winner advised upon negotiations between the Kuwaiti government and the hijackers. Issues covered were allowing the plane to land, fuel, food, access to media, release of hostages, release of convicted terrorists and the possible conviction of the terrorists. Family_Winner's advice coincided with the eventual outcome of the siege.

5. An example taken from [7] considered a negotiation held between two companies discussing a company merger. Issues in dispute were, name, headquarters, chairman, chief executive officer and layoffs. The settlement reached by Brams and Taylor was identical to that achieved using Family_Winner. The results obtained from this example demonstrate the effectiveness of point assignments to show the importance value of an issue to a party, coupled with trade-off equations to assist in the allocation of issues valued closely by the respective parties.

An investigation of these five examples has shown the benefit of Family_Winner for advising upon trade-offs, compensation and the sequencing of negotiations as long as the issues can be described and remain static and points can be allocated to issues. The system cannot develop creative solutions nor (currently) deal with temporal changes. Problems can occur in legal domains where a negotiated settlement conflicts with our notion of justice.

4 Developing On Line Dispute Resolution

4.1 The benefits of On Line Dispute Resolution

[14] state that compared to litigation, Alternative Dispute Resolution has the following advantages: a) Lower cost; b) Greater speed; c) More flexibility in outcomes; d) Less adversarial; e) More informal; e) Solution rather than blame-oriented; and f) Private. On Line Dispute Resolution has additional benefits: g) Disputants do not have to meet face-to-face: an important factor if there has been a history of violence; h) Mediation can occur at any time, with participants located in different countries.

We are now focusing upon developing various on-line dispute resolution systems, including making Split_Up and Family Winner available on-line. Specifically, we are developing systems for the UK building industry and for plea-bargaining in Victoria, Australia.

4.2 Web-based Building Decision Support System

At Glasgow Caledonian University we have commenced a project on the Development and testing of a United Kingdom web-based decision support system for use in improving the consistency and predictability of adjudicators' decisions in building construction disputes. We are building a web-based decision support system by

(a) Combining the records of project partners (The Adjudication Reporting Centre; James R Knowles plc, Construction Contracts Consultants; MacRoberts, Solicitors; and Bishops, Solicitors); electronically publishing these records; creating a standard hub where stakeholders can record adjudication data; and data mining the records;

(b) decision modeling of the domain of building industry dispute resolution by developing a web-based model of legal reasoning in adjudication;

(c) comissioning a tool for predicting the course of building dispute adjudications.

The project has as objectives:

1. The data mining of adjudication records. The decisions of adjudicators are being examined for coherence. The major impact of this action is to replace the largely anecdotal experience of adjudication with a systematic and transparent analysis.

2. The development of new web-based, analytical tools to identify the predictability of decisions involving many variables, some of which depend on legal reasoning, and some on purely statistical analysis. A decision model is being created based on a legalistic approach to adjudication, as derived from over one hundred decisions that have been made by the UK courts. Knowledge discovery is being used in this task

3. Testing the decision model against new adjudications that are being handled by project partners, and the identification of issues where the model aids predictability, and which may be used to facilitate settlement and reduce conflict.

The project will provide an easily accessed, one-stop decision support system with information on procedure and case law which is capable of being used by adjudicators to test reasoning before publishing a decision. The opportunities it will bring include: (1) Ability to test reasoning; (2) Ability to test likelihood of success; (3) Information and guidance on procedure, thereby reducing the danger of procedural error by adjudicators; (4) Up-to-date information and guidance on matters that frequently come to adjudication; (5) Up-to-date information and guidance on case law; (6) Training tool; (7) Reporter on trends.

4.3 Current Research

A joint project in Victoria Australia, between Victoria University, La Trobe University, JUSTSYS and Victoria Legal Aid is developing an On Line Plea Bargaining system to allow prosecutors and defence barristers to negotiate pleas and sentences with regard to criminal offences. A model of sentencing has been developed using Knowledge Discovery from Database techniques.

Smartsettle [21] assists parties to overcome the challenges of conventional negotiation through a range of analytical tools to clarify interests, identify tradeoffs, recognise party satisfaction and generate optimal solutions. The aim is to better prepare parties for negotiation or to support them during the negotiation process. We are working at incorporating Smartsettle strategies into the Family_Winner system.

5 Conclusion

For the past decade, we have developed negotiation support systems in the domain of Australian Family Law. In this article we first discussed our template-based system (DEUS) that informs mediators of the issues in the conflict and the extent of disputation. Split_Up is a knowledge-based system that advices upon BATNAs whilst Family_Negotiator is a hybrid rule-based/case-based system that models Family Law negotiations.

AdjustedWinner is a point allocation procedure that distributes items or issues to the parties that most value the issues in dispute. Family_Winner extends the point allocation procedure through the use of importance values and trade-offs. It provides advice upon structuring a negotiation, and an equitable outcome, given the disputant's preferences.

In evaluating Family_Winner, we noted that disputant's preferences might well conflict with notions of justice. This is particularly true in Family Law, where the interests of children are paramount.

We hence realized certain limitations of bargaining-type negotiation support systems such as Family_Winner. An evaluation of Family_Winner in diverse domains such as enterprise bargaining, company mergers and international disputes has shown that it is useful for advising upon trade-offs, compensation and the sequencing of negotiations as long as the issues can be described and remain static and points can be allocated to issues. The system cannot develop creative solutions nor (currently) deal with temporal changes.

We conclude by discussing how research on negotiation support systems is now focusing upon On Line Dispute Resolution. Examples of current research include the UK building industry and plea-bargaining about sentencing in Australia.

References

[1] Aakhus, M. 2003. Neither Naïve nor Critical: Dispite mediators, impasse and the design of argumentation. *Argumentation: An International Journal on Reasoning*, Kluwer, 17(3).

[2] Alexander, R. 1992. Mediation, violence and the family. *Alternative Law Journal* 17(6): 276-99

[3] Bellucci, E. 2003. *Developing Compensation Strategies for the construction of Negotiation Decision Support Systems.* PHD thesis, La Trobe University, Bundoora 3086, Victoria, Australia

[4] Bellucci, E. and Zeleznikow, J. 1997. Family—Negotiator: an intelligent decision support system for negotiation in Australian Family Law. *Proceedings of the Fourth Conference of the International Society for Decision Support Systems,* Lausanne, International Society for Decision Support Systems: 359-373.

[5] Bellucci, E. and Zeleznikow, J. 1998. A comparative study of negotiation decision support systems. *Proceedings of the Thirty-First Hawaii International Conference on System Sciences.* IEEE Computer Society, Los Alamitos, Cal: 254-262.

[6] Bellucci, E. and Zeleznikow, J. 2001. Representations for decision making support in negotiation. *Journal of Decision Support.* 10(3-4)

[7] Brams, S. J. and Taylor A. D., 1996. *Fair Division, From cake cutting to dispute resolution.* Cambridge University Press, Cambridge, UK.

[8] Faratin, P., Sierra, C. and Jennings, N.R. 2000. Using similarity criteria to make negotiation trade-offs, Proceedings of *Fourth International Conference on Multi-Agent Systems (ICMAS2000),* Boston:119-126.

[9] Fisher, R. and Ury, W. 1991. *Getting to YES: Negotiating Agreement Without Giving In.* Boston: Haughton Mifflin.

[10] Hall, M. J. J., Hall, R. and Zeleznikow, J. 2003. A method for evaluating legal knowledge-based systems based upon the Context Criteria Contingency-guidelines framework. Proceedings of the *Ninth International Conference on Artificial Intelligence and Law,* Edinburgh, Scotland: ACM Press, 274-283.

[11] Hoz-Weiss, P., Kraus, S., Wilkenfield, J. and Santmire, T. E. 2002. An Automated Negotiator for an International Crisis, *Procedings of AAAI-02.*

[12] Ingleby, R., 1993. *Family Law and Society,* Butterworths, Sydney

[13] Jennings, N.R., Faratin, P., Lomuscio, A.R., Parsons, S., Wooldridge, M.J. and Sierra, C. 2001. Automated Negotiation: Prospects, Methods and Challenges, *Group Decision and Negotiation,* 10 (2):199-215.

[14] Katsh, E. and Rifkin, J. 2001. *Online Dispute Resolution: Resolving Conflicts in Cyberspace.* Jossey-Bass, San Francisco Ca.

[15] Nash, J. F. 1953. Two person co-operative games. Econometrica, 21:128-140.

[16] Raiffa, H. 1982. *The Art and Science of Negotiation.* Harvard University Press.

[17] Ross, H. L., 1980, *Settled Out of Court,* Aldine

[18] Searle, D. A., Daniel, T. E. and Rapaport, A. 2001. The information advantage in two person bargaining with incomplete information. *Journal of Economic Behaviour and Organisation.* 44:177-200.

[19] Stranieri, A, Zeleznikow, J, Gawler, M, and Lewis, B, 1999. A Hybrid rule- neural approach for the automation of legal reasoning in the discretionary domain of family law in Australia. *Artificial Intelligence and Law* 7 (2-3): 153-183

[20] Sycara, K. 1998. Multiagent Systems, *AI Magazine 19*(2): 79-92.

[21] Thiessen, Ernest M. and McMahon, Joseph P. 2000. Beyond Win-Win in Cyberspace. *Ohio State Journal on Dispute Resolution,* 15: 643.

[22] Toulmin, S. 1958. *The uses of argument.* Cambridge: Cambridge University Press.

[23] Walton, D. 1998. *The new dialectic. Conversational contexts of argument.* University of Toronto Press.

[24] Williams, G.R., 1983, *Legal Negotiation and Settlement,* West Publishing Co., St. Paul, Minnesota

[25] Zeleznikow, J., Meersman, R., Hunter, D. and van Helvoort, E. 1995. Computer tools for aiding legal negotiation. *ACIS95 — Sixth Australasian Conference on Information Systems,* Curtin University of Technology, Perth, Western Australia: 231-251.

Agency in Legal Reasoning

Ghita Holmström-Hintikka
Department of Philosophy, Boston University
Boston, MA , USA
Department of Systematic Theology, University of Helsinki
Helsinki, Finland
g2h36@hotmail.com

Abstract. Agency is a key component in a trial. Various aspects thereof are distinguished: *mere causation* in contradistinction to two kinds of action, *instrumental-* and *purposive actions*. The *goal directed will* is also taken into account. The model for legal reasoning is based on an interrogative model of truth seeking for sciences, developed by Jaakko Hintikka. The attempt is to build in agency to this model of questioning as a part of a wider project aiming at the development of a model for legal argumentation.

1 Introduction

This work falls into the framework of the "Fenno-Scandic school" of action logic in combination with legal philosophy then branching to Jaakko Hintikka's work on logic and argumentation. Central in this group was Stig Kanger of Uppsala University. (See eg [13], [14], [15], [16], [17].) Well known in the community of legal philosophers is also Lars Lindahl from Lund University (See [18].). From Finland Ingmar Pörn and me myself may be seen as members of this same school. (See e.g. [19], [20].). Although founding this tradition of action theory, Kanger stayed with a Do-operator which mainly was a two place relation. Only in his last few papers in this area did he include the idea of a three place operator, still remaining though with an unanalyzed 'Do-concept'. Lindahl as well, in developing a deontic model including actions, in his remarkable book [18] stays with the unanalyzed two place 'Do-operator'. This holds for Pörn as well [19], [20]. Further developments of my own contributions to the field, in addition to my book, [5], can be found in [7] and [9].

In this paper I concentrate on legal reasoning as (it should be) performed in courts. In so doing I acknowledge that actions and agency play a significant role in the evaluation of agents. A brief presentation of the basic features in the action theory created in my book, *Action Purpose and Will: A Formal Theory* is thus in order. The concepts and their logical connections will then be used utilizing a variant of the model of truth seeking in science, the Interrogative Model, developed by Jaakko Hintikka, [2], [3], [4]. Into a modified version of this model I shall build my own Action Theory, [5].

In evaluating, criticizing and judging people we often have their actions and intentions in mind. They are what our judgments are all about. Fundamental distinctions to be made, however, are on the one hand between *mere causation* and *action*. The latter in turn divides into *instrumental action* and *purposive action*. Not being intentional, mere causation, or just causing, is *not* an action in any respect. One additional component to be taken into account is the will; *goal directed will* I name it. In the model of legal argumentation, of which this paper is a part, I suggest a method to be used in court of law by judges and jury members. This

Ghita Holmström-Hintikka, 'Agency in Legal Reasoning' in D. Bourcier (ed.), *Legal Knowledge and Information Systems. Jurix 2003: The Sixteenth Annual Conference*. Amsterdam: IOS Press, 2003, pp. 31-40.

model is based on questions and answers and consequences of them. The underlying model is the said Interrogative Model.

In court of law, whether it is a matter of criminal law or law of torts, the judge has to argue from given evidence to a right conclusion. The verdict and possible penalty will be dependent on his skills. If a jury is involved the same holds for it, from given testimonies, facts found e.g. in analyses at the crime lab etc. its task is to reach the right conclusion.

2 Causing, Acting and Willing

2.1 *Conceptual Framework*

Before continuing our discussion we need to fix our terminology. First, when we talk about *agents* we have in mind individuals such as persons, computer aided robots, God or collectives such as associations, business companies, societies. Agents may be involved in at least agent causation and willing. Agent causation may be purposive, i.e., intentional, as in *actions* or not on purpose, unintentional, as in *mere causation.* Being un-purposive mere causation or simply *causing* shall not be considered an action at all. Actions in turn fall into *instrumental action* and *purposive action.* Both categories have an element of purpose imbedded into them. To move sand in ones shoes constitute an example of mere causation. An additional component to be considered is the *goal directed will.* These concepts were created and discussed in depth in my book, [5] and can be presented only briefly here.

In what follows I shall use the following notation:

a, b, c, ..., x, y, z	as constants and variables for agents
m, n, p, q, r, ...	as variables for conditions (states of affairs)
'$\sim$', '$\vee$', '&', '$\rightarrow$', '$\leftrightarrow$'	are the usual Boolean operators for negation disjunction, conjunction, (material) implication, (material) equivalence
'$\exists$' and '$\forall$'	are the usual existential and universal operators
C, E, A, W	are used as operators for *mere* causation, *instrumental* action, *purposive* action and *goal directed will,* respectively. They operate over individuals as well as over conditions

2.2 *Definitions and Bridging Principles*

Using these tools we can construct the following three-place and two-place relations:

1. *Mere causation,* C(x,m,r), for agent x the means m suffices to obtain the result r (to appear, remain, disappear).

2. *Instrumental action,* E(x,m,r), by means of m the agent x sees to it that the result r obtains (appears, remains, disappears).

3. *Purposive action,* A(x,r,p), the agent x sees to it that r obtains (remains, ...), for the purpose that p.

4. *Goal directed will,* W(x,p,q), the agent x wills that p for the further goal that q (i.e., aiming that q).

In an un-analyzed form in everyday language we seem to use the shorter two-place relations for 'causing', 'seeing to it', 'seeing to it on purpose', 'have a purpose' and 'to will'. They can and should, however, be analyzed by means of quantifiers in terms of the corresponding three-place relations. For instance 'x causes it that r' means that 'some means m suffices for x to cause it that r'. In an analogous way quantifiers are used to quantify into contexts governed by the operators E, A, W:

(1.1)	$C(x,r) =_{df} mC(x,m,r)$
(2.1)	$E(x,r) =_{df} mE(x,m,r)$
(2.1.1)	x sees to it that r, iff x sees to it that r by some means
(3.1.1)	$AN(x,r) =_{df} pA(x,r,p)$
(3.1.1.1)	x sees to it that r on purpose iff there is some purpose for which x sees to it that r
(3.1.2)	$NA(x,p) =_{df} \exists rA(x,r,p)$
(3.1.2.1)	x has the purpose that p iff x does *something* for the purpose that p
(4.1)	$W(x,p) =_{df} \exists qW(x,p,q)$
(4.1.1)	x wills that p iff there is some further goal q such that x wills that p for the further goal that q (aiming at q)

Note that AN(x,r) stands for 'x sees to it that r on purpose' and NA(x,p) 'x has the purpose that p'.

The concept of 'will' I use as a technical term and have accepted Harry Frankfurt's thought ([1], pp. 7 ff.) that

> [an agent's] will is the notion of an effective desire - one that moves (or will or would move) a person all the way to action. (*Ibid.*, p. 8.)

The will thus described I name *goal directed* will and consider it a three-place relation between an agent x, the object p and the aim, i.e., further goal q as stated in the formula (4.1). This relation, as a matter of fact, forms the connection between will and purpose as postulated in the important *bridging principle* (AxWA):

(AxWA)	$\exists qW(x,p,q) \leftrightarrow \exists rA(x,r,p)$
(AxWA.1)	x wills that p aiming that some q (for some further goal that q) iff x sees to it that some r for the purpose that p

In other words x wills that p, which is the object of his will, iff he does *something*, not necessarily p, for the purpose of fulfilling his will, i.e., for the purpose that p.

In analogy with the axiom above there are axioms which form the *bridging* principles between instrumental actions and purposive actions:

(AxEA)	$\exists mE(x,m,r) \leftrightarrow \exists pA(x,r,p)$
(AxEA.1)	x sees to it that r by some means iff x sees to it that r for some purpose that p

In other words x sees to it that r iff x sees to it that r on purpose. From here and the definitions (2.1) and (3.1.1) we conclude that

(EA.2)	$E(x,r) \leftrightarrow AN(x,r)$

Further bridging principles are presented in my book [5].

All the relations mentioned above are supposed also to be conditions. This observation becomes meaningful as we move to iterated and higher order relations, the agent sees to it that she sees to it, sees to it that he wills, wills that he sees to it etc. When m,n,p,q,r,... are conditions in themselves, we can substitute for each of them another condition, even a three-place or two-place relation of acting and willing. Thus, we can express the judge's will in relation to the defendant:

W(d,W(x,r,s),q),
the judge (d) wills, aiming at punishing the defendant (q), that the defendant (x) wills that he becomes a better person (r) for the further goal that he ceases to commit crimes (s).

3 Argumentation and the Interrogative Model

A child crossed a lively trafficked street along the pedestrian's path towards green light. A private driver comes speeding along the street into the crossing against red light. The child is hit by the car and killed. This tragic example from real life may function as our model example.

The newspapers write about it, people ask about it, the authorities wonder. The case proceeds and becomes a typical legal case where by means of factual argumentation justice is sought for the parties involved.

Wonder is the first step towards truth seeking. When we wonder we start asking questions such as "Who drove the car?", "What was his speed?", "Did the girl walk towards red light?", "What is the speed limit for the street H?", "Was the driver under the influence?", "Was there a sight constraint?"

The model I shall present here has its roots in Hintikka's *interrogative* model for truth seeking in scientific theory and argumentation. The model has been further developed by several philosophers in Finland (Sandu, Hiipakka, Sintonen, Mutanen, Halonen) and in the United States (Bachman), to mention a few. My own work is calculated to develop this model towards legal philosophy, especially legal argumentation.

Initially the model assumes true answers but by means of a bracketing procedure one can scrutinize false answers and their consequences. Unfortunately I have no space here to explain the bracketing procedure, as important as it is in legal contexts including the hearing of witnesses. (For a further presentation, see. [3]. See also [10].)

Following Hintikka we shall envisage a game theoretical model where the actors are the *Inquirer* and the answerers, the *Oracle* or *Nature*. The task as an Inquirer may be divided among several agents, a fact which becomes plain for instance in a trial where the prosecutor and the defense lawyer share the task of finding the truth. *Oracles* in a trial may be the witnesses, w_1, ... or expert witnesses, ew_1,... the police in the street, the forensic laboratory ...

The method is a book keeping method where the questions by Inquirer to the Oracle are written in a Beth type table. In an American court room this task is taken care of by the trial secretary. The answers, the true answers are written in the left column of the table. In the right column the ultimate conclusion C_U and possible falsity preserving statements are written down. The initial premises, IP, e.g. Betty was hit by the red car, and new premises P_1,P_2,... e.g. Betty was killed, the breaking distance was m meters, as well as logical inferences, LI, sometimes also named conclusions, C, made from them, all come on the left hand side. Questions and answers bring in *new information* to the reasoning, i.e., argumentation and they are called *interrogative moves*, IM. When this new information or inferences drawn there from is of *legal* nature we shall talk about *legal moves*, LM. The interrogative model is obviously a dialectic method with its roots in Socrates. The modern variant covers almost

Table 1:

1.	If a driver drives faster than 80 km/h then he is speeding
2.	This driver drove with the speed of 100 km/h
3.	This driver was speeding

Table 2:

		T	C
1.	If the driver drives faster than 80 km/h then he is speeding	(IM)	C_U
2.	This driver drove with the speed of 100 km/h	(IM, or: w1)	
3.	100 km/h is faster than 80 km/h	(tacit)	
4.	This driver was speeding	(LI, 1, 2, 3)	
5.	The one who is speeding shall be punished with fines	(LM, or: ew)	
6.	This driver shall be punished with fines	(LI, 4, 5)	

all logical models but myself I have applied and developed it in the field of legal reasoning. Thus, the talk about legal moves constitutes an addition to Hintikka's model. So does the introduction of action logic.

Table 1. gives a good picture of the model in its simple form. A single argument consists of one or more premises and a logical inference based on the laws of logic.

This syllogism turned into the interrogative table gives us by far more information when at each move we also spell out the Oracle. Notice also that the tacit knowledge has to be spelled out as in 3 in table 2.

4 Questions about Questions

4.1 Definition

Questions may be defined as the Inquirer's request to the Oracle. "See to it that I know *whether* (or *that*) . . . " (Cf [2], p. 22 f.) For instance when the Counselor asks "What happened in the intersection?" she d*e facto* expects to be informed (get to know) that the red car drove through red lights.

In the interrogative method we distinguish two kinds of questions, "big" *main* questions and "small" *operative* questions which are needed to help to solve the problem. When a big question i.e., a principal question has gotten its final solution it can later function as an operative question in a new argument. In the case law system this is a familiar procedure, for instance cases which get their final solution in the Supreme Court function as precedents in future similar cases in lower courts.

We also make a distinction between 'yes-no questions' and 'Wh-questions' in both "principal" and "operative" questions. The 'Wh-questions' are "what?", "who?", "which?", "why?" and "how?". The "yes-no questions" result in a branching tree, the answers to the "wh-questions" bring in new information. It is permitted to ask a question only if the *presuppositions* have been established. For instance "When did you give your husband a flower?" is permitted only if the answerer has a husband. The answers on the "yes-no questions" establish which one of two possible branches is the right one.

I have, as I said, developed Hintikka's model in three respects and keep applying it into legal matters. 1) I have introduced the legal moves (LM) and everything that follows, in the category of questions and answers in the legal field. For instance "the one who breaks the law shall be punished", 2) the Socratic tree as a model of Socratic dialectic, 3) the introduction of action logic developed by myself.

4.2 Socratic Dialectics

'Hostile witness' is a concept familiar to us through American court movies. A hostile witness is usually the opponent's witness who is likely to be unwilling to cooperate and to share information. The method of cross-examination is used, 'yes-no questions' are asked. "Answer the question 'yes or no'!"

In my view the Socratic dialectic either-or method may be represented by a branching tree. Even the modern scientific and legal investigation has its roots in the Socratic dialectics. When the learned man asks his questions they would be in the form of "When somebody helps, should we say that ... or is it ... ?" We can see him build the interrogative tree where in each node there are two branches. The given answer is added to the existing positive branch and will form the foundation for a new question. Since this was presented in earlier papers of mine, I shall not go further into it here. (See, e.g., [10].)

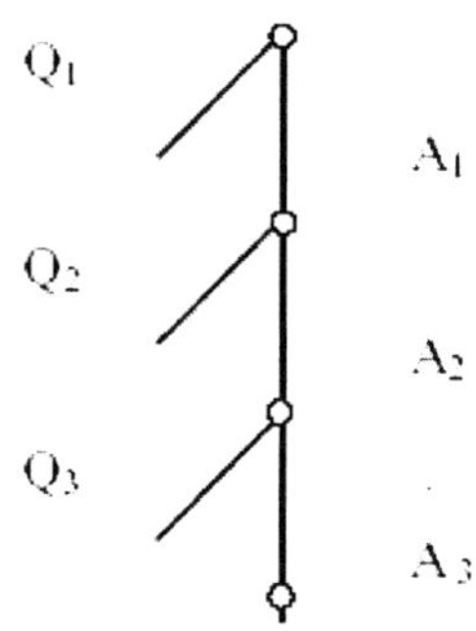

5 Actions in the Interrogative Model

We are now entitled to ask how our action concepts fit into the interrogative model and then we shall think in particular of the legal expansion thereof.

Let us assume that the case reaches the court of law. For the sake of the continued process (and for the sake of the title of the crime), it is important that we analyze the agent causation somewhat closer. We assume two agents, 1) the driver $a$in the red car and 2) the girl Betty who was killed, b. Now we may ask what Betty did and we shall see that

(5.1.1) For Betty it sufficed to walk into the street (m_1) to be killed (r_1)
(5.1) $C(b, m_1, r_1)$
(5.2.1) By walking by the green lights (m_2) Betty made sure that she entered the intersection (r_2)
(5.2) $E(b, m_2, r_2)$
(5.3.1) Betty entered the intersection (r_2) for the purpose of reaching the other side (p_1)
(5.3) $A(b, r_2, p_1)$
(5.4.1) Betty willed that she reached the other side (p_1) for the further aim that she goes to her school (q_1)
(5.4) $W(p_1, q_1)$

In a similar way we may spell out the activities of the driver.

(5.5.1) For the driver speeding (m_3) suffices to kill the girl
(5.5) $C(a, m_3, r_1)$
(5.6.1) By speeding (m_3) the driver sees to it that he reaches the intersection (r_2)
(5.6) $E(a, m_3, r_2)$
(5.7.1) The driver sees to it that he reaches the intersection (fast) (r_2) for the purpose of proceeding fast (p_2)
(5.7) $A(a, r_2, p_2)$
(5.8.1) The driver wills that he proceeds fast (p_2) aiming at reaching his destination fast (q_2)
(5.8) $W(a, p_2, q_2)$

Now we can bring this section of the court protocol into the table form (Table 3). In Table 3 in our example we have one single straight path which bridges to the ultimate conclusion. If we assume a split path as a consequence of a disjunction (or implication) there is the option that one of the paths either closes by contradiction or else remains open. The other obviously bridges to the ultimate conclusion on the right. An open path, as indicated in Table 4 line n+3, provides us with a counterexample. One simple example where we obtain a split path is the possibility expressed as an answer to a question: "The driver either caused it that Betty is dead, $C(a, m_4, r_1)$, *or* he saw to it that she is dead by speeding, $E(a, m_3, r_1)$. In pursuing these two paths we proceed as before, but now we have to apply these rules to two separate paths. Let us assume for instance that this happens in our table on line n, see Table 4.

The bracketing method enables handling of contradictory situations should they occur at any stage in our argument. We proceed backwards along the table and using the interrogative method, inquire each step in the argument. If and when we find the weak spot, the lie or even a mistakenly adopted theory, we bracket this answer and every further step in which it plays a role. (For further discussion see e.g., [3], [8], [10].) Different ways of dealing with new information which may then and otherwise occur, is that it always can be construed as answers to questions.

One additional observation we want to make is the following: As a consequence of our action analyses we can distinguish, not only the actions but also the questions to which the separate agency concepts give an answer. Mere causation answers questions about

"who?" and "what?" and "how possible?"; "who caused what?" and "what made it possible?". Instrumental action in turn answers questions about "who?", "how?" and "what?" In addition to answering the "who?" and "what?" questions purposive action also gives an answer to "why?". Finally, the will concept is capable of giving an answer also to "what for?", in addition obviously to "who?", "what?" and "why?"

A final note, but an important one needs to be made. We have shown that this driver was reckless but we have not shown that he killed the girl on purpose. In other words he did not

Table 3:

		T	C
1.	Betty is dead	IP	
2.	C(b, m_1, r_1) For Betty it sufficed to walk into the street (m_1) to be killed (r_1)	P_1 (IM)	C_U
3.	C(b, r_1)	(LI, 2)	
4.	m_1 & r_1	(LI, 2, 3)	
5.	C(a, m_4, r_1) For the driver driving towards red lights (m_4) suffices to kill Betty (r_1)	P_2 (IM)	
6.	C(a, r_1) The driver caused it that the girl is killed (r_1)	(LI, 5)	
7.	m_4 & r_1	(LI, 5)	
8.	E(a, m_3, r_4) By speeding (m_3) the driver sees to it that he hits the red lights (r_4)	P_3 (IM)	
9.	m_3	(LI, 8)	
10.	r_4	(LI, 8)	
11.	The one who kills another person shall be punished	(LM)	
12.	The driver shall be punished	(LI, 6, 11)	
13.	A(a, r_4, p_2) The driver sees to it that he reaches the intersection fast (r_2) for the purpose of proceeding fast (p_2)	P_4 (IM)	
14.	∃pA(a, r_2) the driver drove fast to the intersection on purpose	(LI, 13)	
15.	E(a, r_2) the driver drove fast to the intersection	(LI, 13)	
16.	If somebody kills another person on purpose (with the purpose of killing) he shall be punished for murder	(LM)	
17.	a did not kill on purpose	P_5 (IM)	
18.	If somebody causes another person's death out of recklessness he shall be ...	(LM)	
19.	∼E(a, A(a, r_2, p_2), r_5) By means of reaching the intersection fast (r_r) for the purpose of proceeding fast (p_2) the driver did *not* see to it that he was careful (r_5)	P_5 (IM)	
20.	The driver shall be punished for causing Betty's death out of recklessness	(LI, 17, 19)	
		C_U	

Table 4:

n	E(a, m_3, r_1)	∨	C(a, m_4, r_1)
n+1	E(a, m_3, r_1)		m_4
n+2	∃pA(x, r_1, p)		r_1
n+3	open path		bridge to C_U

see to it that the girl was killed although he caused it.

6 Future Perspectives.

There has been a vast discussion about agents' intent. The charges against a defendant are often dependent on whether criminal intent, *mens rea,* a guilty mind, can be shown or not. How to argue about the defendant's possible *mens rea* is a matter for the two attorneys and a future paper and shall not be dealt with here.

References

[1] Harry G. Frankfurt, Freedom of the Will and the Concept of a Person. In: *The Journal of Philosophy,* **68.** No. 1, (1971), pp. 5-21.

[2] Jaakko Hintikka, *The Semantics of Questions and the Questions of Semantics,* (Acta Philosophica Fennica, **XXVIII**, No. 4), 1976. North-Holland Publishing Company, Amsterdam.

[3] J. Hintikka, and Bachman, J. *What If... ? Towards Excellence in Reasoning,* ISBN 0-87484-964-0, Mayfield Publishing Company, Mountain View, California, 1991.

[4] Jaakko Hintikka, *Inquiry as Inquiry: A Logic of Scientific Discovery,* ISBN 0-7923-5477-X, Kluwer Publishing Company, 1999.

[5] Ghita Holmström-Hintikka, *Action, Purpose and Will: A Formal Theory* ISBN 951-9264-12-4, (Acta Philosophica Fennica,.Vol. **50**), Helsinki, 1991.

[6] Ghita Holmström-Hintikka, Evidence, Experts and Legal Reasoning. In: G. Holmström-Hintikka, (ed.) Legal Argumentation, *Communication and Cognition,* Vol **28**, No 1, 1995. pp. 7-36.

[7] Ghita Holmström-Hintikka, Actions in Action, In: G. Holmström-Hintikka and Tuomela, R., *Contemporary Action Theory, Vol I: Individual Action,* ISBN 0-7923-4752-8, Synthese Library Vol **266,** 1997, pp. 109-134.

[8] Ghita Holmström-Hintikka, Expert Witnesses in the Interrogative Model, *Computing and Informatics,* Vol. **20**, 2001, pp. 555-579.

[9] Ghita Holmström-Hintikka, Stig Kanger's Actions and Influence. In: [11],Vol. II, ISBN 1-40200111-8, Synthese Library, Vol. **304**, 2001, pp. 185-204.

[10] Ghita Holmström-Hintikka, Questions about Answers. In: T. Childers and Majer, O., (eds.), *The Logica Yearbook, 2002,* ISBN 80-7007-172-9 Filosofia, Prague, 2003, pp. 99-108.

[11] G Holmström-Hintikka, S. Lindström and Sliwinski, R., *Collected Papers of Stig Kanger with Essays on his Life and Work,* Vol. I and Vol. II, ISBN1-4020-0021-9 and ISBN 1-4020-0111-8, Kluwer Academic Publishers, 2001, Synthese Library, Vol**, 303, 304**.

[12] Helle Kanger, *Human Rights and Their Realization,* Reports of the Research Project Models for Justice, Department of Philosophy, University of Uppsala,**1**, 1981.

[13] Stig Kanger, New Foundation for Ethical Theory, First published , Stockholm 1957, Reprinted in: R. Hilpinen (ed.) *Deaontic Logic: Introductory and Systematic Readings, Dordrecht (*Reidel, Synthese Library), 1971, pp. 36-58. Reprinted in [11], pp. 99-119.

[14] Stig Kanger, (together with Helle Kanger), Rights and Parliamentarism, In: R.E. Olson and Paul, A.M., (eds.), *Contemporary Philosophy in Scandinavia,* Baltimore (Johns Hopkins Press), 1972, pp. 213-236. Reprinted in [11], pp. 120-145.

[15] Stig Kanger, Law and Logic, *Theoria,* **38,** 1972, pp. 105-236. Reprinted in [11], pp. 146-169

[16] Stig Kanger, Some aspects on the Concept of Influence, In: *Filosofiska smulor tillägnade Konrad Marc-Wogau, 75 ar,* Uppsala, 1977, pp. 12-23. Reprinted in [11], pp. 170-178.

[17] Stig Kanger, On Realization of Human Rights , In: G Holmström-Hintikka and A.J.I. Jones (eds.), *Action, Logic and Social Theory. Dedicated to Ingmar Pörn on the Occasion of His 50th Birthday,* Helsinki (Acta Philosophica Fennica, **38**) 1985, pp. 71-78. Reprinted in [11] pp. 179-191.

[18] Lars Lindahl, *Position and Change,* D..Reidel Publishing Company, 1977, ISBN90-277-0787, Synthese Library, Vol 112.

[19] Ingmar Pörn, *The Logic of Power*, Basil Blackwell, Oxford, 1970.

[20] Ingmar Pörn, *Action Theory an Social Sciences,* D. Reidel Publishing Company, Dordrecht, Holland/Boston, 1977.

Legal Abductions

Giovanni Tuzet
University of Paris XII, Paris, France
University of Turin, Turin, Italy
tuzetg@hotmail.com

Abstract. This paper deals with the role of abductive inference in legal reasoning. Both in the determination of the relevant facts and in the determination of their legal consequences abductive inference plays a crucial role, being the first step of such reasoning tasks. Two kinds of legal abduction are distinguished: an *explanatory* one aiming at the reconstruction of the relevant facts and a *classificatory* one aiming at a legal conceptualization of those facts. We concentrate on the first kind, stressing the similarities it has with scientific abduction, notably on the concern of truth. We claim that legal abduction is truth-directed, justice being in the first place *epistemic justice*.

1 Charles S. Peirce and Abduction

Charles Sanders Peirce (1839-1914) calls *abduction* the inference suggesting an explanation. In his early writings instead of *abduction* he speaks of *hypothesis* – see e.g. W1: 180, 266 ff. (1865); W1: 362, 430 ff. (1866); W3: 323-338 (1878). At that time his main purpose is to distinguish, in a kantian way, ampliative from non-ampliative inferences. *Hypothesis* and *induction* are ampliative inferences while *deduction* is non-ampliative, being merely explicatory. The point being the difference between ampliative and non-ampliative inferences, in his early writings Peirce does not always draw a clear distinction between *hypothesis* and *induction*. Yet he says that induction determines a general character while hypothesis permits the knowledge of causes (W1: 428; cf. e.g. CP 5.272-276, 2.624). Nonetheless, he more often uses *hypothesis* to denote a classificatory reasoning, depending on a syllogistic scheme, than a causal, explanatory reasoning. But in his later writings he makes a clear threefold distinction between *abduction*, *deduction* and *induction* – see e.g. CP 7.162-255 (1901); CP 5.14-212 (1903). This threefold distinction follows the methodological principles of scientific inquiry according to him. Every scientific inquiry is constituted by three inferential steps: first, by abduction we suggest an hypothesis explaining a fact; second, by deduction we determine the conceivable consequences of the hypothesis; third, by induction we test the conceivable consequences of the hypothesis verifying whether they correspond or not to real consequences[1].

To sum up for our purposes, *hypothesis* denotes in Peirce's early writings a kind of *classificatory reasoning*, while in his later writings *abduction* denotes an *explanatory reasoning*.

2 Legal Abduction

Legal adjudication presents at least two kinds of abduction. If we take abduction in the proper *explanatory* sense, as being (i) the inference which goes from effect to cause, the 'fact-finding question' in adjudication is a kind of abductive reasoning: from the known facts to the unknown, making hypotheses on what happened. If we take abduction in the *classificatory* sense

[1] Cf. especially [7]. On the logical and semiotic models involved in Peirce's theory of inference see [30].

Giovanni Tuzet, 'Legal Abductions' in D. Bourcier (ed.), *Legal Knowledge and Information Systems. Jurix 2003: The Sixteenth Annual Conference*. Amsterdam: IOS Press, 2003, pp. 41-50.

of hypothesis, as being (ii) the inference which classifies some actual facts under a type of fact, also the 'rule-finding question' in adjudication is a kind of abductive reasoning: it goes from the characters of the facts accounted for by abduction (i), to the type of fact those characters belong to. This means, in other terms, that abduction (ii) finds the *rule* or the principle that articulates that type of fact and its normative consequences (if fact-P has occurred, then consequence-Q is due). *Legal abduction* in a broad sense is the combination of abduction (i) and (ii).

Following such an abductive phase, the inference that determines the legal consequences of the relevant facts, is, in the main, a *deduction*. In a strict sense, it is the normative phase of legal reasoning: legal deduction determines the consequences that *ought* to follow from the facts ascertained according to some rule or principle. (A deductivist account of legal reasoning, as for example Neil MacCormick's, captures the inference of legal consequences but not the inference of the relevant facts, which is, in the main, abductive[2]).

A warning must be taken. According to Peirce's inferential methodology, no inference by itself is a sufficient condition of knowledge: abductive conclusions in particular need to be tested by further inferential steps (a deductive determination of their conceivable factual consequences, an inductive procedure of testing those consequences). So, in particular, the 'fact-finding question' is in the main an abduction but not an abduction only. This being understood, let us say something more on the two kinds of abduction we sketched.

3 Legal Abduction (i): The Fact-finding

Legal reasoning about the facts has the nature of abduction: it should set out an hypothesis providing, or at least suggesting, a causal explanation of the known effects. It is not false to claim that abduction is the core of the legal process – as Benjamin Cardozo ([5]: 129) said: "the controversy relates most often not to the law, but to the facts"[3].

That the legal process has at his first step an abductive nature, it is a suggestion we take from the writings of Patrick Nerhot, whose very thesis is the likeness of legal and historical inquiry. He has widely shown ([25, 26]) that legal and historical methodology are quite proximate[4]. Both legal and historical inquiry aim at stating the truth of what happened, inferring its causes from its effects – that is, in our opinion, starting from an abductive inference. The problem is that on trial there is usually no possibility to reproduce the facts experimentally, so as to test them by an induction using quantitative methods (cf. CP 2.758-759). They are, as Christopher Hookway ([17]: 50 ff.) calls them, *lost facts*. In general such an hypothesis as the hypothesis concerning the legally relevant facts cannot be proved directly, neither statistically nor experimentally. But it does not follow from that that abduction has no relevance for legal reasoning. A legal-historical hypothesis may be supported by other evidence related to it and capable of proving it indirectly. In the first place, the general aspects of a disputed event can be explained according to some rules connecting general causes to general effects. In the second place, the particular aspects of the event can be reconstructed starting from general assumptions and adding to them any evidence and evaluation concerning the case at hand. Even if a legal-historical hypothesis cannot be directly tested, it can yield a justified belief if it is based on indirect, and adequate, evidence[5].

[2]Cf. [23], chap. 2 (*Deductive Justification*) and chap. 3 (*Deductive Justification – Presuppositions and Limits*).

[3]On legal fact-finding cf. recently [28, 1, 32]).

[4]On historical methodology cf. CP 2.511, footnote 1. It is true that the first Peirce conceives of historical abduction in the somewhat strict terms of archeological method, but the late Peirce develops a richer account of documentary evidence (cf. CP 2.625, CP 7.162-255).

[5]Cf. [33]: 1562-1563 and [28]: 1648) on the notion of *ancillary evidence*. For a general survey of the problem

4 Legal Abduction (ii): The Rule-finding

It is sometimes said it is more difficult to admit the relevance of abduction for the 'rule-finding question'. The rule-finding cannot be naturalized, according to some legal scholars[6]. Yet we believe that the processes leading to the determination of the rule to be applied should be analyzed. Which are the logical and psychological processes involved in the 'rule-finding'?

The expression 'rule-finding' may be misleading: that which is found is not a certain rule immediately, but a rule starting from the characters of the case in hand. Such a case is classified according to some legal concept. Legal rules usually consist in the relation between a legal concept and its normative legal consequences. (To put it differently, between a type of fact and a normative consequence following from it). So a fundamental step to the determination of the legal rule to be applied is the finding of the legal concept instantiated by the case. This finding has an abductive character, starting from the legally relevant factual characters connoting the case. Be the case S presenting the characters P1, P2, P3. If a legal concept M corresponding to such characters exist, the case will be classified as an instance of that concept. This classification is not deductive, but abductive. To be more precise, it is an *hypothesis* in the logical sense given by Peirce to the term 'hypothesis', that is a *classificatory* inference substituting a more general predicate to other predicates less general: if the case S has the characters P1, P2, P3, and the legal concept M has such characters, the case S has the legal character M (cf. CP 2.461-516, 2.704 ff.). At that stage, according to the rules in which such a concept is contemplated, the normative consequences following from that concept should be deduced. Obviously, a problem could be the want of a concept adequate to the particular characters of the case, and the want of a corresponding rule. In such an eventuality, the abduction will have the form of an analogical abduction (cf. CP 6.40, 1.65, 1.69), or it will be a highly creative abduction, producing a new legal concept and a new corresponding rule.

Concerning in particular the *common law* systems, some similar considerations could be developed bearing on the process of determination of a principle of judgment relative to a range of precedents: from the analysis of precedent decisions a rule is abduced, then its consequences are deduced, finally these consequences are tested by induction relatively to other cases[7].

5 Fact-finding in Science and Law

We will concentrate on the first kind of abduction: the one which covers the 'fact-finding question'. We can compare abduction in science and abduction in law, sketching out three similarities. They concern respectively the *explanatory*, *truth-seeking*, and *public* nature of abduction.

(I) Legal abduction is the inference which goes from an effect, legally relevant, to its cause, providing for the *best explanation* of the known effect (as science does). The expression 'inference to the best explanation' denotes indeed a more complex process than the process of finding an hypothesis[8]. It comprehends the evaluation of the hypothesis, so as to choose between rival hypotheses. Legal abduction at the first stage is merely the inference

see [16], especially chapters 9 and 12.

[6]"Peirce's abduction is a powerful instrument to build empirical hypotheses, and it is extremely doubtful that the very concept of an empirical hypothesis could work with a legal (or moral) rule" ([12]: 264, footnote 51). – Notice that the expression 'rule-finding' is narrower but not inferentially different from the larger 'law-finding' – cf. [27].

[7]See [6]. Cf. [14].

[8]Cf. [15, 22, 19].

suggesting an explanation. But in its *ripe* sense it is the inference providing the best explanation of what happened.

(II) It could be said that legal adjudication must only evaluate the *evidence* produced by the parties, and must not push the inquiry beyond that limit. It could be argued in this way that legal abduction does not aim at finding the truth (as science would do). It could be claimed that legal abduction should rather account for the evidence, and not for truth.

So, to scientific abduction another model of inquiry could be opposed, the one whose end is not to find the truth, but only to evaluate the evidence. According to some legal scholars, this model of inquiry is more akin to legal inquiry. This opinion is largely based on the distinction between *adversary model* and *inquisitorial model* of legal process. The fact that the adversary model has today a larger diffusion supports the opinion that truth is not the end of legal process, its goal being otherwise the sole evaluation, by an impartial judge, of the evidence produced by the parties. The distinction between the two models cannot be disregarded, but we believe it to consist in putting different constraints on the patterns of inquiry. What changes is the *breadth* of the inquiry, so to speak, and not its principal *goal*, that is the *statement of truth*, even if in the adversary model some moral, political and legal principles restrain the patterns of investigation. Still the judicial decision should be based on the facts ascertained.

That from an institutional point of view. From a conceptual point of view, we believe the opposition between truth and evidence, or truth and proof, to be a false one. If *evidence* is required, it is required so as to *state the truth*. The same applies to proof[9]. A *proof*, is a proof of the *true*. How can we plead such a conceptual claim? We can draw some paradoxical consequences from the opposition between truth and proof. For example, to be a true one, the opposition between truth and proof should imply that certain proofs hold good while being false. It should likewise imply that certain proofs hold good while allowing the inference of some false consequence, or while being inferred from a false premise. Essentially, we can reformulate the Moore's paradox. Such a paradox has been made famous by a passage from Ludwig Wittgenstein's *Philosophical Investigations* (second part, X). It concerns the relation between reality and belief, the paradox being, in our reading, that a conceptual difference such as the difference between reality and belief implies nevertheless a certain connection between the two, so as to make some statements contradictory as the following:

1. *It rains but I believe it does not rain.*

We can reformulate the Moore's paradox regarding the relation between truth and proof:

2. *We have the proof of* p *but* p *is not true.*

Or:

3. *We have no proof of* p *but* p *is true.*

These paradoxical statements, as (2) and (3), are such in virtue of the conceptual relation between truth and proof. They confirm our intuition that a proof is ultimately a proof if and only if it does account for truth.

Three objections could be raised indeed to this argument[10]. The first is a *legal* one: civil proof and criminal proof have different standards. In a criminal case, the relevant fact should

[9] Which is the difference between proof and evidence? Technically, proof may be considered as the effect of evidence – see for instance [4]:1215-1216 according to which 'the effect of evidence' means 'the establishment of a fact by evidence'.

[10] Thanks to Martin P. Golding and François Lepage for drawing our attention on the first and second objection, respectively. Furthermore, we take the opportunity for thanking the two anonymous referees of a previous version of this paper.

be proved 'beyond reasonable doubt'; while in civil cases the standard is less high. This is true, but it does concern the pragmatics of legal inquiry, so to speak, and not the conceptual relation between truth and proof: independently of the standard, a proof is always taken as a proof of the true. No one, both in civil and criminal cases, would ever claim to have a false proof of the fact he is trying to prove. The second objection is a *logical* one: on a certain logical conception of proof, (2) and (3) are not paradoxical. They could be stated as follows: (2') If we have the proof of p but p is not true, then the system is not sound; (3') If we have no proof of p but p is true, then the system is not complete. This is true for a syntactic conception of proof, we suspect, being false or pointless for a semantic conception of proof, as the legal conception is: what matters in a legal context of proof are the facts accounted for, not the strictly logical properties of the proofs or the properties of the system they belong to. The third objection is a *metaphysical* one: (2) and (3) would be not paradoxical if truth be intended as metaphysical truth. It could be the case, given the distinction between epistemology and metaphysics, that we have no proof of $p$but $p$is true. This cannot be denied by our realist intuitions. In fact, our argument does not claim the reduction of truth to proof: on the contrary, it claims that a proof is a proof if and only if it does account for truth. So, on the conceptual priority of truth over proof, there is room for a realist conception of truth consistent with the principle that unproved or unknown truths could not determine a legal judgment.

To sum up, these objections do not undermine our intuition that a proof is a proof of the true, at least in the legal context. Moreover, any constraint on the patterns of legal inquiry does not alter the meaning and goal of the latter. *Truth is the main goal of legal inquiry and abduction.*

Apart from that argument on truth and proof, a current objection to legal abduction is the following: if for example a footprint and some traces of blood and hair are found, and if they correspond to footprints, blood and hair of, say, Theodore, then we could argue by abduction that Theodore was there; but it could be well exist another man with those physical characteristics[11]. Thus, is abduction an invalid reasoning? No, or at least not for this reason. Because in the example just made the problem concerns the evidence and not the reasoning. The conclusion is not secure because the evidence is not adequate.

Anyway, abduction never yields certainty. It is a probable inference, that is an inference determining conclusions whose truth does not necessarily follow from the truth of the premises (cf. W2: 22). But this is not a check: it is indeed a principle of responsibility. The knowledge of the uncertainty of abductive conclusions, means the responsibility for their inference. The knowledge of the lack of certainty of a certain piece of reasoning, means the impossibility of concealing an arbitrary decision under the shield of logic. The shared knowledge of the hypothetical nature of a certain conclusion, means the impossibility of claiming it as necessary.

(III) Legal abduction (at least in the adversary model) is public as scientific abduction is: according to a fallibilist approach in epistemology, centering on the public debate of arguments, we should say that the adversary model offers many more truth-warranties than a 'private' inquiry does according to the inquisitorial model[12].

In fact, the adversary model, which seems in other respects to separate legal and scientific abduction, has *publicity* as its main character: the evidence is produced on trial, in the public

[11]Cf. e.g. [18]: 406-407.

[12]He who has rightly denounced the misunderstanding of the opposition between adversary model and truth-seeking, is among others [8]: 362 ff. in particular), its main claim being that truth is to be determined less in investigation than in debate. On the opposition between truth-seeking and adversary system, see for example [11], chap. VI (*The "Fight" Theory versus the "Truth" Theory*); cf. [13].

debate of the parties. This is a fundamental difference from the inquisitorial model, where the legal inquiry can be carried on secretly by the authority, being admitted as relevant for the final decision the evidence collected *privatim* by the authority, regardless of its being discussed on trial. This public dimension is a strong similarity between legal and scientific abduction: the method of science defended by Peirce requires our beliefs to be discussed by the community of the inquirers (see e.g. CP 5.378, 5.407).

So we are able to comprehend which is the limit of the comparison between abduction and police investigation. Many peircean scholars insisted on such a theme[13]. But abduction as reconstruction of what happened is less a private investigation, the hunch of a particularly skillful detective, than a public confrontation of hypotheses. It can certainly happen that the more ingenious and brilliant hypothesis is the one resolving a case, but any hypothesis should be publicly evaluated according to some shared criteria and principles. The trial is the means of a public reconstruction of the disputed events. It is not decided by the genial hunch of a detective, nor by the absolutely private investigation of an authority.

It could be objected indeed that we are speaking of what follows abduction, that is of the process of verifying or falsifying the hypothesis, instead of speaking of abduction as hypothesis suggestion; this is not false, but such an objection would stay again on the quite romantic idea of a private hunch, regardless of any principle of method (cf. CP 2.634-635, 7.220, on the *criteria* of hypothesis formulation and selection). In fact, at point (I) we spoke of legal abduction as hypothesis evaluation and not only as hypothesis suggestion.

What has often been claimed about the logical structure of legal decision, is the practice of inverting the decision and its reasons. It is not only a practice of certain legal systems which admit the reasons of a decision to be made public after the decision is made public; it is also, according to some scholars, a practice of reasoning. That is, the practice of finding the premises after the conclusion is selected. This inversion was noticed by John Dewey in his celebrated article of 1924, *Logical Method and Law* (MW 15: 65-77)[14]. According to him, we generally begin with some vague anticipation of a conclusion (or at least of alternative conclusions), and then we look around for reasons and premises supporting it. It could be replied that a chronological priority is not a logical priority. As Neil MacCormick has rightly noticed, it does not make sense to insist on the inversion between reasons for decision and decision, or in other words between the context of discovery and the context of justification: in law, what makes a conclusion acceptable is its justification, regardless of the way it has been discovered at first[15]. Be it a logical priority, from Peirce's point of view it would be 'sham reasoning'[16].

So, both the reconstruction of the events and the justification of decision are public and publicly made through the debate of the parties. On the other hand, that the parties are more interested in their own success than they are in the discovery of truth, it is obvious. But it is no less true that the *judgment* must not concern the personal or political interests of the parties, but their arguments and the evidence produced, determining the truth-value of such arguments and evidence.

Even if it is utterly meaningless, or at least unrealistic, to hope for a collaborative spirit

---

[13]Cf. most of all [29]. That legal reasoning is quite different from police investigation is clearly shown by those legal scholars working on legal decision and justification: the legal decision is "perhaps a uniquely public and published form of reasoning" ([23]: 7).

[14]On Dewey's legal thought – compared to coeval 'legal realism' – see [24].

[15][23]: 15-16. Cf. [2]: 38 ff. for an examination of MacCormick's thesis and a comparison between justification of judicial decision and scientific testing.

[16]Reasoning from the conclusions desired is contrary to truth and logical validity – "it is no longer the reasoning which determines what the conclusion shall be, but it is the conclusion which determines what the reasoning shall be. This is sham reasoning" (CP 1.57).

between the parties, in any case *the judgment should be determined in the observance of truth*. Even if the parties do not aim at a shared determination of truth, even if there is no community of inquirers as in science, the goal of the investigation remains the same.

Justice should be in the first place *epistemic justice*. By that, we mean that a judicial decision is a right decision if it is determined on the basis of the facts ascertained. Where legal rules prescribe certain consequences to follow from the instances of a certain type of fact, and where the fact-finding ascertains such instances, there is no *political justice* capable of legally prevailing on the acquired knowledge. Here, justice follows from truth, and not the contrary.

Indeed, the prevailing of epistemic justice on political justice should be almost a triviality, but in recent years the contrary has often been claimed, that is that justice is essentially political justice[17]. If this claim is intended as general, it is completely at variance with the spirit of the legal process. A more subtle objection could be the following: especially in civil cases, the process is a form of politically-oriented and authority-based problem solving. We should reply as follows: the idea of a problem solving regardless of the state of things to be settled is a very difficult one to grasp. Even if a case might be settled without an historical inquiry determining what really happened, it is obviously impossible to settle a case without *knowing* the subject matter of the controversy. What is true of the case is a fundamental cognitive component of a good problem solving, and, at least in this weak sense, justice is necessarily epistemic justice.

But we are not completely satisfied with this weak sense of epistemic justice. Especially for criminal cases, we believe that epistemic justice has a strong sense consisting in the normative goal of a true reconstruction of what happened[18]. We do not accept the idea of political justice prevailing on epistemic justice because the first and more important goal of the process is the statement of truth, independently of its political convenience. As many important scholars recognize, the process has a *cognitive function* and the political interests cannot dispose of it[19].

We have to recognize at most that the determination of truth is not a *sufficient* condition of justice, even if it is a *necessary* condition of it. Essentially, a judicial decision is a right one if (i) factual premises are true and (ii) normative premises are morally acceptable. Now, concerning the first condition, justice follows from a true account of the facts. There cannot be justice without truth. There cannot be a right decision on the basis of a false reconstruction of what happened or matters.

In observance of the truth, those legal consequences should be determined which normatively follow from the facts ascertained. Only in the determination of those consequences some political considerations could be allowed, if and only if the law itself leaves to the judge a faculty of choosing between more or less slightly different normative consequences.

Finally, we can sum up our comparison between legal and scientific abduction in the following points:

(i) legal abduction in its ripe sense provides for the best explanation of what happened;

(ii) concerning the relation of truth and proof, their opposition is a false one, because a proof is a proof of the true, and a limitation of the patterns of investigation does not change its goal;

[17] See e.g. [31, 20, 21]. Less recently, [10].

[18] "Factfinding in a legal context has, as a principal goal, an "epistemic objective": the generation of findings that are *accurate* descriptions of events and that are *warranted* by the legally available evidence" ([33]: 1526).

[19] Cf. for instance [9]: 1-3, 133, 157).

(iii) at least in the adversary model, legal abduction is public as scientific abduction is;

(iv) if it is true that the parties on trial are in conflict, it is no less true that the judgment should regard the truth or falsehood of their arguments, and not their political convenience.

We believe these points to testify in favor of the relevance of abduction for legal inquiry. If we are justified in speaking of *legal abduction*, then, the main point being the determination of truth as necessary condition of judgment, we are finally justified in claiming that, in law and for legal inquiry, *justice follows from truth*.

Abbreviations

CP *Collected Papers* of C.S. Peirce, 8 vols., ed. by C. Hartshorne, P. Weiss (vols. 1-6), and A. Burks (vols. 7-8), Harvard University Press, 1931-1958. For example, CP 5.189: volume 5, paragraph 189.

W *Writings of C.S. Peirce: a Chronological Edition*, 6 vols. published, ed. by M. Fisch et al., Bloomington, Indiana University Press, 1982-. For example, W1: 210: volume 1, page 210.

MW *The Middle Works* of J. Dewey, 1899-1924, ed. by J.A. Boydston, Carbondale and Edwardsville, Southern Illinois University Press, 1976-1983. For example MW 3: 111: volume 3, page 111.

References

[1] Abimbola, K. (2001), *Abductive Reasoning in Law: Taxonomy and Inference to the Best Explanation*, Cardozo Law Review, vol. 22: 1683-1745.

[2] Anderson, B. (1996), *"Discovery" in Legal Decision-Making*, Kluwer Academic Publishers, Dordrecht.

[3] Bessone, M. and Guastini, R. (eds.) (1995), *La regola del caso*, Cedam, Padova.

[4] Black, H.C. (1891) *Black's Law Dictionary*, Sixth Edition, West Publishing Co., St. Paul (Minn.), 1990.

[5] Cardozo, B.N. (1921), *The Nature of Judicial Process*, Yale University Press, 1991.

[6] Downard, J.B. (2000), *The Common Law and the Forms of Reasoning*, International Journal for the Semiotics of Law, vol. 13: 377-406.

[7] Fann, K.T. (1970), *Peirce's Theory of Abduction*, Martinus Nijhoff, The Hague.

[8] Ferrua, P. (1995), *Contraddittorio e verità nel processo penale*, in Bessone and Guastini (1995).

[9] Ferrua, P. (1997), *Studi sul processo penale*, III, Giappichelli, Torino.

[10] Frank, J. (1930), *Law and the Modern Mind*, Peter Smith, Glouchester (Mass.), 1970.

[11] Frank, J. (1949), *Courts on Trial. Myth and Reality in American Justice*, Princeton University Press, 1973.

[12] Gianformaggio, L. (1997), *'Like' – 'Equal' – 'Similar': Are They To Be Treated Alike?*, in E. Garzón Valdés, W. Krawietz, G.H. von Wright, R. Zimmerling (eds.), *Normative Systems in Legal and Moral Theory*, Duncker & Humblot, Berlin.

[13] Haack, S. (2003), *Truth and Justice, Inquiry and Advocacy, Science and Law*, Associations, vol. VII: 103-114.

[14] Hage, J. and Sartor, G. (2003), *Legal Theory Construction*, Associations, vol. VII: 171-183.

[15] Harman, G. (1965), *Inference to the Best Explanation*, The Philosophical Review, vol. 74: 88-95.

[16] Hempel, C.G. (1965) *Aspects of Scientific Explanation. And Other Essays in the Philosophy of Science*, The Free Press.

[17] Hookway, C. (2000), *Truth, Rationality, and Pragmatism*, Clarendon Press, Oxford.

[18] Iacoviello, F.M. (1995), *I criteri di valutazione della prova*, in Bessone and Guastini (1995).

[19] Josephson, J.R., Josephson, S.G. (eds.) (1994), *Abductive Inference*, Cambridge University Press.

[20] Kelman, M. (1987), *A Guide to Critical Legal Studies,* Harvard University Press.

[21] Kennedy, D. (1997), *A Critique of Adjudication (fin de siècle)*, Harvard University Press.

[22] Lipton, P. (1991), *Inference to the Best Explanation*, Routledge, London.

[23] MacCormick, N. (1978), *Legal Reasoning and Legal Theory*, Clarendon Press, Oxford.

[24] Mendell, M. (1994), *Dewey and the Logic of Legal Reasoning*, Transactions of the Charles S. Peirce Society, vol. XXX: 575-635.

[25] Nerhot, P. (1994), *Diritto-Storia*, Cedam, Padova.

[26] Nerhot, P. (1995), *La vérité en histoire et le métier d'historien*, Quaderni fiorentini, vol. XXIV: 11-138.

[27] Pound, R. (1960), *Law Finding Through Experience and Reason*, University of Georgia Press.

[28] Schum, D.A. (2001), *Species of Abductive Reasoning in Fact Investigation and Law*, Cardozo Law Review, vol. 22: 1645-1681.

[29] Sebeok, T.A. and Eco, U. (eds.) (1983), *The Sign of Three: Holmes, Dupin, Peirce*, Indiana University Press, Bloomington.

[30] Tiercelin, C. (1993), *La pensée-signe. Études sur C.S. Peirce*, Éditions Jacqueline Chambon, Nîmes.

[31] Unger, R.M. (1986), *The Critical Legal Studies Movement*, Harvard University Press.

[32] van Andel, P. and Bourcier, D. (2001), *Serendipity and Abduction in Proofs, Presumptions, and Emerging Laws*, Cardozo Law Review, vol. 22: 1605-1620.

[33] Walker, V.R. 2001, *Theories of Uncertainty: Explaining The Possible Sources of Error in Inferences*, Cardozo Law Review, vol. 22: 1523-1570.

A Map-Based Expert-Friendly Shell

Pamela N.Gray* Xenogene Gray†
*School of Law University of Western Sydney, Parramatta Campus
Parramatta, NSW, Australia
pgray@csu.edu.au
†Grays Knowledge Engineering
Telopea, NSW 2117, Australia
xen@grayske.com

Abstract. eGanges is a map-based, expert-friendly legal expert system shell that allows construction of nested rule or procedure maps, with various glosses of nodes in the maps. Gloss options include links between nodes in the same map and between parallel maps. The shell has facilities to navigate and interrogate maps, as well as functionality in processing interrogation input. A sample of the Vienna Convention is used to illustrate features of an application of the shell.

1 Introduction

A map-based, expert-friendly, legal expert system shell, eGanges (electronic glossed adversarial nested graphical expert system), has a design that is based on a template of rule-oriented or procedure-oriented expertise or intelligence. The template is derived from the jurisprudential model of 3d legal logic [1 - 4]. The theory of 3d legal logic reifies legal logic so that it is suited to object-oriented programming, interactive visualisation of legal logic, and concrete learning. eGanges is an object-oriented Java program.

Although the theory of 3d legal logic was developed as legal knowledge engineering methodology, its jurisprudential model is theoretically independent of computer technology: in its electronic or non-electronic form, it may be useful for understanding, schematising, teaching and managing rule-oriented or procedure-oriented domains. The reification requires notional three dimensional space, but it has permitted eGanges to be designed with simpler, navigable two dimensional graphics. The eGanges interface further simplifies the reification.

Knowledge engineering design graphics, in eGanges, are ostensibly part of the expert system itself. This provides transparency. Navigable River maps with eGanges functionality, permit users to see the precise nature and extent of the expert knowledge, while at the same time seeing exactly how this knowledge is applied to a particular case. The construction and consultation interface is shown in Graphic 1.

2 Construction Task

In order to build a legal expert system using eGanges, a legal knowledge engineer must construct logic graphics in the form of rule or procedure maps in the River window and Questions in the Question window and answers on the Answer buttons. The builder may also detail glosses through the gloss menu or in the Note window. The Build button in the Options menu allows the user to develop: (1) nested tributaries of River rule/procedure maps, (2) questions

Pamela N. Gray and Xenogene Gray, 'A Map-Based Expert-Friendly Shell' in D. Bourcier (ed.), *Legal Knowledge and Information Systems. Jurix 2003: The Sixteenth Annual Conference*. Amsterdam: IOS Press, 2003, pp. 51-60.

and glosses that pertain to antecedents or procedural points on the rivers, (3) possible answers to the questions, and (4) notes that pertain to the questions.

In constructing an eGanges application, there must be adherence to the jurisprudential model of 3d legal logic. First, the final consequent of a field of rules must be specified. For instance, a final consequent of the rules of United Nations Convention on Contracts for the International Sale of Goods (known as the Vienna Convention) might be 'enforcement entitlement', as in the River window in Graphic 1. The main rule that establishes this final consequent may then be drawn.

Rules are represented in a map by a method of standardisation and then interlocking at identified points of overlap. Standardisation of rules requires the formalisation of each rule as a conditional proposition, i.e. as 'if (antecedent(s)) then (consequent)' statements. Following standardisation, where an antecedent in one rule is the same as the consequent in another rule, or more than one rule has the same consequent or antecedent, there is a point of overlap that identifies how the rules may be locked together. In Graphic 1, 'Net remedy' is both an antecedent in the main rule and the consequent of three secondary rules that particularise buyer and seller remedies respectively. These secondary rules are not mutually exclusive alternatives. Some alternatives are. Graphically, the locking together forms a tributary structure.

Rule maps use nodes to represent antecedents and consequents, or procedural points. The antecedent nodes in a rule are joined by lines that indicate a conjunction relationship between them. Where an antecedent or consequent in one rule is identical to an antecedent or consequent in another rule, one node is used to represent both, as a node where the rules intersect. Every node label must be unique. A good design will keep the label short.

The flow from antecedent(s) to consequent is represented by a directional arrow, as in a logical relationship or a flowchart, giving to the tributary structure, the attribute of a river. No matter how extensive and complex the tributary system, the direction of flow always aids its navigation. Where an antecedent in one rule is a consequent in a second rule, then the flow downstream in that second rule joins the flow downstream in the first rule. Similarly, procedural sequences may be standardised and locked together at overlapping points.

Where several rules share the same consequent, they form a fan of alternative ways of establishing the consequent, as a more complex confluence. The fan captures single or multiple disjunctions, with one or multiple Vs. There may be one or more antecedents in a fan river. If there is more than one, like non-fan rivers, they are connected by 'and' links.

When an antecedent in one rule is identical to the consequent in a second rule, then the second rule effectively defines the antecedent in the first rule. A tributary rule map is hierarchical. Prima facie, what is upstream defines what is downstream. However, this is not always in the sense of general concepts being downstream and particular concepts being upstream toward the watershed. Granularity of the antecedents may be irregular, so that one rule stream may contain general concepts in some of its antecedent nodes as well as particular concepts in some of its other antecedent nodes. The exercise of lawmaking power determines not only the antecedents and consequents of the rules but also the relationships between them, their definitions, and the spread of abstract and concrete terms in the rules.

However, the more upstreams there are for an antecedent, the more particularised is that area of expertise. A rule map may be developed as an hierarchical structure with a primary or main stream, from whose antecedents defining secondary streams may arise; any secondary rule flows into a mainstream antecedent. From the antecedents of such secondary streams, defining tertiary streams may arise, and so on up into the fine detail of the watershed of the system. In eGanges, colour-coding of the hierarchy aid navigation.

In common law, the rules run out at the far reaches of antecedents, the material facts. Beyond that, the facts of precedent cases are examples of how material facts are established.

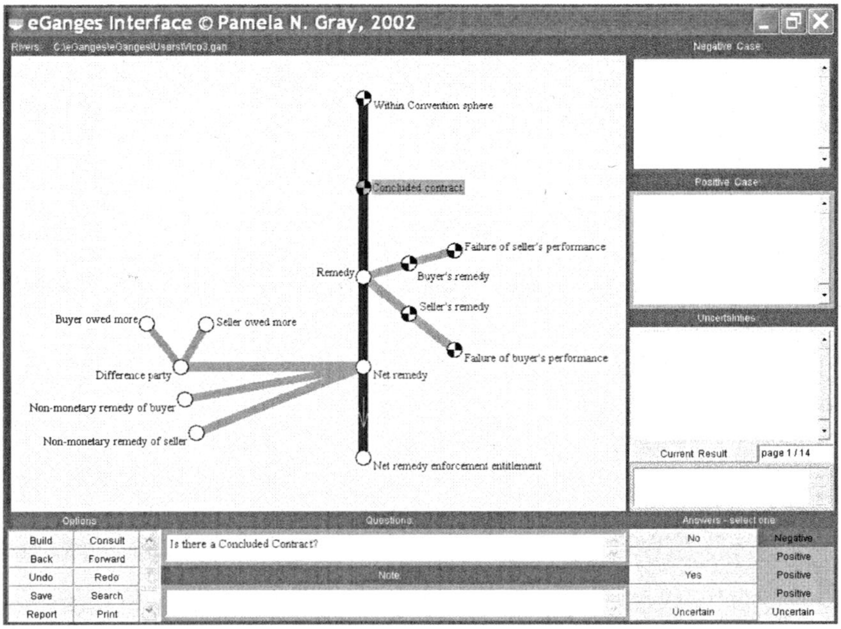

Figure 1:

Examples may be incorporated into the river system with an appropriate text gloss indicating that they are examples only in a fan or spectrum of possibilities. A fan of examples may include a fan to cover unspecified examples, for future specification.

The consequent of the main stream is the final consequent or result of the system. Just as backward and forward chaining indicate the direction of reasoning for a knowledge or decision tree, so a river system may be navigated upstream or downstream. However, rule logic or river procedure logic always flows downstream. All rules or procedural sequences flow directly or indirectly to the final result.

The rules could be represented as an and/or tree, but the river structure is a truer representation of interlocking rules; it also distinguishes the 'and' and the 'or' aspects of rule logic by different structures. The 'and' structure better facilitates labelling of nodes.

If a river system, such as the Vienna Convention, is too vast and complex for the whole of it to be viewed at once, then the solution is to nest the rivers. The Rivers window in Graphic 2 contains a rule map that represents streamlining of some of Part II of the Vienna Convention; it deals with the formation of a contract. This rule map in Graphic 2 is nested, like a sub-system, in the antecedent 'Concluded contract' in Graphic 1. Soccer ball nodes indicate a nested sub-map. In the nested map, an antecedent becomes a consequent. Nesting navigation may proceed as a two way system, through many levels of nesting, as a kind of metamorphosis, from an antecedent to its transformed state as a consequent, and back from consequent to antecedent. The deeper the nesting, the higher the streams.

Sometimes a field of expertise is a composite of many rules, and various strands have to be separated for the purposes of building an application. Any implied rules must also be expressly stated to complete the system of rules. Question/Answer processes apply the rules to a user's situation. Rule maps [1] provide a check list for ensuring all necessary and sufficient antecedents have been presented; they are a basis for identifying where there are alternative ways of establishing an antecedent or a consequent. They are also a basis for identifying antecedents that are in issue. Comprehensive extended legal arguments, and their sequence for linear presentation, may also be designed from the framework of rule maps.

3 Map Processing - Functionality

A system of adversarial heuristics applies to rule maps. These adversarial heuristics determine the processing of user input in relation to the Questions and Answers associated with the rule maps. In eGanges, the adversarial system is accessible through:

- 3d lists
- question and answer logic and
- current result.

3.1 3d Lists

In an adversarial field, there are two corresponding rivers that represent (1) the positive set of rules that supports the positive case, and (2) the negative set of rules that supports the negative case. This is adversarial correspondence. In a procedural domain, a positive procedure leads to a procedurally positive result and a negative procedure leads to a procedurally negative result.

A simple example of adversarial correspondence (as distinct from conventional logic) that applies in the legal domain, is: if a then b (jurisprudential positive) and if not-a then not-b (jurisprudential negative). Put simply, if there is an agreement then there is a valid contract and if there is no agreement then there is no valid contract. These are adversarial propositions that are both true law by virtue of the lawmaking authority that has pronounced them so, expressly or impliedly.

Legal experts and authorities may state a rule expressly in its adversarially positive or negative form. Whatever is stated expressly in its positive form can be restated in its corresponding negative form. In all the positive and negative rules, if there is more than one antecedent, then the antecedents are linked by ‘and’ connections. Procedural points are similarly linked by ‘and’, to indicate proceeding downstream.

However, some antecedents are neutral. This is represented by the simple example: if c then d and if not-c then d. Usually, neutral nodes are all positive; there is no corresponding adversarial negative rule. Neutral nodes can be represented as a set of single antecedent positive rules in a fan with a common positive consequent. For example, in contract law, an enquiry by the offeree as to the meaning of an offer, is a neutral antecedent. Whether or not such an inquiry has been made, or is uncertain to have been made, the parties are still on foot with the ultimate positive result that there is a valid contract. This is the reason why eGanges has five possible answer buttons: one negative, three positive and one uncertain.

A positive case only wins if all positive antecedents or procedural points in the positive river system are established. There may be inconclusive negative antecedents in a positive case as these may be matters of unnecessary fan alternatives. If there is a positive fan, then all of its streams must fail before the negative consequent arises. A positive rule with conjunctions has a corresponding negative fan of disjunctions. A negative rule with conjunctions has a corresponding positive fan of disjunctions.

Subject to the constraints of any fans that provide the positive case with alternatives, if any negative antecedent is established, then there is a partially negative but conclusive result. Thus, all the antecedent elements of a concluded contract must be present in a particular case to establish a concluded contract; if one or more of these antecedents is missing, a concluded contract can not be shown.

Every negative antecedent has two possible consequents Severally, the negative antecedents have a common partially negative but conclusive result that can be represented in a pole fan; jointly they have a wholly negative result. If all negative antecedents are established in a particular case, then there is a wholly negative final result. This is illustrated in Graphic 3. A set of negative rules is identified by its pole characteristic. If either the wholly or partially negative case is established, then the negative case wins. The strength of a negative case can be shown by the number of negative antecedents that have been established.

In practice, a user's case, may be hindered by uncertainties. Thus, to complete the model, there is a third set of rules that corresponds in structure to the positive and negative rivers, namely, the uncertain river system. Uncertain antecedents, like negative antecedents, also have two possible consequents, that can be represented in a river that corresponds with the positive river and in a pole fan, respectively. If all uncertain antecedents are established, then there is a wholly uncertain case. However, subject to fan alternatives, if any uncertain antecedent is established, then there is a partially uncertain case. It is possible to show the uncertainty strength in a case by the number of established uncertain antecedents.

In the legal domain, uncertainties are included in settlement advice that might resolve a conflict. For both the positive and negative cases, uncertainties are risks of losing. They are more likely to support the negative case, because the positive case usually carries the burden of proof. For the positive case to win in a civil court action, subject to any fan constraints, every uncertainty must be proved to be positive on the balance of probabilities. In a criminal case, usually the prosecution must prove that every uncertain antecedent is, beyond a reasonable doubt, actually a positive antecedent. As long as the party with the negative case can keep an antecedent uncertain when the standard of proof is applied, the uncertainty will prevent the positive case from winning, even though no negative antecedent has been established. The party with the negative case wins by virtue of the uncertainties that are not found to be positives.

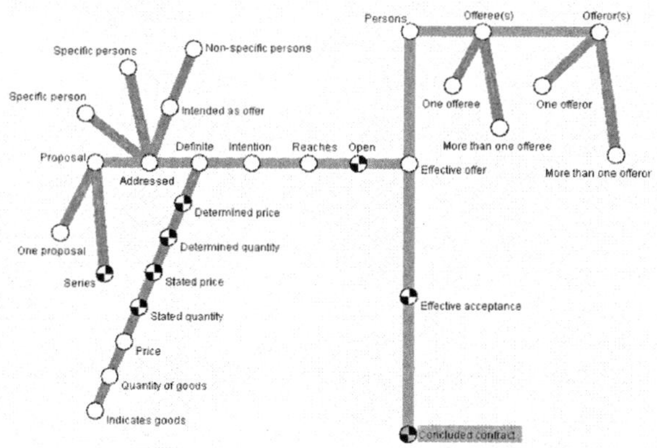

Figure 2:

As illustrated in Graphic 3, notional three dimensional space is required for the symbolic sphere that contains the full adversarial structure of rules. Triad links are used to show the corresponding negative, positive and uncertain antecedents in the negative, positive and uncertain tributary structures; the spectral connection or continuum of the three antecedents is also represented by the triad link. For example, the negative sector of a triad may have 'no offer', the positive sector may have 'offer' and the uncertain sector may have 'quasi-offer'.

The notional north pole represents a partially negative but conclusive result and the notional south pole represents a partially uncertain result. Pole streams connect negative antecedents to their common consequent or negative pole result, and uncertain antecedents to their common consequent, the uncertain pole result. Typically, pole rules have only one antecedent which is also an antecedent in the tributary structure that has a wholly negative or wholly uncertain final result.

In Graphic 3, two presuppositions of the system of rules, are connected by a boundary ring: (1) there is an initial triad, consisting of three alternative antecedents, that is the start of the system and (2) there are five possible end results in the sphere of rules, namely:

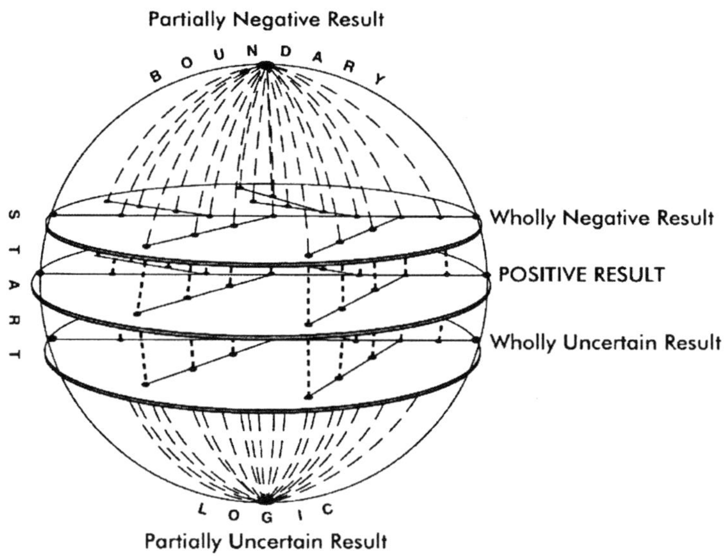

Figure 3: Sphere of river logic

The sphere of rivers confines the combinatorial explosion of possible cases. The positive river system is placed in the central position, as it has no pole streams. It may be larger than the negative and uncertain river systems if it has neutral antecedents.

In eGanges, three dimensional graphics are not used; they are thought to be too complicated for navigation. Instead, there are three windows: Negative case window, Positive case window and Uncertainties window, each of which will list appropriately antecedents that are established in a user's case. A two dimensional rule map in the eGanges Rivers window indicates the paths for establishing a final outcome of a user's case; the river to be constructed by the builder of an eGanges application, is effectively the positive river. However this two dimensional river map works *in tandem* with the Case and Uncertainties lists to implement the full system of adversarial rules.

3.2 *Question and Answer Logic*

In a consultation, a left click of the mouse on an antecedent node in the Rivers window produces, in the question window, a question that can be answered by the user. The eGanges design distinguishes factual negation from adversarial negative. The answer buttons are aligned to show which factual answer will support which adversarial case: positive, negative, or uncertain. After the user selects an answer, by a left click on the requisite answer button, the antecedent label is listed appropriately, in the Negative Case window, the Positive Case window or the Uncertainties window. These lists indicate the second premises in an extended set of *modus ponens* arguments, where the first premise is the relevant rule.

Once antecedents are established for the user's case, interim and final conclusions, by way of deduction, are available as the current result. At any time during a consultation, the user can see how many points there are, if any, for each adversary or side, and how many uncertainties there are.

Usually, there will be three alternative answers, each positioned appropriately by the application builder, on the negative, positive, and uncertain buttons: yes, no and uncertain. In accordance with the rules of law, sometimes a yes answer will support the positive case, and sometimes it will support the negative case. Likewise, a no answer may sometimes be adversarially positive or negative. To avoid an uncertain answer, the Note window, may have an advice from the builder to answer further questions upstream to clarify the situation; otherwise an uncertain answer produces a node label in the uncertainties list. If a node is neutral, all three alternative answers, yes, no and uncertain, will support the positive case and will appear on the three positive answer buttons.

The order in which antecedents are placed in a rule is sometimes determined by the sense required for questions. A temporal sequence may be required. For instance, an offer comes before its acceptance. A question, "Has the offer been accepted?", presupposes that there has been a question answered positively: "Was an offer made?" If a negative answer has been given to the effect that no offer has been made, so that the current result is immediately a conclusive negative, then, from this time on, questions will assume that no negative antecedent has been established. Further questions may assume that there is an offer even though input has established otherwise. A user may wish to proceed in this way in order to ascertain how strong the negative or uncertain case is.

The label on an antecedent node in the Rivers window is the label that appears in a list following the selection of an answer. The labels are appropriate to the positive case. For example, in a contract application, the label 'Offer' in the negative list, means that there is no offer; in the positive list it means that there is an offer.

For a contract node label, 'No rejection', meaning no rejection of an offer, a direct question will take the negative perspective: Has the offer been rejected? The negative answer is yes and if this answer is given, then the label 'No rejection' will appear in the Negative case window. However, this means that there is a double negative: there is not no rejection, meaning there is rejection. When the user requests a Report on the consultation, then the Report will print beside the label 'No rejection', the question that was asked and the answer that was given.

A user may change an answer that has been given, by selecting the node label from the positive, negative or uncertainties lists. A left mouse click on the requisite node, produces in the Rivers window the rule map that contains that node, and the node question in the Question window with the alternative answers to it on the answer buttons. The selection acts as a back button, so that the lists are also navigation aids that permit the user to reconsider or change an answer. A different answer may then be selected and the list windows will be adjusted accordingly. To move an antecedent from one case window to another, the answer must be changed appropriately.

3.3 Current Result

The Current result button permits the user to obtain confirmation of the current result during the consultation of an application, as follows:

1. If there is a negative antecedent in the Negative case window, then the current result is negative.
2. If there is an uncertain antecedent in the Uncertainties window, and no negative antecedent in the Negative case window, then the current result is uncertain.
3. Until all the necessary and sufficient positive antecedents are established for the positive result, a current result can not be positive. However, the current result may be tenuously positive, with the interim result of 'unanswered'.

If the user does not use the current result button, then the current result is available by understanding the significance of the Case and Uncertainties entries. Negative antecedents or points in the Negative case list produce a conclusive result that overrides uncertainty. Inconclusive fan negatives and uncertainties remain in the Positive Case window until there is a sufficient accumulation of them to activate a pole rule. Then they shift to the appropriate Negative Case or Uncertainties window.

4 Glosses

Glosses or commentary may be added by the builder in two ways: (1) as strata logic or (2) as question notes

A right click of the mouse on an antecedent or procedural node in a river map will permit the user to build or consult glosses associated with that node. Questions may also be glossed through the Note window.

4.1 Strata logic

It is possible to build three types of expert system: (1) rule or procedure systems which apply only rules and/or procedures, (2) expanded rule and/or procedure systems that include inferences from the rules or procedures, (3) critical expanded rule and/or procedure systems that include inferences from the rules or procedures, and further critical information about the rules and/or procedures and/or any inferences from them. In any of these systems, various commentary may be relevant as strata logic. eGanges gloss facilities allow the builder to add strata of commentary about an antecedent node. Available gloss types are:

Text: this information might contain the natural language definition of the selected node's label, the natural language statement of the rule or procedure in which the node is located, and authorities for the definitions and rule statement. Inconsistencies, alternative definitions and statements, critical comment, or reform views, might be included.

Spectrum: the spectral continuum of negative-positive-uncertain triads may set out information about the content of each sector. A triad spectrum may range from negative to positive to uncertain, to reflect the adversarial structure, or it may range from positive to uncertain to negative, to reflect a gradation of quantity or quality. Gradation may clarify adversarial sectors and the location of gaps in the law. For instance a rule that provides for a minimum quantity, such as one peppercorn places 1-n peppercorns in the positive sector, zero peppercorns in the negative sector and anything between zero and 1 in the uncertain sector. Continuity of a spectrum may be the basis for legal argument.

Inter-node links: sometimes there is a relationship between triads that are on different rivers in the same river system. For instance, in law, the triads of misrepresentation and mistake could be glossed and linked as a double spectrum so that fine distinctions between sectors can be clarified.

Parallel river links: there may be rearrangements of river systems to suit different perspectives or purposes of users. For instance, rivers of contractual strategy may be created from the rules of contract law. A gloss link may be created to permit a consideration of other reconstrued or relevant river systems as a parallel logic.

File links: a gloss link to another file or program may be created. For instance, in tax law, mathematical calculations may be required; at the relevant node, a link to a calculation program might be provided.

Thus related information may be included in an application at a precise point of relevance. The uncertain sector of a spectrum gloss may show possibilities discussed in obiter dicta, or as a matter of speculation based on meaning, common knowledge, empirical observation or hypothesis. Extended legal arguments may have elements of gloss arguments about what the rules mean, why they are rules or what the rules ought to be. Gloss content may be interwoven into the presentation of arguments. Thus gloss information is available for understanding the law, appreciating the nature of a question and its possible answers, and formulating heterostatic argument for judicial or political development of the rule system.

4.2 Question Notes

The Note window may be used in two ways: (1) it may provide output such as advice about questions or the best order for answers, or (2) it allows users to enter data, such as evidence detailing proof of an antecedent.

5 Consult

The Consult button enables the user to consult an application by (1) navigating the nested River tributaries, (2) accessing the glosses, questions and notes, (3) providing input by selecting from the available answers and receiving feedback, following the input, in the Negative Case, Positive Case, Uncertainties and Current Result windows and (4) providing input in the Note window for the purpose of recording the user's evidence or other information for the consultation report. A Report of the consultation lists the antecedent labels that have been recorded in the positive, negative and uncertainties windows together with their questions, the user's answers, Note advice, Note data input, unanswered nodes, and current result. A person consulting an application may be precluded from accessing the build menu, while a builder may be precluded from accessing a particular consultation.

6 Conclusion

The shell is suitable for short or protracted sessions of application construction, maintenance or consultation; applications may be useful pro tem. eGanges satisfies the design criteria recommended by Meister [5]: its interface is simple, easy to learn and concrete. Yet the ostensible simplicity of eGanges, can capture the three dimensionality of extensive and complex rule-oriented and procedure-oriented expertise. The preparation of a nested map presupposes a science of legal choice.

References

[1] Gray, P.N., 'Explanatory Rule Maps', *Computers and Law Journal for the Australian and New Zealand Societies for Computers and the Law* No.50, pp.11-13, December 2002.

[2] Gray, P.N., *Artificial Legal Intelligence*, Dartmouth Publishing Co., Aldershot, England, 1997.

[3] Gray, P.N., 'Scaling Up To A Three Dimensional Graphic Trace' in Ciampi, C., Socci Natali, F. and Taddei Elmi, G. (eds), *Verso Un Sistema Esperto Giuridico Integrale*, Cedam, Padua, Italy, 1995.

[4] Gray, P.N., *Choice and Jurisprudential Systems*, University of Sydney LL.M. thesis, 1990.

[5] Meister, D., *Psychology of System Design*, Elsevier, Amsterdam, 1991.

CATMInE Computer Assisted Trade-Mark Infringement Evaluation

Pierre Renaux
GREYC - UMR 6072
Université de Caen
Caen, France

Abstract. In forensic Machine Learning, information systems are not easy to use due to many constraints. Knowledge generally comes from laws and their use is represented by decisions. The whole data requires several parses in order to obtain a structured database on which decision tools can be applied. This study presents the use of machine learning tools to assist the lawyer in nominative trade-mark infringement evaluation. The domain formalism and database are obtained from the JURINPI database which regroups thousands of cases in the trade-mark domain. The use of a neural network and of Sammon's non-linear mapping provides a development of datas with designed decision tools for trade-mark infringement evaluation : CATMInE (Computer Assisted Trade-Mark Infringement Evaluation). This web-oriented application requires little technical knowledge on machine learning and displays a readable and concise information.

1 Introduction

context : This paper suggests a system dedicated to problem resolution on some machine learning concepts. Trade-Marks represent the company in consumer's mind and thus have important economical issues. There are many registrations and checking for their validity becomes difficult. This work is done by legal advisors for trade-marks owners in order to make the most of their trade-marks portfolio.

motivation : This working context, less studied, represents an important task for lawyers and data is still increasing. Working with it is not complete as it could be for other application areas as business or medicine [2].

The central claim for this research activity is to provide machine learning tools for legal advisors, where behaviour isn't built on imitate human decision making, as expert systems, but rely on case based learning. As far as, applying these tools mustn't imply knowledge on the used machine learning algorithms .

contribution : CATMInE answers to the presented motivations by offering a decision process for nominative trade-mark infringement. This system uses a database and tools where maintenance can be done without the help of the machine learning expert. The whole system is also designed as knowledge repository and provides users an Internet access to the system.

organisation : First, this study presents the nominative trade-mark infringement database and the features extracted to exploit it. Next, pre-hypothesis and their results for knowledge representation in CATMInE are presented.

Pierre Renaux, 'CATMInE - Computer Assisted Trade-Mark Infringement Evaluation' in D. Bourcier (ed.), *Legal Knowledge and Information Systems. Jurix 2003: The Sixteenth Annual Conference*. Amsterdam: IOS Press, 2003, pp. 61-70.

Table 1: Types, tags, and available information used for trade-mark infringement storing.

Information	tags	expressions
Reference	<REF>	*M19950787* or a date *M* = Marque *1995* = year *0787* = order in the year
Jurisdiction	<DOC>	level *place (Court)*, date
Decision's date	<DAT>	*Year-Month-Day*
Parts	<PART>	*Plaintif1; ...; Plaintif n/Dfence1;...*
Trade-Marks	<MARQ>	*Trade-Mark1; Trade-Mark2*
Analyse	<ABS>	*Infringement (YES)*
registration numbers	<OBJ>	*1546621;910560*
Products and services	<CL>	*CL01, CL02* *CL01 CL25*
Referenced judgement if it is needed	<LIEN>	*level place (Court), date* or a reference : *M19950787*
Complete decision	<TXT>	*About decision...*

The third section gives an overview of CATMInE and its functionalities developed to assists the lawyer during a trade-mark infringement search or study. Finally we present the experimentations and a brief discussion on the system's evolution.

2 Application Area

The domain for this research activity is the french trade-mark infringement case-law. It is taken from the online database JURINPI which offers two major interests. First, it is a real database (as opposed to an artificially created one) and second it is partially represented within an XML structure.

2.1 The Trade-mark Infringement Evaluation Task

The trade-mark domain is growing up. For a company, its trade-marks reflect its identity to consumers, for targeted products and services. Having an opponent that uses a similar trade-mark for the same products or services becomes a commercial constraint. The deformed trade-mark could confuse a standard consumer, and the society would loose market activities.

To protect their rights, societies ask for intellectual and industrial property law protection in order to increase the value of their trade-marks portfolio. In case of a trade-mark infringement, the resolution can be done by a court. The taken decision is then inserted into JURINPI.

The JURINPI database represents a part of this case-law[1] and offers an access for consulting, from the Internet, to a legal advisor, for a consideration.

2.2 JURINPI : Database u

The JURINPI database is built on a XML structure to represent decisions. A decision can be seen as a form. The XML structure is composed of 19 tags. Only 10 tags are used for nominative trade-mark infringement. The remaining tags are designed to comply with patent case-law and database indexation. Table 1 describes tags and available information used to represent the nominative trade-mark case-law.

[1] it represents french patent cases law too

In this structure, many elements are difficult to extract. First, in the case analysis, the verdict is not the only information expressed. The information consists of case summaries. Moreover, in nominative trade-mark infringement, two types of verdict are possible : reproduction (total or partial) and counterfeit. The first deals with infringement seizure. The second case corresponds to our targeted research domain. Finding the verdict implies complex mechanisms in order to be extracted.

On the same principle, the "Owner/Trade-Mark", "Trade-Mark/Product and Services", or "Trade-Mark/Registration Number" associations are not easy to establish : enumeration order in the XML structure is not respected for all the tags. The only way to do it is to analyse each case completely in order to validate or to correct the computed associations.

3 Domain Hypothesis

Completing this research activity on the JURINPI database implies the extraction of relevant information to establish a computational structure. The aim is to define linguistic features in order to apply machine learning tools on it.

To establish if a trade-mark imitates another, it is necessary to compare them on their whole aspect in order to find if a risk of infringement exists between them. As the domain is the nominative trade-mark, it is possible to consider a trade-mark as words. So comparing them is exactly as finding common properties on words.

To define a case law, we calculate similarities on the way trade-marks are written, the graphemic aspect, and the way trade-marks are pronounced, the phonemic aspect. These similarities came from an expert know-how and, are calculated, in way of characters, between two trade-marks in the graphemic and in the phonemic representation. So we can establish comparison points on character similarity, phoneme similarity, graphemic string, phonemic string and co-positioning strings for graphemic and phonemic aspect. All these elements came from a large study of case-law, and, from elements used by court to apply laws. These values are next stored in a linguistic similarity vector (one per pair of trade-marks) for future treatments.

For example, if we study the pair of trade-marks (GOLF PLUS, GOLF'US)[2] for graphemic level, we can observe :

- GOLF PLUS is composed of all the characters from GOLF'US, GOLF'US contains 6 characters from the 9 of GOLF PLUS
- GOLF is the longest string common to the two trade-marks
- GOLF is the opening word of the both trade-marks

At the phonetic level, parsing is identical, but applied on the phonemic transcription of the trade-marks pair. This transcription is obtained by using a contextual rules translator. Using a phonemic lexica to translate trade-marks is not possible. Trade-marks are commonly neologisms (a neologism is never present in a lexica). So using a rule based translator is more efficient : easy maintenance, neologism representation and acronyms pronunciation integration are possible.

Another aspect of this research area deals with the different court levels. Applied to french courts, the first court level, Tribunal de Grande Instance is less important than the Cours

[2]Golf House (ste, Italie) versus P. Schmidlin, imitation infringement, Tribunal de Grande Instance, Paris (Ch.03), 01/09/1999

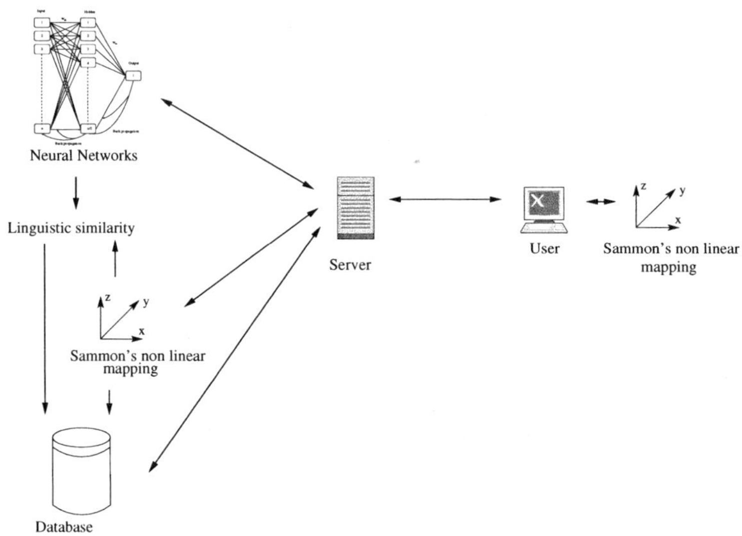

Figure 1: CATMInE's dependencies diagram

d'Appel, which is also less important than the Cours de Cassation. By this relation between levels, the more important the hierarchy, the more the decisions weigh over lower court

This hierarchy justifies the modelling necessity of nominative trade-marks infringements, using case-law. The infringement risk evaluation, needed to prevent law suite between trade-marks, is obtained on a case based learning process, put into practice by a neural network [7]. With the previous definition, having an expert system for this evaluation does not comply with the court's level principle.

4 Computer Assisted Trade-Mark Infringement Evaluation

4.1 Overview

CATMInE software was developed by myself during a Research and Development project between our industrial partner Breese & Majerowicz and the University of Caen by the way of Thomas Lebarbé. It uses the two hypothesis presented before, and can work on any case-based legal system, as the United Kingdom one, just by changing the contextual rules translator and case-base (it also implies a learning process on this case-base). It can be used by the way of a web server application. The designed software is presented in diagram 1, p.64

4.2 First use of CATMInE : Evaluating a Risk of Infringement

Evaluating a risk of infringement between two nominative trade-marks is obtained by computing the linguistic features from the pair of trade marks given in input (see 3). This evaluation depends on graphemic and phonemic similarities. It also depends on the studied country. The phonemic translation and learning database are adapted to the targeted country. Results are then stored in a linguistic similarity vector, one per country.

When features have been computed, it is possible to compare the input case to the whole case-base with the neural network, which has been previously tuned. Result is expressed by

Figure 2: Screen shot of infringement risks evaluation between Velux and Faelux for the french jurisdiction

a score varying from 0 to 100 (near 100, high risk; near 0, low risk). Figure 2, presents this kind of infringement evaluation for the pair of trade-marks (Velux,Faelux)[3].

Moreover, with the linguistic similarity vector, the system is able to display the input case among the whole. This representation is obtained with three proximity case-law mappings. These graphics are drawn using the Sammon's non linear mapping algorithm ([1], [3]) which allows to project a set of points (one per decision) from an n dimensional space to an m one, where $m < n$ and spatial distances are preserved as much as possible. With this algorithm, the software can produce a map of the case-base where the user can observe the surrounding cases in order to study on which grounds the decision has been taken for nearby cases. Observation can also be done on a selected court level or city. Figure 3, page 66 shows the phono-graphemic[4] map (there is one for each graphemic and phonemic aspects) on the french case base. Red cross represent cases where infringement evaluation concludes to yes, blue ones correspond to a negative decision.

By gathering the surrounding cases on the mapping, CATMInE produces a summary of the comparisons by finding the five most similar decision for each mapping. From this list, the lawyer can obtain the text of decision in order to study on which grounds the decisions were taken in order to target his study as best as possible.

---

[3] V KANN RASMUSSEN INDUSTRI A/S (Ste, Danemark) and VELUX FRANCE (SA) versus S.N.C. FAELUX DI FANTINI SERGIO EC (Ste, Italie), Cours d'Appel, PARIS (CH.04), 25/02/2002

[4] combined graphemic and phonemic features

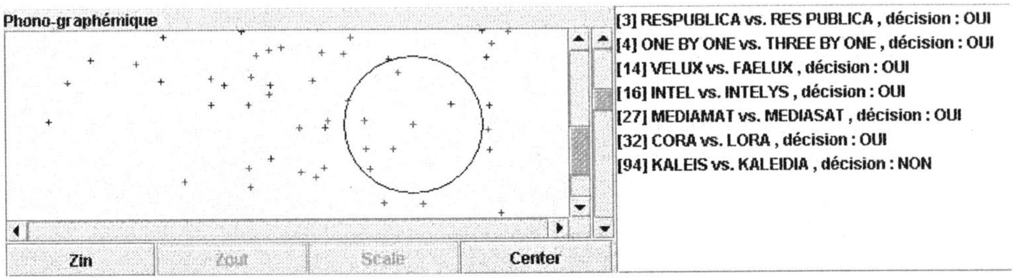

Figure 3: Phono-graphemic map for the (Velux/Faelux) infringement evaluation on the french jurisdiction

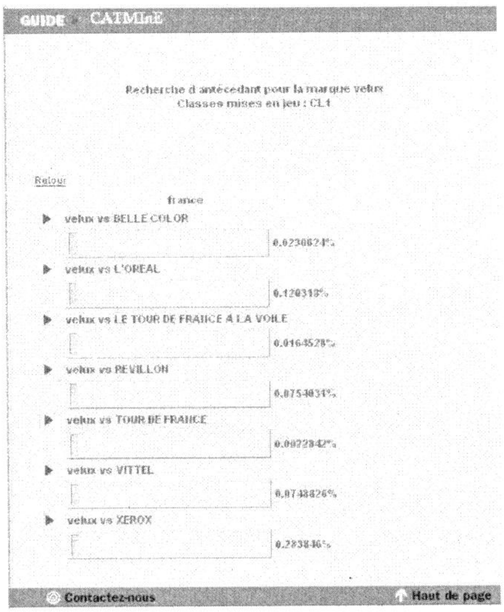

Figure 4: List of antecedents extracted by similarity from the french case base for the trade-mark Velux on the First class of products and services.

4.3 Second use of CATMInE : Sorting a List of Antecedents

Finding a list of antecedents aims to find out if a new trade-mark generates a strong infringement risk with existing ones, for the same or similar targeted products and services. This search usually represents long investigations but is simplified by the use of the CATMInE's database.

By querying the database, it is possible to obtain the whole list of trade-marks for the targeted products and services.

The linguistic similarity vector is computed for each trade-marks pair (composed of the new trade-mark and one from the query) and their infringement risk evaluated by the neural network (this is the same method as the one used for comparing trade-marks). Results of this action is the list of all the trade-marks (sort by name), for the targeted products and services, and their potential infringement risk with the trade-mark given in input.Figure 4, page 66 presents results for a kind of search.

4.4 Third use of CATMInE : Doctrinal use

An interesting point, in this way of using CATMInE, is the evaluation of a recent decision. The neural network tells the degree of similarity with case-law. This provides new tools for the lawyer to study and explain the decision with the mapping.

The second point is to study, globally, the case base evolution through time. If the system is regularly updated with new decisions, it becomes possible to have a look on decisions given by a court. It is also feasible to study jurisdiction's sudden changes : finding forewarning elements in order to anticipate them by observing the Sammon non linear mapping.

5 Discussion

CATMInE corresponds to new tools in the domain of Artificial Intelligence applied to Law. From this research in the domain of computer assisted decision process, some problems emerged and are presented here.

The first problem is of a semantic order. The aim is to use in the decision making the semantic similarity between trade-marks. For example, if we study the trade-marks pair "new man" and "new boy", the surface linguistic similarity wouldn't argue to infringement. But in this case there is infringement due to semantic similarity between "man" and "boy". A way to solve this problem could be a user specification during the input of the case.

A second problem is the automatic language detection. For registering a new trade-mark, it is possible that the rules for translating the trade-mark into its phonemic equivalent are not adapted. To illustrate, it is possible to register an english trade-mark in France (and in the same way a french trade-mark in England). The system will use the french's transcription rules to produce the phonemic representation. So, this transcription might be false : the final 's', for example, wouldn't be transcripted and may change the phonemic similarity with the other trade-marks. This constraint implies that the legal advisor defines which rules the system should apply for each word of the trade-mark.

The third problem is based on the length of the compared trade-marks. If one is bigger than the other, the system should integrate features in order to reveal it during the learning process.

Last, the fourth problem refers to the neural network which could be replaced by another decision process in order to explain the elements which conclude to an infringement and trace the decision process. This point refers to my research activities and is briefly presented in the next section.

6 Evolution

The previous section highlights that a neural network could not explain its decision. The hypothesis was to replace it by another decision process as decision tree.

C4.5rules[6] was the first tested algorithm, with defaults parameters. Its results were not good enough. It generally produces 1 rule and a default one, for sometimes the same targeted decision. Its average error rate is around 35%. Experiments show that c4.5 usually use the default rules to classify a new example. In this way, decision explanation is not powerful.

The next section presents a part of my research activity : quality measures applied to decision tree in an further version of CATMInE, named DETMInE.

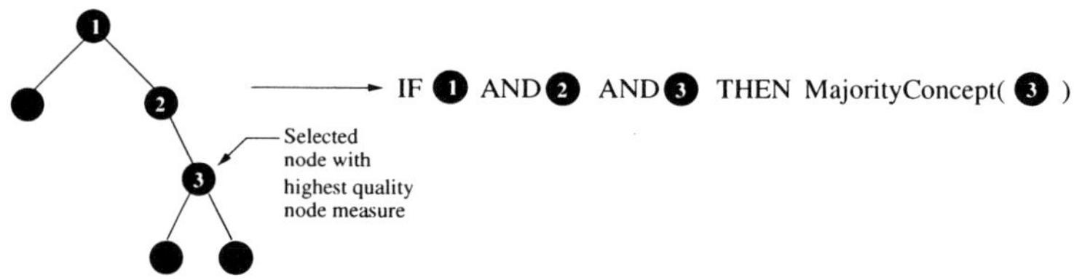

Figure 5: rule construction.

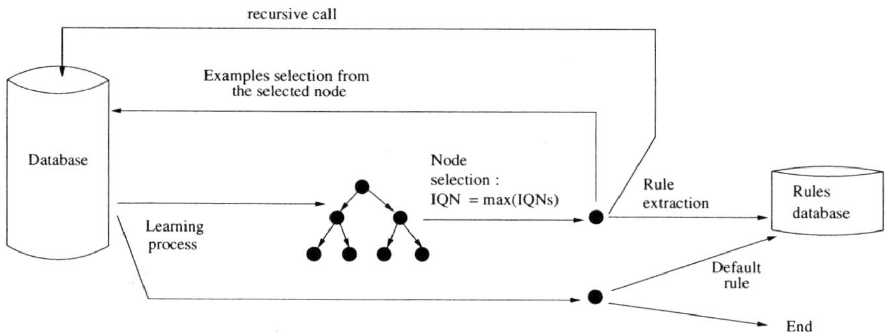

Figure 6: Recursive algorithm for rules selection.

6.1 Decision Tree for Trade Mark Infringement Evaluation

The working hypothesis was to classify majority examples with simple rules and complex examples with complex rules. So, by using a quality node measure on decision tree[5], the hypothesis can be developed. This quality node measure depends on three parameters :

1. the weigh of the node in the tree (number of associated examples to the node)
2. an impurity measure normalised between 0 and 1
3. a damping function which depends on the depth of the node in the tree

First, the decision process builds a decision tree form the learning database. Next it searches the node which presents the highest quality node measure. A rule is then produced from the selected node as presented in the diagram 5, p.68. The associated examples are deleted from the learning database and the highest court's level is extracted from the deleted examples. The court's level is then associated to the rule as an extended information.

Last, the algorithm rebuilds a new decision tree from the rest of the learning database and extract other rules in the same way, until the decision tree is reduced to a root node. This root node will then represent a default case to apply if no rule is available.

This algorithm is summarised in the diagram 6, p.68.

When a new example is studied, the court level will be used in case of conflicts between rules : if two rules are available for this new example, the algorithm selects the rule which presents the highest court's level. If available rules have the same level, the selection is then made on their highest level's population.

Table 2: Ten-fold Cross Validation's error rates.

Experiments	Neural Network Accuracy	DeTTMInE Accuracy
Experience 1	60%	60%
Experience 2	80%	70%
Experience 3	90%	80%
Experience 4	70%	70%
Experience 5	70%	70%
Experience 6	70%	80%
Experience 7	80%	60%
Experience 8	70%	70%
Experience 9	70%	60%
Experience 10	60 %	70%
Average	72%	69%

6.2 Experimentation

The goal of these experiments is to compare the neural network accuracy to the DeTTMInE's one. Their accuracy is estimated using a ten-fold cross validation([4]). Accuracy of the learned classifiers are summarised in the table 2. In the overall, the neural network seems to be slightly better than the decision tree algorithm for only 3%. But the induced rules, by the new algorithm, offer explanations to lawyer in many ways. First it can produce all the examples that satisfy this rule (examples extracted during the learning process). Those examples can be used by the lawyer for a better understanding of the studied example. It can also show a rule, and so features that are relevant for the suggested decision.

Another important result is related to the number of produced rules and their use. In opposition to c4.5, DeTTMInE produces around twenty rules and uses around fifteen of them. So, explanation of new examples is not justified with a default rule, but by a set of rules that satisfy the objectives of explanation and information needed by CATMInE for the decision making.

7 Conclusion

The presented system, CATMInE, uses machine learning algorithms to provide support for trade-mark infringement evaluation. First a neural network for a quick infringement evaluation between two trade-marks, and next a N-dimensional case based mapping for observing the surrounding cases and trace the decision process. The evolution on the decision process offers the ability to explain a comparison or antecedent search without changing the application and represents a starting point for further research.

The guidelines for this work allows a legal advisor to study infringement risk between trade-marks without machine learning expert. The effectiveness of the comparison/visualisation system was tested and validated onto two case-bases : a french one and an english one.

CATMInE was designed for our industrial partner Breese & Majerowicz. Available on the Internet, it allows a knowledge repository for available country. The multi-lingual aspect supports infringement evaluation on any available country, European community and maybe more.

Professionals who use CATMInE, show the interest to have simple and explanatory tools at their's disposal, able to assist them daily and was demonstrated in May 2003 at the International Trade-Mark Association annual meeting (INTA'03).

References

[1] J.W. Sammon, A nonlinear mapping for data structure analysis, IEEE Transactions on Computers, vol. 18, pp 401-409, 1969

[2] S. Ivkovic, J. Yearwood and A. Stranieri, Visualizing Association Rules for feedback within the legal system, ICAIL03 proceeding, pp 214-223, 2003

[3] Biswas G., Jain A.K., and Dubes R.C., Evaluation of projection algorithms, IEEE Transactions on Pattern Analysis and Machine Intelligence, vol. 3, pp 701-708, 1981

[4] Petrak J., Fast Subsampling Performance Estimates for Classification Algorithm Selection, ECML, Workshop, 2002

[5] Fournier D., Thèse, Etude de la qualité de données à partir de l'apprentissage automatique. Application aux arbres d'induction, Université de Caen - Campus II, 2001

[6] Quinlan J. R., C4.5: programs for machine learning, isbn : 1-55860-238-0, publisher : Morgan Kaufmann Publishers Inc., 1993

[7] McCulloch W.S. and Pitts W.H., A logical calculus of the ideas immanent in nervous activity, Bulletin of Mathematical Biophysics, vol. 5, pp115-133, 1943

GoldminePower: Decisions in Governmental Process Design

Evert van Heel* Tom M. van Engers†
*postbus@e-vanheel.demon.nl
†Leibniz Center for Law,
Faculty of Law, Universiteit van Amsterdam
Amsterdam, The Netherlands
vanengers@lri.jur.uva.nl

Abstract. The success of governmental policy depends much on the success of governmental services. Governmental services in its turn depend much on governmental processes. Governmental processes therefore are a determining factor for the success and especially the justification of governmental behaviour. Process design is an important means of realising good en well-performing governmental processes. Governments raise specific demands and wishes in the field of process design, such as transparency and justification of policy. The process design method applied should consequently reflect these important aspects of governmental process design.

A reasonable assumption is that quality of (governmental) processes is related to the degree in which the involved process design decisions have been made explicit, and the degree in which the explicit decisions have been accounted for. In this paper we introduce a proposition for a new governmental process design approach called GoldminePower. This approach has the specific governmental requirements (the process's legal bases and the need for transparency and justification) as starting point. A strong focus will be put on explicit design decisions during governmental process design. The application of this method is not limited to public administration. Non-governmental organisations could also benefit from more transparent and justifiable process design.

1 Governmental Issues[1]

In this section we would first like to stress the importance of processes for governments. We do this by showing almost all governmental problems are process-related. The importance of processes for governments implies the importance of process design. That is why in the second sub-section we consider demands and wishes governments could and should have in the field of process design.

1.1 Process Related Governmental Problems

Most well-known problems with governmental policy tend to be process related. This becomes clear when studying a recent Dutch manifest of the committee "Belgen doen het beter [1]" ("Belgians perform better") in which the success of Dutch governmental policy is compared to the policy of other European states. In table 1 an overview of Dutch governmental problems from this manifest is given.

[1] ≪Johnny's in the basement / Mixing up the medicine / I'm on the pavement / Thinking about the government . . . ≫ (Bob Dylan – Subterranean homesick blues)

Evert van Heel and Tom M. van Engers, 'GoldminePower: Decisions in Governmental Process Design' in D. Bourcier (ed.), *Legal Knowledge and Information Systems. Jurix 2003: The Sixteenth Annual Conference*. Amsterdam: IOS Press, 2003, pp. 71-80.

Table 1: Some Dutch governmental problems

NR	Problem Kind	Problem	Description / Background	Possible process aspects
1	Budgeting	Huge costs of Dutch social security	The social security institute "Uitvoeringsorgaan WerknemersVerzekeringen"(UWV) is very expensive. This institute is the consequence of a merger between a large number of similar institutes for unemployment and illness insurance. The services of the UWV are carried out in processes that stem from those former institutes and that mainly have been kept unchanged.	Not integrating and (poor) maintaining redundant processes looks to be the cause. BPR necessary
2	Planning	Waiting lists in health care	The waiting lists in the Dutch health care institutes are notorious. There are many supposed causes amongst which lack of data exchange between institutes.	Unclear and inconsistent policy and unclear responsibilities of the different parties that are involved in the underlying services / processes might be a cause. BPR necessary
3	Quality	Citizens safety	The solve percentage of crimes in Holland is low. This is stated to be the main cause why a huge percentage of the Dutch citizens don't feel safe. One of the causes is said to be the lack of data exchange between police departments.	Crime resolving processes need to be improved BPR necessary
4	Quality	Errors in health care	Research has shown that on a yearly base about 90.000 hospital intakes are due to avoidable medication errors. These errors could have been avoided if the doctors had access to all of the patients' medical data	Processes need to be improved BPR necessary
5	Quality	Food safety	Holland lately has suffered a lot of food crises like the BSE-crisis the Pigs-plague, the Foot-And-Mouth-crisis and the Birds-plague. There is a need for more transparency in the food chain processes here.	Different services / processes have different goals and don't work together very well BPR necessary
6	Quality	Dealing with terror	Data exchange between for instance the Dutch intelligence service and the police departments is no good.	Terror preventing and resolving processes need to be improved BPR necessary

This list is far from complete and could easily be extended with other Dutch and non-Dutch governmental problems. In most cases it will be easy to link those other governmental problems to process shortcomings as well. So maybe the best way for governments to improve their governing is improving their governmental processes.

1.2 Governmental Demands and Wishes in the Field of Process Design

In the previous sub-section we showed governments have a lot to gain by good process design. This can lead to well-performing processes and solved governmental problems.

Now we will consider the demands and wishes governments should have in the field of process design. In section 2 we'll unfold a design method that satisfies these demands and wishes. As governmental demands we consider requirements that stem from legislation or that are for other reasons specific for governments, wishes stem from other sources like good management. In table 2 our list is displayed.

2 GoldminePower Method

The central idea in this paper is to address the issues from section 1 with a method that combines two promising methods from literature. Both methods "Goldmine"[[2][2]] and "Power"[[3][3]] make the same kind of claims: "Better, cheaper and faster" than common practice. We observe that current process modelling approaches are focussed on business process redesign issues and optimization of existing processes rather than establishing a transparent representation of the temporal aspects that are essential to law enforcement and other forms of legal

Table 2: List of governmental requirements for process design

Requirement	Description
Legal base and justification	For all governmental actions (this includes every step in a governmental process) there must be a legal base, so that they can be justified.
Transparency	There are no specific juridical reasons to strive after transparency (governments must be able to justify a specific case, but then it is sufficient to refer to the involved legislation). But although governments in general don't have to justify process design decisions and the working of its processes, good reasons exist for governments to indeed strive after transparency. The first reason is that the governmental processes can be justified to politics, which will create support for the government's policy. The second reason is that case-justification can be faster, cheaper and easier done, since any process step in a transparent process knows its origins in legislation
Effectiveness	"Obtaining as much as possible effect with as little as possible effort" It is good management to strive after effectiveness. Just like businesses governments have limited budgets. In process design achieving more effectiveness means that indicators must play an important role. It must be clear which indicators represent the effects we want to measure, how these indicators must be measured, which results are expected, etc.
Efficiency	"Obtaining all required goals at the right time" This is also important in good management. If not enough budget is available this may conflict with the effectiveness wish. In process design terms efficiency has a lot to do with the sequence order in which process steps have to be carried out, so it is important that design decisions about this are made explicit.
Flexibility	Legislation in democratic countries is very often subject to change. It is therefore very important to governments that they can easily change their services and processes that are results of legislation. In process design to achieve flexibility it is very important that all design decisions that have led to a process implementation have been stored so that they can be re-used.

reasoning.

Besides the other things we are convinced to be lacking in current process design approaches this feature, being able to contain transparent relationships between process models and the legal sources it originates from, is essential for a modelling approach applicable to the governmental processes.

First we have to say something about the scope of the new combined "GoldminePower" method as compared to the Power method. The Power method focuses on declarative aspects in source text (For instance: "A person older than 17 is an adult".).

The Power method does not focus on procedural and temporal aspects in the used source texts. The final integrated Power model in UML/OCL format therefore needs extra procedural knowledge when it is used to create an application. Such an application for instance needs to know what its goals should be; this information should be available in the design of the business process in which the application that is to be developed plays a role. The GoldminePower method focuses on procedural aspects to use them for process designs. So GoldminePower can perfectly be used additional to the Power method.

In this section the combined method GoldminePower is explained in a step-by-step manner.

2.1 From Legislation to Legislation Design Decisions

The way legislation documents are transformed to a formal model in GoldminePower is very similar to way this is handled in Power. Consider the example in figure 1.

The first step in the Power method is to register the structure of the documents. In GoldminePower structure blocks and references in legislation documents are found in exactly the same way as is done in the Power method. In the example the structure block kinds "Law", "Chapter", "Article" and "Sentence" are found.

After this the text in the sentence structure blocks is scanned for process design decisions which are registered in the Goldmine business knowledge format. More specific the text is scanned for:

LawY
Chapter 1
Article 1.1 Intentions and definitions
This law is meant to make people happier.
A person older than 17 is an adult.
Article 1.2 X
Anyone can order the town hall to perform X for him or her.
The town hall floor manager then will do A.
B will also have to be carried out.
B may not be done before A is finished.
...

Figure 1: A legislation example

- Existence of process (sub) steps
- Properties of process steps (data, triggers, indicators, actors, ...)
- Order relations of steps
- Priorities of indicators on process steps (policy rules)

This scan is additional to the scan that is used in the Power method. Where the Power method is constructing an ontology using an OCL/UML notation and therefore is noun-oriented (Types are mostly nouns), the GoldminePower is verb-oriented (Steps are mostly verb-phrases).

The thus created "Translated" GoldminePower design decision models are Power-like combined into one "Integrated" GoldminePower legislation design decision model. Just like in the Power method these steps can be supported by natural language processing software [4]. Also just like in the Power[3] method found unclearness in legislation can serve as feedback to legislation drafters.

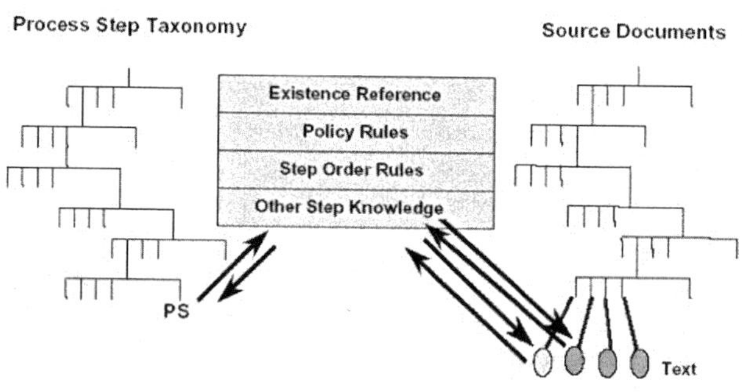

Figure 2: View on the Goldmine business knowledge representation

In figure 2 a view on the Goldmine "Business knowledge" is given. The Goldmine claim is that all that is needed to implement a (workflow) process can be stored in this business knowledge representation and that this knowledge is easy to maintain, especially if also traceability to and from source documents is realised.

This format is in the GoldminePower method used for the "design decision models". The decisions are located in a taxonomy of process steps. In table 3 we can see a design decisions model for process X from figure 1.

As the reader can see the design decisions are easy to understand and to maintain.

Table 3: A design decisions model

Design Decision Nr	Decision Kind	Content	Parent	Source /Why
1	Step existence	X is a governmental process		Law Y, Article 1.2, first sentence
2	Step existence	A is a sub-step	X	Law Y, Article 1.2, second sentence
3	Step existence	B is a sub-step	X	Law Y, Article 1.2, third sentence
4	Order of sub-steps	B must be carried out unconditional after A	X	Law Y, Article 1.2, fourth sentence
5	Other step knowledge	Public_Order is a trigger	X	Law Y, Article 1.2, first sentence
6	Other step knowledge	Happiness is an indicator of X	X	Law Y, Article 1.1, first sentence
7	Other step knowledge	Happiness-after must be greater than happiness-before	X	Law Y, Article 1.1, first sentence
8	Other step knowledge	The town hall floor manager is the actor	A	Law Y, Article 1.2, second sentence
....				

2.2 *Supporting Legislation Drafters Using a Generated Process Design from Legislation Design Decisions*

Each single design decision from the legislation design decisions model is easy to understand for any reader. However, to see what the effect of all business knowledge as a whole is this model is no good. A Petri-net [5] like semantic network is much better equipped to serve as a validating view. This is also known from a study on formal representation format [6] where scenarios prove to be better equipped to validate a model than rules. And this is probably why drawing/case tools (ABC, Visio, Rose, Mega ...) process simulators (Testbed, bWise,...), and workflow engines (Staffware,..)use formal network representations for process design models [7].

In the Goldmine method is the knowledge that is needed for constructing a formal network representation from out of the design decisions is called "modelling knowledge". This typically is the knowledge that a human process designer uses to apply new facts from documents or experts in the process design. In doing so there is a risk that the facts that have led to the process design are not registered. A slight change in those facts might result in a big change in the formal network representation(s). When design decisions are not present in an explicit format Business Process Redesign can be a big effort.

The human process designer's task must not be under-estimated. But since modelling knowledge is almost constant (It only changes if important modelling conventions change) it is something that can be done by a computer. This is one of the main ideas in the Goldmine project. In Goldmine an algorithm is described for producing a process design in an all-information-containing network representation (The "integrated process description" in figure 1) from out of a design decisions model. A prototype that applies such an algorithm was not included in the Goldmine research but was used nevertheless. This prototype also can export views on the design for MS Visio[7].

The existence of a very good version of such a design generator is essential to the Goldmine and GoldminePower methods. In the rest of section 2 the existence of a perfect generator is assumed. Starting from a design decisions model this generator can produce (any model view on) a process design in less than 1 second.

In figure 3 a view on the meta model for a process design environment is given.

The dark blue (dark grey) rectangles in figure 3 represent abstract classes. The light blue (medium grey) rectangles represent knowledge objects that are present in the design decisions

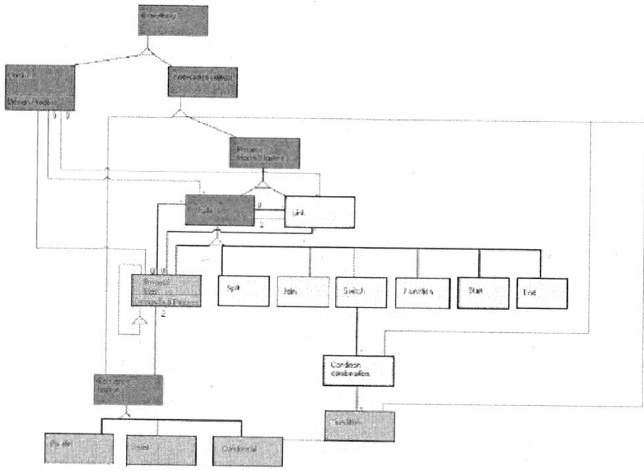

Figure 3: A view on the meta model for a process design environment

model. The yellow (light grey) rectangles represent objects that are generated because they are needed for a formal network representation.

Having different views on a process design is also a very important aspect of Goldmine and GoldminePower. The town hall floor manager would like to see a view on process X that gives his own work in a very detailed format, and all other steps in a global format. He has got an extra requirement saying he would like to see all town hall floor activities "swim-laned". A workflow engine will want another kind of view as an interface, and is not interested in details that are not workflow-supported.

Views can of course also differ in graphical knowledge representation (See figure 4)

Here you see three examples of style views in which formal network descriptions can be displayed and which the perfect generator is able to deliver. The left-hand style view represents the format for the integrated process descriptions that is used in the Goldmine prototype.Characteristics of the left hand style representation:

- A process step always has one incoming and one outgoing flow
- Decomposition like in IDEF3 [8]
- Unlike IDEF3, but after Brand & v.d. Kolk [9], XOR (switch/junction) and AND (split/join) objects. IDEF3 uses OR and AND. The OR has the drawback that the number of flow instances is uncertain.
- Level start and end markers (Can be suppressed in the Goldmine prototype)
- Dummy process steps (Can be suppressed in the Goldmine prototype)

The top style view represents the CSC Catalyst [10] process view representation. Finally the right-hand view represents a style one could adopt after studying Brand & v.d. Kolk.[9]

Now back to supporting legislation drafters. From the legislation design decisions model a legislation process design can be generated. When performed by a perfect generator this action only fails if inconsistent design decisions exist.

An example is given in Table 4. These inconsistent design decisions are of course important input to legislation drafters. In most cases however, the generator will be able to make an

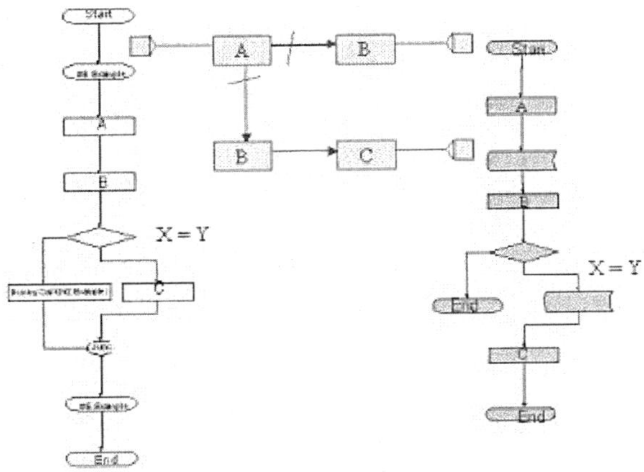

Figure 4: Possible graphical view representations for the same design decisions model

Table 4: An example of inconsistent design decisions

Design Decision Nr	Decision Kind	Content	Parent	Source /Why
1	Step existence	X is a governmental process		Law Y, Article 1.2, first sentence
2	Step existence	A is a sub-step	X	Law Y, Article 1.2, second sentence
3	Step existence	B is a sub-step	X	Law Y, Article 1.2, third sentence
4	Order of sub-steps	B must be carried out unconditional after A	X	Law Y, Article 1.2, fourth sentence
5	Order of sub-steps	A must be carried out unconditional after B	X	Law Z, Article 3.2.1

integrated process description for which relevant views can be exported to and validated by a case tool or a process simulation tool (like Testbed, bWise ...)[7].

Note that the generator includes all modelling knowledge. If for instance in table 4 decisions 4 and 5 are not present the generator must implement a default order for sub-steps A and B. (Simultaneously, In alphabetical order, ...).The most important feedback for legislation drafters we expect will come from optically reviewing the generated process models. A human legal expert can for instance see that process steps are missing, inconsistent, redundant or in an illogic order. The involved legal expert will get his views in a format to which he is most familiar [11]. His remarks will lead to a changed set of design decisions and afterwards in changed design model views.

For further validation a simulation tool can produce valuable information for legislation drafters. If for instance change in legislation was meant to generate a cheaper governmental service, a process design view in simulator environment might show the changed process is more expensive instead of cheaper.

2.3 Adding Local Design Decisions

(Parts of) government processes might be carried out in a local institute that has its own policy, wishes and demands with regard to its processes. To get the total process design this business knowledge has to be added to the legislation design decisions model. This can again be done by scanning documents with institutional policy, but also by making new design decisions based on business economical considerations or common-sense. In table 5 we skipped the incorrect design decision 5 from table 4 and added two local design decisions. This seemed to make sense after consulting some town hall documents and a local town hall floor manager.

Table 5: Added local business knowledge

Design Decision Nr	Decision Kind	Content	Parent	Source /Why
1	Step existence	X is a governmental process		Law Y, Article 1.2, first sentence
2	Step existence	A is a sub-step	X	Law Y, Article 1.2, second sentence
3	Step existence	B is a sub-step	X	Law Y, Article 1.2, third sentence
4	Order of sub-steps	B must be carried out unconditional after A	X	Law Y, Article 1.2, fourth sentence
5	Step existence	"Sending a welcomes gift" is a sub-step	X	Institutional policy, page 1, third paragraph
6	Order of sub-steps	"Sending a welcomes gift" is carried out Parallel with A	X	Because A is the first official step and we don't want any delay in the total process
7	.....	...	..	..
...				

After all local business knowledge has been added the total design decisions model is finished.

2.4 *Validating the Total Set of Design Decisions Using a Generated Process Model*

In figure 5 a possible view is given on a generated process model from the design decisions model in table 5. This kind of graphical representation is the kind that is used in the Goldmine thesis (see 2.2.). Within the same graphical representation kind still a lot of views on a process model design are possible depending on the perspective the reader (Man or machine) is interested in. Possibly step A has been decomposed whereas the reader is not interested in the details of step A.

Just like in 2.2. experts have to look at the total design model views to detect mistakes or less optimal design decisions (Maybe an unconditional sub-step of A which existence is based on a legislation design decision has the same purpose as a conditional sub-step N (Based on a local design decision) of X that occurs after B.

A simulator can help validating the behavior of a process model. If from legislation design decisions are present saying TotalTime is an indicator for this process and the maximum TotalTime is 4 days, and from local design decisions it is clear that step A on an average will cost 1 day and step "Sending a welcomes gift" on an average will cost 2 weeks, the simulator might show that the process model does not satisfy the governmental demands.

In this case the total design decisions model could be improved by skipping step "Sending a welcomes gift" as a sub-step of X, and adding a design decision on step A saying step A is a trigger for a local process called "Sending a welcomes gift".

2.5 *Implementing the Validated Process Model*

After the process model has been designed and validated in an iterative way the generator can provide a workflow engine tool[7] interface with a view on the process model that is necessary that makes sense to the workflow engine. During execution of any process step of

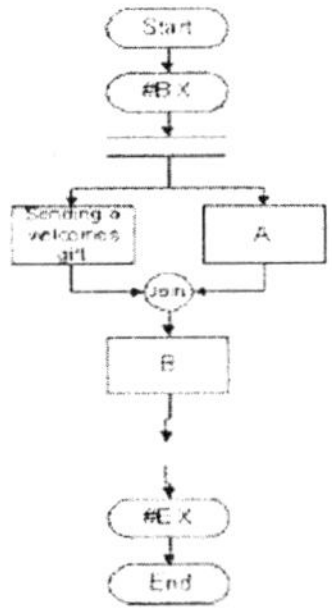

Figure 5: Possible design view

the workflow process the source of the design decisions that have led to or influenced the have current task can be re-found and re-used.

For the more difficult tasks the process can be supported by modules that have been developed with the Power[3] method. The implemented process model has to be monitored on its indicators so that for instance the intended mean values can be re-evaluated. This might lead to a changed design decisions model, and afterwards to a better process model design and a better performing implementation.

3 Research Plans

We plan to test two major hypotheses which are surrounded by many questions and definitions. The first hypothesis we feel needs testing is:

H1: *The degree of (accounted for) explicit design decisions is an indicator for process quality.*

We hereby give the most important definition: Explicit design decision == *a decision about the existence of a process (sub step), about the order in which sub steps of a process (sub step) have to be carried out, or about a property of a process (sub step) that is explicitly mentioned in the process design.* For the H1 research we will investigate as many as possible governmental processes. Possible design decisions formats will be part of the research. Research after process quality indicators will also be done. For this the list of judgement criteria[2] for process designing that is a result from the Goldmine project will be a starting point.

The second and last hypothesis that will be tested is:

H2: *The GoldminePower method for implementing (changes in) governmental policy into governmental processes should be widely recommended.*

We would like to try the GoldminePower method on a real project that is initiated by a planned change in legislation. This has the advantage that the quality of the involved governmental process can be measured before and after the business process redesign project. The research for H2 will include all possible computer support to the method.

4 Conclusions

Governmental problems are mostly process related, and might be solved when the involved processes are improved by means of excellent process design that satisfies all governmental requirements in the field of process design. The GoldminePower method promises to provide this. Governments could get more grip on their process related problems because of the transparency brought by the method. All decisions that lead to a process implementation are made explicit and are accounted for. This makes processes and changes in legislation easy to maintain. Design decisions can also include decisions on indicators for which the process has to be optimised thus helping to create optimal performing processes. Process designs could be validated even by politicians since the GoldminePower method can provide audience centred views[11] on process designs.

The GoldminePower method therefore is a very promising set of ideas. Because of the great interest governments have in solving their problems it is very important that the proposed method is researched as soon as possible. We hope governments will be very eager for supporting the planned GoldminePower research.

References

[1] February 2003,Een kwestie van uitvoering, Vernieuwingsagenda voor de presterende overheid, site http://www.kennisland.nl/kennisland/binaries/KLsite/actueel/publicaties/Een_kwestie_van_uitvoering.pdf

[2] van Heel,E.J.,2000,Goldmine-A KT approach to workflow process designing, MSc thesis Cibit, Utrecht

[3] van Engers,T.M., Kordelaar,P.J.M., den Hartog, J., Glassée, E.,2000, POWER: Programme for an Ontology based Working Environment for modeling and use of Regulations and legislation. In proceeding of the 11th workshop on Database and Expert Systems Applications (IEEE) Eds. Tjoa, Wagner and Al-Zobaidie, Greenwich London, ISBN 0-7695-0680-1, pp. 327-334.

[4] Ron van Gog, Tom M. van Engers,2001,Modeling legislation using natual language processing, Proceedings of the 2001 IEEE Systems, Man, and Cybernetics Conference, available at http://www.lri.jur.uva.nl/~epower/publications/modleg.pdf

[5] van der Aalst,W.M.P.,1996,Petri-net-based Workflow Management Software, Proceedings of the NFS Workshop on Workflow and Process Automation in Information Systems, Athens, Georgia

[6] Tom van Engers, Liesbeth van Driel and Margherita Boekenoogen,2002, The effect of formal representation formats on the quality of legal decision-making,Legal knowledge and information systems-JURIX 2002: The fifteen annual conference,ISBN 1-58603-299-2, page 63

[7] W.D. van Dommelen, S.M.M. Joosten, M.C.J. de Mol, H. de Zwart,1999,Vergelijkend onderzoek hulpmiddelen beheersing bedrijfsprocessen, EAP, Apeldoorn, downloadable from: http://www.anaxagoras.com/publicaties/vohbb.htm

[8] Richard J. Mayer,.Christopher P. Menzel, Michael K. Painter, Paula S. deWitte, Thomas Blinn, Benjamin Perakath, 1995, IDEF3 Process Flow and Object State Description Capture Method, full report downloadable from: http://www.idef.com/idef3.html

[9] Brand, N.A. & van der Kolk, J.R.P., 1997, Werkstroomanalyse en –ontwerp, Het logistiek vriendelijk ontwerpen van informatiesystemen, Kluwer bedrijfsinformatie, ISBN 90 267 2100 5.

[10] CSC process thread, see Allen, P., & Frost, A. ,1998, Component-Based Development for Enterprise Systems: Applying The Select Perspective, Cambridge University Press, ISBN 0-521-64999-4 paperback.

[11] Abeysinghe, G.K., Henderson, P., Phalp, K.T. and Walters,>=1997, R. An Audience Centred Approach for Business Process Reengineering, see http://www.ecs.soton.ac.uk/~rjw1/papers/method/method.pdf

A Use Case Analysis of Legal Knowledge-Based Systems

Thomas F. Gordon
Fraunhofer FOKUS
Kaiserin-Augusta-Allee 31, 10589 Berlin, Germany
Thomas.Gordon@fokus.fraunhofer.de

Abstract. A number of important use cases for public administration ("e-governance") applications of legal knowledge-based systems are identified. For each use case, a data flow model is developed showing processes and document types sufficient to implement the use case. Our main goal is to identify document types which, if standardized, would enable a modular set of interoperable components for building legal knowledge-based systems.

1 Introduction

This paper provides a high-level process analysis of the major **use cases** of legal knowledge-based systems, with a focus on public administration applications. Our analysis is based in part on prior work by the ePower project [4, 5] and the survey of AI methods and tools for supporting legal argumentation by Bench-Capon, et. al., in [1]. Use cases are a software engineering modeling and diagramming technique, standardized as part of the Unified Modeling Language. Use cases are very high level models showing how different kinds of actors interact with a system to carry out tasks. They are useful for helping to get an overview of the desired functionality of the complete system and are an "essential tool" for identifying requirements [6].

Figure 1 is a UML diagram showing all of the use cases we have identified. There are five main kinds of actors participating in these use cases: *legal analysts* (lawyers) and *knowledge engineers* (computers scientists) work together to build formal, computer models of legislation; *clients* (citizens or businesses) consult *advisors* (such as lawyers or tax consultants) take part in a structured dialog, for example to apply for social benefits or a building permit, with a *public agency*. Both the advisor (or the client) and the public agency use these models and other resources to analyze the issues of a case and to generate arguments.

The following section present process models showing the document types and processes required to implement each use case. In doing this, our main goal is to identify document types which, if standardized, would enable a modular set of interoperable components for building legal knowledge-based systems. Ideally, appropriate industry standards for the document types in these processes would enable components to be used together and allow consumers to freely choose products for each of the components. Presumably competition would help to improve quality and reduce prices while the availability of several competing products for each component would provide public administration and other users with a measure of security protecting their investments.

Thomas F. Gordon, 'A Use Case Analysis of Legal Knowledge-Based Systems' in D. Bourcier (ed.), *Legal Knowledge and Information Systems. Jurix 2003: The Sixteenth Annual Conference*. Amsterdam: IOS Press, 2003, pp. 81-90.

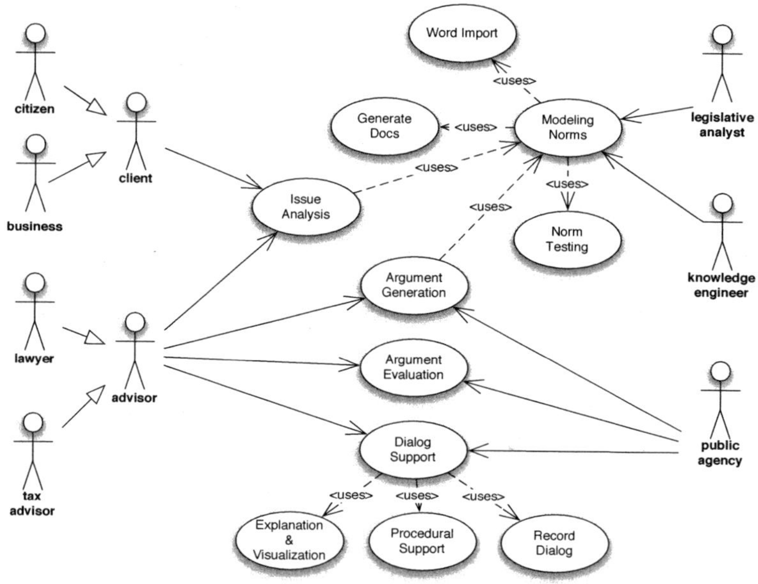

Figure 1: Legal Reasoning Uses Cases

2 Modeling Norms

Let us begin with the Modeling Norms use case. Here the task is to interpret and analyze legal sources, such as a piece of legislation, a regulation or some case law, to produce a high-level formal model of the concepts and norms in the sources. For our purposes here, it does not matter what knowledge representation methods are applied for this purpose. Figure 2 show the data flow diagram[1] for norm modeling.

There are two starting points in this data flow chart. You can start at the bottom, with an empty norm model, and simply begin to create a model. If, for example, the models are being created using UML/OCL, as in the ePower methodology, this could be done using one of the many CASE tools for UML. Presuming you have a structured, marked-up version of the legislation to be modeled, using for example the MetaLex XML document schema for legislation [2], you can start at the top by generating partial models from this structured document and then integrating these models. For example, the ePower workbench provides a tool for generating models from MetaLex files, using a natural language parser to identify concepts and relations.

Please note that the processes in this and the following data flow diagrams, such as Generate Model and Integrate Model in Figure 2, are not assumed to be performed completely automatically. Rather, the way these processes are performed is left completely open during this analysis. At one extreme, the process could be performed completely manually, in some conventional way. More ambitiously, ICT tools can be imagined which could assist a human user in performing these tasks. Most advanced would be full automation, but this is clearly beyond the state of the art for many if not most of the processes discussed in this paper.

[1]To be precise, we use UML Activity Diagrams as data flow diagrams.

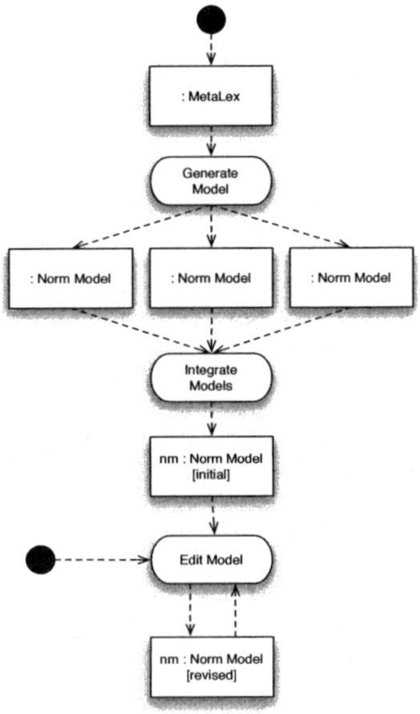

Figure 2: Modeling Norms

3 Word Import

The ePower workbench also provides a tool implementing the Word Import use case from Figure 1. The data flow diagram for the Word Import use case is shown in Figure 3.

The structure parser converts a Microsoft Word version of a piece of legislation into MetaLex, which is an XML Schema for legislation and other legal texts. The structure parser depends on the structure of the Word document having been previously marked up by applying paragraph and character styles from a particular Word template. This conversion process is made necessary by the wide spread use of Microsoft Word to draft legislation. Perhaps some day this will be done using XML editors, making this conversion process unnecessary. The Check References process of the Word Import use case makes sure that all cross references in the legislation are correct, or at least do not refer to non-existing sections or paragraphs.

In the discussion so far we have identified three document types which are candidates for a standardization effort: 1) the Word Template for marking up legislation using Microsoft Word; 2) An XML document schema such as MetaLex for marking up the structure of legislation using XML; and 3) some document type for models of norms. More will follow below.

4 Model Testing

Figure 4 is the data flow diagram for testing norm models. This is the first process to use argumentation, which will be explained shortly. The input to the process is some representation of a case and the norm model. The diagram illustrates the testing process for a single case, but this process usually would be iterated for some set of test cases. A case here should consist at least of the legal facts of the cases, that is the facts in terms of the legal terminology (or "ontology") used by the norm model, the legal issue or issues to be decided and the outcome or decision. For decided court cases, the outcome would be the actual decision reached by the court. But for testing models of new legislation the test cases may be "hypotheticals" with

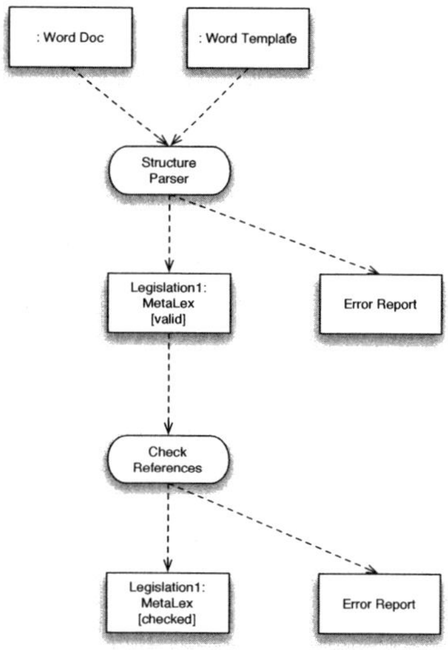

Figure 3: Word Import

the desired outcomes given the policy behind the legislation.

Now we explain the use of argumentation in this process. We do not restrict the norm models to logical representations, let alone to representations in monotonic logics such as first-order predicate logic (FOL). Rather, we want to also support models which use, for example, case-based reasoning or some kind of defeasible (nonmonotonic) logic. The problem here is to find a way to make the results of reasoning with such heterogenous models somehow comparable and interoperable. Our proposed solution is to have each kind of model explain its reasoning as a set of arguments in a standard format. Each argument instantiates an argumentation schema, where each kind of model can define its own schemas.

The Generate Arguments process applies the model to the facts of the case to try to resolve the issues of the case. Essentially, the issues are interpreted as queries to be posed to the model. The model may generate conflicting arguments, pro and contra some resolution of an issue. The task of the Apply Arguments process is to link up these arguments into an argumentation graph. The Evaluate Arguments process then labels the arguments, or the propositions in the premises and conclusions of the arguments. These labels record whether the argument or proposition is *acceptable* (i.e. to be considered proven or "true" given all the arguments made). The Check Results process then compares the decision of the case with the labels of the issues in the argument graph to determine whether they are consistent or compatible.

The precise form and semantics of legal arguments, argument schemas, argument graphs is an active area of research [7, 10, 15]. But all approaches fit the abstract process model presented here. Again, our goal here is not to solve these research problems but to identify document types and processes which (eventually) should be standardized. Here we see the need for standards to represent cases, norm models, arguments and argument graphs.

One important advantage of this process model is that it is easily extensible to cover reasoning with **multiple norm models**. Many legal problems can only be resolved by considering a multiple sources of norms. For example, a cross-border commercial transaction between parties in Germany and The Netherlands might be regulated by The United Nations

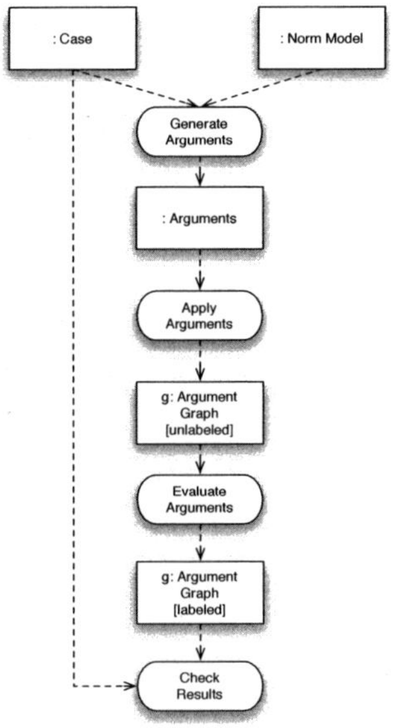

Figure 4: Model Testing

Convention on the International Sale of Goods[2] (CISG), laws of the European Union and the national laws of both countries, not to mention case law about all of these legal texts.

This completes our presentation of the use cases for modeling norms, except for the Generate Docs use case. This is about generating documentation of norm models from templates and style sheets in various output formats, such as HTML, PDF, or even Word. Since document generation is well understood and well supported by industry standards, we have omitted a more detailed discussion to save space.

5 Issue Analysis

Let us turn our attention to the more interesting use cases in which clients with the help of their advisors interact with public agencies, beginning with Issue Analysis. To illustrate the issue analysis use case, let us use the following hypothetical from [3]. A client comes into an attorney's office and tells the following story:

At the place where I work, our bookkeeper didn't give me my paycheck. Instead she signed my name on it, cashed it an left town. I asked my boss for a new check but he said he already paid me. Is he right that he doesn't owe me my wages?

Although from a common sense perspective the client's story and problem are quite clear, the problem is to identify the legal issues, if any. To do this, the story needs to be interpreted in light of knowledge of one or more areas of substantive law. Is this a commercial law problem, a labor law problem, or perhaps some kind of tort? (Or perhaps more than one of these.) That is, the lawyer needs to use his knowledge of the law to first try to narrow in on one or more areas of law which might be relevant. Then, for each of the selected areas of law, the common sense terms of the client's story need to be mapped into the technical legal terms. Branting shows the result for the US Uniform Commerical Code:

[2]http://www.cisg-online.ch/cisg/conv/convuk.htm

Under Article 3 of the Uniform Commercial Code, is a payor's obligation to a payee discharged by a negotiable instrument if the negotiable instrument is paid to a third party over a forged signature?

Only after the problem has been reformulated in this way can we begin to use some model of the selected legal domain to try to begin to analyse the legal issues and generate arguments for the client.

Although Branting's example is about a private legal conflict, the problem is just as relevant in the context of e-governance and the electronic delivery of public services. One of the goals of e-governance is to provide one-stop shops for citizens on the Web. Supposing that the vision is to provide a wide variety of government services backed by legal knowledge-based systems, how shall the citizen find out which of the many services is relevant for his or her problem or "life event"? The person at the front-desk of the one-stop shop has the role of the advisor in this scenario and faces the same issue identification problem of an attorney or other legal advisor.

Figure 5 is the data flow diagram for the issue identification process. (Incidentally, this process is called "theory construction" in [1], but since this term is also used for the process of creating a theory explaining a set of precedent cases I prefer "issue identification" here.) There are two main tasks in this process, finding models and interpreting the story of the client. We imagine there to be a library of models, including metadata indexing the models. For each model selected, the story interpretation task translates the story into legal facts and issues.

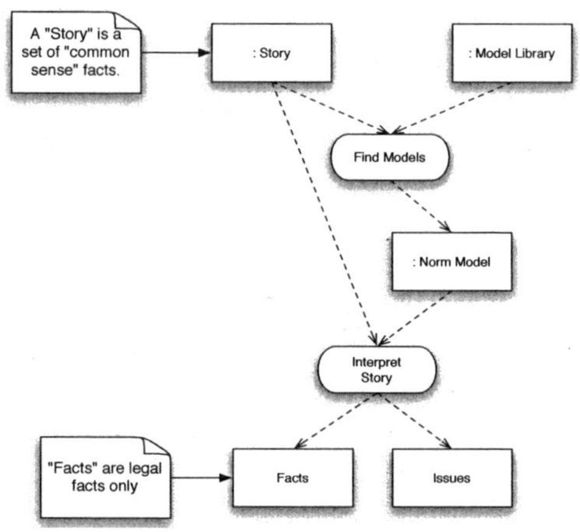

Figure 5: Issue Identification

Document types of the issue identification process which might be suitable for standardization include the norm models, and representation of the legal facts and issues. Legal facts and issues were also a part of the case document type discussed previously, so these should be represented in an integrated fashion, as part of the same document type. The story document, on the other hand, does not seem suitable for standardization, since it is simply the story as told by the client in natural language.

It is not clear how far we can go in providing ICT support for finding models and interpreting stories. Surely some support can be provided, but these are very difficult tasks requiring a great deal of both common sense knowledge and legal expertise.

6 Argument Generation

The next use cases to discuss are for generating and evaluation arguments. Figure 6 is a data flow diagram for argument generation. It is similar in some ways to the model testing process discussed previously. Instead of a test case, we have the legal facts and issues which were identified by the previous process. Instead of a decision or desired outcome, some representation of the **interests** of the client are input into the process. These are used to evaluate and select arguments supporting alternative decisions or outcomes, rather than restricting attention to a single desired outcome prematurely. The argument selection process also take into account the prior state of the dialog, recorded in an argument graph, and features of the audience, to make use of rhetorical skills. The result of the argument construction process is a set of selected arguments and a updated argumentation graph including these arguments.

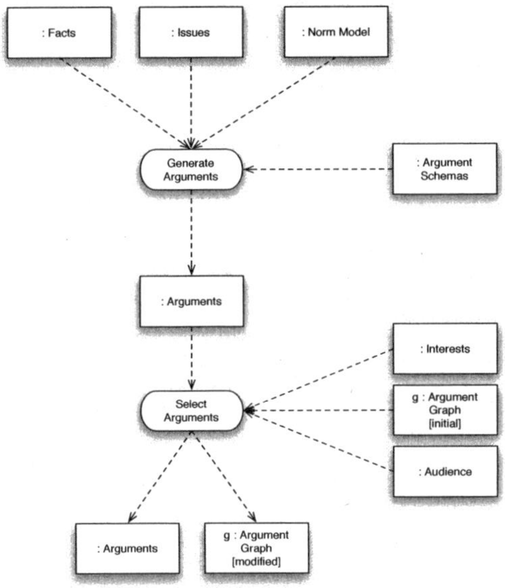

Figure 6: Argument Generation

There are no new document types in this process, assuming that legal facts and issues are part of the document type for cases. An exception is possibly the document type for argument schemas, which appears here for the first time. Perhaps argument schemas should be a part of document type for domain models. There seems no pressing need to standardize the representation of interests and the audience, so long as there are no tools or methods for using these representations to select arguments. We are not aware of research results in this area.

7 Argument Evaluation

Figure 7 is a data flow diagram for the argument evaluation process. It is deceptively simple. It takes a set of arguments and the prior state of an argument graph, extends this graph with the new arguments and updates the labels of the graph. This process may make use of the argument application and evaluation processes of the model testing process discussed previously. Although not shown in the diagram, a model of **metanorms** for resolving conflicts between norms will be used by this process. Famous examples of such norms include *lex specialis* (prefer the most specific norm) and *lex superior* (prefer the most authoritative norm). But there is a lot of hand waving going on here, since as mentioned previously this is an active area of research. There is as yet no consensus on the form (syntax) or semantics of argumentation graphs. No new document types appear in this process.

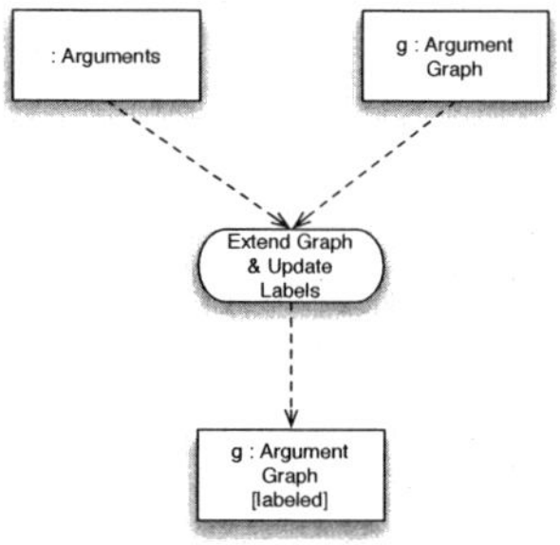

Figure 7: Argument Evaluation

8 Discourse Support

This nearly completes our discussion of the legal reasoning use cases. It remains only to discuss discourse support. We do not have data flow diagrams for the discourse use cases ready for this paper. Although my colleagues and I have done some work in this area [8, 9, 13] some effort is required to bring this prior work up to date and to integrate it into the general framework presented here. However some general requirements already seem quite clear. The discourse support system must support the use of formal, structured protocols for various kinds of dialog types [17], such as critical discussions, deliberation and negotiation. These protocols will make use of rules of procedure [14], which themselves ideally would be modeled in the same way as substantive areas of law. In the e-governance context, there may be specific administrative procedures to take into consideration. The discourse support system will need to manage the state of the dialog, keeping a record of the moves (speech acts) made and their effects. This includes managing the so-called **commitment stores** of the participants, so that we know who made which assertions of facts. These commitment stores are not only for helping to prevent the participants from contradicting themselves, but also for such mundane purposes as allowing information provided on forms to modified. Finally, the discourse support system should provide tools for presenting and visualizing arguments and argument graphs [12, 16], to make them more understandable without requiring users to become familiar with formal languages.

9 Conclusion and Future Work

The main goal of the work presented here has been to identify document types which, if standardized, would enable a modular set of interoperable components for building legal knowledge-based systems. Rather than taking a technology-driven approach, by starting with existing legal knowledge-based systems and looking for common document types, we have taken a requirements-driven approach here, starting with e-governance use cases. In conclusion, the following document types have been identified:

- A Microsoft Word template for marking up legislation and other sources of norms using Word;
- A markup language and exchange format for legislation and other sources of norms;
- A knowledge representation language and exchange format for formal models of norms;
- An exchange format for legal cases, including facts, issues and decisions;
- An exchange format for arguments and argument graphs; and
- Possibly a representation language and exchange format for argument schemas, if this is not part of the language for norm models.

We have conducted a survey of proprietary formats, research prototypes and proposed or emerging standards for these document types. Unfortunately, there is no room to present the results of this survey here; we will try to publish this research in another paper soon. For now, we can only say that our conclusion is that the legal knowledge-based systems industry is still in a very early stage of development.

References

[1] Bench-Capon, Trevor, James Freeman, Hanns Hohmann and Henry Prakken "Computational Models, Argumentation Theories and Legal Practice." Argumentation Machines; New Frontiers in Argument and Computation. Eds. Chris Reed and Timothy J. Norman: Kluwer Academic Publishers, 2003. 85-120.

[2] Boer, Alexander, Rinke Hoekstra, and Radboud Winkels. "Metalex: Legislation in XML." Legal Knowledge and Information Systems (Jurix 2002). Eds. T. Bench-Capon, A. Daskalopulu and R. Winkels: IOS Press, 2002. 1–10.

[3] Branting, L. Karl. "An Agenda for Empirical Research in AI and Law." ICAIL Workshop on the Evaluation of Legal Reasoning and Problem-Solving Systems. Eds. Karl Branting and Steffi Brüninghaus. Edinburgh: International Association of Artificial Intelligence and Law, 2003. 28–35.

[4] Engers, Tom M. van, Rik Gerrits, Margherita Boekenoogen, Erwin Glassée and Partries Kordelaar "Power: Using UML/OCL for Modeling Legislation – an Application Report." International Conference on Artificial Intelligence and Law (ICAIL 2001). Ed. Henry Prakken. St. Louis, 2001. 157–67.

[5] Engers, Tom M. van, and Margherita R. Boekenoogen. "Improving Legal Quality – an Application Report." International Conference on Artificial Intelligence and Law (ICAIL 2003). Ed. Giovanni Sartor. Edinburgh: ACM, 2003. 284–92.

[6] Fowler, Martin, and Kendall Scott. UML Distilled – a Brief Guide to the Standard Object Modeling Language. 2nd ed: Addison Wesley Longman, Inc., 2000.

[7] Gordon, Thomas F., and Nikos Karacapilidis. "The Zeno Argumentation Framework." Proceedings of the Sixth International Conference on Artificial Intelligence and Law. Melbourne, Australia, 1997. 10-18.

[8] Gordon, Thomas F. The Pleadings Game; an Artificial Intelligence Model of Procedural Justice. Dordrecht: Kluwer, 1995.

[9] Gordon, Thomas F., and Oliver Märker. "Mediation Systems." Online-Mediation. Neue Medien in Der Konfliktvermittlung - Mit Beispielen Aus Politik Und Wirtschaft. Eds. Oliver Märker and Matthias Trénel. Berlin: Edition Sigma, 2002. 61-84.

[10] Greenwood, Katie, Trevor Bench-Capon, and Peter McBurney. "Towards a Computational Account of Persuasion in Law." International Conference on Artificial Intelligence and Law. Ed. Giovanni Sartor. Edinburgh: ACM, 2003. 22–31.

[11] Johnson, Peter. Legal Knowledge-Based Systems in Administrative Practice and Electronic Service Delivery (E-Government), 2000.

[12] Kirschner, Paul A., Simon J. Buckingham Shum, and Chadd Carr, eds. Visualizing Argumentation: Software Tools for Collaborative Education and Sense-Making. London: Springer-Verlag, 2002.

[13] Mochol, Malgorzata. "Discourse Support Design Patterns." Online Dispute Resolution – Legal and Technical Aspects. Eds. Arno R. Lodder, et al. Edinburgh, 2003. 61-74.

[14] Prakken, Henry, and Thomas F. Gordon. "Rules of Order for Electronic Group Decision Making – a Formal Methodology." Collaboration between Human and Artificial Societies. Ed. Julian A. Padget. Springer Lecture Notes in Ai. Berlin, 1999. 246-63.

[15] Prakken, Henry, Chris Reed, and Douglas Walton. "Argumentation Schemes and Generalisations About Evidence." International Conference on Artificial Intelligence and Law. Edinburgh, 2003. 32–41

[16] Rowe, G. W. A., C. A. Reed, and J. Katzav. "Araucaria: Marking up Argument." European Conference on Computing and Philosophy. Glasgow, 2003.

[17] Walton, Douglas N. The New Dialectic : Conversational Contexts of Argument. Toronto; Buffalo: University of Toronto Press, 1998.

Knowledge Management for Legislative Drafting in an International Setting

Alexander Boer Radboud Winkels Rinke Hoekstra Tom M. van Engers
Leibniz Center for Law
Faculty of Law, Universiteit van Amsterdam
Amsterdam, The Netherlands
{aboer, winkels, hoekstra, vanengers}@lri.jur.uva.nl

Abstract. The processes of drafting consistent and coherent legislation and upholding and applying valid law are getting more and more complicated. In this paper we sketch the components of an integrated Knowledge Management architecture for Legislative Drafting and deployment of legislation in an international setting and discuss problems conceptual mismatches in legal vocabulary of competing legislative authorities. Such a support environment should at least provide the following functionalities: Management of references, version management, management of subsumption structures between concepts and norms, access to similar legal documents for 'best practices', and access to guidelines or norms about drafting. We identify the key problem of managing a large and complicated repository of legislation as the problem of comparing (models of) legislation.

1 Introduction

Increasing legal convergence between governments in the European Union, and traffic of people over borders of jurisdictions, leads to an increased interest in the problem of comparing and harmonizing legislation. Administrations need to know and understand legislation of friendly governments to be able to assist citizens and reduce negative consequences of movement. Global companies offer products and services in many jurisdictions at the same time, and the product or service has to meet the provisions of all jurisdictions in which it is offered. Different regulations can lead to differences in competitiveness for the product or service; For a financial product, for instance, it is considered important to qualify for tax deductions that make the product more attractive. For a medical product it is important to know whether it can be sold over the counter without a prescription.

This attention for comparing legal systems is evidenced by the number of consultancy firms that advertise their knowledge of multiple jurisdictions to companies. In addition, there are a number of initiatives – often initiated outside the Computer Science and Law community – for constructing international legal ontologies that expose the subsumption relations between legal vocabulary in multiple jurisdictions (e.g. [9]).

As a result the processes of drafting consistent and coherent legislation and upholding and applying valid law are getting more and more complicated. ICT has the potential of supporting both the government and citizens in dealing with this increasing body of law; In the E-POWER project[1] we tried to provide such support. A necessary precondition for ICT support is the electronic availability of legal documents from multiple sources in a structured and standard format. That is why we developed METALex XML[2] (cf. [1]), and try to convince

[1]IST project 2000-28125.
[2]See http://www.metalex.nl

Alexander Boer, Radboud Winkels, Rinke Hoekstra, and Tom M. van Engers 'Knowledge Management for Legislative Drafting in an International Setting' in D. Bourcier (ed.), *Legal Knowledge and Information Systems. Jurix 2003: The Sixteenth Annual Conference*. Amsterdam: IOS Press, 2003, pp. 91-100.

legislators and legal publishers to adopt or facilitate it.

We also tried to use the available E-POWER ontologies for comparing 'similar' legislation from different jurisdictions. Employees of the Dutch Tax and Customs Administration – a member of the consortium – are increasingly confronted with requests that require them to understand European regulations and directives, and regulations of other EU member states, and they need to react to consequences of increased movement of people, products, and money between EU member states and increased harmonization between tax authorities in Europe.

In this paper we present some conclusions from our work on these subjects and try to sketch the components of an integrated Knowledge Management architecture for Legislative Drafting and deployment of legislation in such an international setting, based on an open source METALex RDF repository. We will discuss problems of conceptual mismatches in legal vocabulary of competing legislative authorities. We identify the key problem of managing a large and complicated repository of legislation as the problem of comparing (models of) legislation.

2 Computer-assisted Legislative Drafting

Existing legislative drafting support software (cf. generally [5]; LEDA, Solon, LexEdit, Enact, etc.) is usually structured in accordance with legislation that regulates legislative drafting. This represents one important set of requirements for legislation, but many others are not explicitly taken into account. LEDA, for instance, included access to CD-ROM databases with existing legislation for reference purposes. Another category of software that claims to assist legislative drafting are legislative 'databases' or Content Management Systems (CMS; e.g. [4]). These projects stress that legislative drafting is a complex knowledge management task requiring access to many legal sources, but lack a coherent perspective on the role these other legal sources play in legislative drafting and offer nothing but norms about drafting to support decision making.

Most legislation builds on existing legislation and legal vocabulary. Legislative drafters take into account: information from the legislation to be replaced/amended (e.g. to decide on a transitory regime[3]); legislation that regulates legislative drafting; legislation that will interact with the new legislation; similar legislation from other jurisdictions; known alternative regimes from literature (or political discourse) relevant to the proposed legislation; information on external costs of changing to the new regime; and information on internal costs of changing affected (internal) business processes, decision support systems, knowledge management systems, training materials, etc.

In our view a knowledge management system for legislative drafting consists of a content management and a decision support component. We classify relevant relations between legal sources as follows:

Jurisdiction and Legislative Competence Legislators are restricted by higher and lower normative systems (municipal, provincial, national, EU, UN etc.; cf. the *lex superior* principle for resolving conflicts) and "connected" by open borders to other normative systems. Proof of legislative competence, and obligation to implement a directive, are very common reasons to cite other legislation.

Norms about drafting Legislation is structured in accordance with legislation that regulates legislative drafting. This legislation may itself change as a result of legislative drafting, of

[3]See http://www.lri.jur.uva.nl/ rinke/leidraad/leidraad.htm for a manual (in Dutch) about transitory legislation designed by our department.

course. In addition, judgments of advisory councils (e.g. a "Council of State") on previous drafts of the same law, or drafts of other laws, may be important (cf. [13]).

Language Legislation is sometimes designed in multiple language versions that must remain consistent.

Time Versions are important in deciding what is valid law for a particular case (legislation applicable at the time, and the *lex posterior* principle). Versions in time may be cited. Temporal relations between legal sources always exist, obviously.

Domain Legal sources may express norms about the same thing, and these norms may be in apparent conflict (resolved by the *lex specialis* principle). Legislation may use vocabulary classifying the domain from other legislation by citing it.

Comparability Any legal source considered 'best practice' in some sense or any alternative versions of legislation with which it can be compared to establish preferences.

Voermans ([13]) notes that the user-unfriendliness of knowledge representations make it unattractive to check the "deontological consequences of a draft". We are not convinced. Given the amount of effort involved in drafting legislation, evaluating consequences, adapting systems and business procedures, and training civil servants, there is no viable argument from efficiency to avoid the formalization step if that results in better legislation. There is a very good reason to formalize at this stage: it makes all next steps less costly. In the fiscal context of E-POWER, for instance, new legislation has direct consequences for software that processes submitted information and detects fraud.

3 A Framework for Comparing Legislation

Evaluation of legislation is central to the task of legislative drafting: To build a knowledge management system for legislative drafters one needs to understand how legislation compares to its alternatives. Generally, a rhetorical comparison compares a thing A (the *primum comparandum*) to a thing B (the *secundum comparatum*) on the basis of a common quality C (the *tertium comparationis*): A is like B with respect to C, or A is as C as B. The comparison is limited to a common quality, or a limited number of common qualities, that are, or should be, known in advance.

Similar regulations are compared for a number of different purposes, and in most cases of comparison the surrounding legal system is assumed to be the same. We distinguish 3 types of comparison of regulations:

Comparison of alternatives Proposals for a regulation addressing the same problem are compared to judge which one is better according to preconceived norms of analysis.

Vertical comparison in time Versions of the same regulation in time are compared to determine the effects (costs and benefits) of changes of legislation on behavior, products, etc.

Horizontal comparison between jurisdictions Two regulations addressing 'similar' things in different jurisdictions are compared to inform others about the effects (costs and benefits) of moving themselves, their property, products, or services over the borders of a jurisdiction.

Costs and benefits for stakeholders are quantified and ranked with a variety of evaluation criteria, sometimes called "norms of analysis". Norms of analysis are the norms used to distinguish good from bad norms (cf. generally [8, 7] in taxation context), and represent the values the legislator has committed itself to. These values can take the form of a preference scale that can be used to rank things. To distinguish good from bad legislation, one has to deal with the additional problem of aggregation of norms in regulations, and the aggregation of the results of application of multiple norms of analysis. Tax neutrality, for instance, is a norm of analysis that postulates that taxation should not create avoidance behavior. Tax neutrality is also a norm for distinguishing good and bad combinations of legislation in the context of migration; In this form it postulates that two jurisdictions that allow free movement between jurisdictions should try to minimize differences in tax pressure.

Comparative analyses made by scholars in Comparative Law that reveal "interesting" differences between regimes are usually based on "functional" similarity[12]. To create useful computerized support, the implicit evaluation criteria used to decide what difference is interesting, and what alternative is better, must be made explicit. If multiple criteria are used, and the ranking or composition of those criteria is omitted in a misguided attempt at modesty or 'objectivity', the comparison only results in "differences" without a judgment. Two variations of this "functional" character of similarity can be distinguished:

Outcome similarity Two regimes can be considered similar if they cause similar interesting outcomes for the group of agents affected by the respective regimes.

Intention similarity Two regimes can be considered similar if they are both intended by the legislator to cause similar interesting outcomes for the group of agents affected by the respective regimes.

If you make assumptions about the effect of codified norms on behavior without validating them, you are confusing intended outcome with actual outcome (cf. [2]).

4 A Knowledge Management System for Legislative Drafting and Deployment

A Knowledge Management System for Legislative Drafting is in essence a Decision Support System – just like expert systems that assist in applying the law. Legislative drafting is decision making. The simplest norms of legislative drafting we are interested in are the *formal* criteria of legislation for legislative drafting. These – and procedural norms to some extent – can be automatically applied. *Substantive* criteria (restricting the content of norms) work as norms of analysis – they serve to choose between alternatives – and are approached as source material for decision support features.

We designed a knowledge management architecture for METALex based on a content management component and a decision support component. The content management component takes care of formal criteria, document-, and conceptual and evaluation model management. Because formal norms can also be amended, and old legislation can never be expected to meet the newest criteria, formal norms are decaratively expressed and not hardwired into procedures. The decision support component uses evaluation models declaring norms of analysis to assist in decision-making for legislative drafters as well as designers of expert systems and tutoring systems. The decision support system helps to deconstruct comparative arguments for legislative drafting, and exposes norms of analysis, questionable assumptions, and overlooked counter-examples.

4.1 Content Management with MetaLex XML

The *formal* requirements of for instance the Netherlands' Regulation for Legislative Drafting (Aanwijzingen voor Regelgeving; AR) can be encoded in a normative XML schema on top of METALex, or using an XSL verification sheet for METALex. However, the application of more complex norms of analysis requires insight into the *context* of the draft legislation within the body of legislation as a whole: both on a syntactical level and at a semantical level.

The METALex XML standard for legal sources provides a generic and easily extensible framework for encoding of the structure and contents of legal and para legal documents in XML (See [1]). It differs from other existing metadata schemes for legal documents in two respects; it is language independent and it aims to accommodate uses of XML beyond search and presentation services. The same content can be written down in one METALex document using multiple languages or in different documents using jurisdiction-specific sets of XML tags. By providing structure to legal texts, METALex facilitates search and filtering on legal documents. The use of four date attributes provides a comprehensive way to determine the validity and activity of any part of a legal text: date-enacted, date-repealed, date-publication and date-effective. These metadata enable automatic generation of current and past versions of legal texts, and control automatic resolution of references (to known persons, bodies or definitions of legal concepts) and citations (of structural elements of a text) over different versions.

A METALex-based CMS will allow for browsing and retrieval, publishing, import/ export to- and from open and proprietary formats. Most importantly, it can make explicit the structure of and relations between (elements) of regulations. This greatly enhances the possibilities for legislative drafters and end-users alike for version management and reference resolution, across languages, and through time.

Information about legal sources, including concepts, evaluation models, extensions to describe the content of regulations in a logic-based framework, and indices for advanced search techniques, is specified in RDF (W3's Resource Description Framework XML). The RDF data model is convenient because it is very expressive, and can be trivially serialized as XML or SQL for relational databases; Both are key technologies for CMS's.

METALex is transparent with respect to other XML-based languages, which makes it highly suitable for integration with existing Semantic Web standards (See Figure 1). In the context of harmonization and comparison of regulations, this means METALex can be built upon to venture beyond the mere syntactical aspects of legislation. The use of METALex and semantic web technologies within a CMS enables the classification of documents by role, authority, jurisdiction and competence, as well as conceptual model and evaluation model management.

4.2 Concepts in RDF and Open Borders

To illustrate the problem of open borders between jurisdictions we can take an example from the agenda of European Parliament; A recent initiative by the Hellenic Republic concerning the application of the "ne bis in idem" principle (double jeopardy; nobody shall be prosecuted twice for the same criminal offense) in EU treaties and proposes a total of 23 amendments to clarify what the "same criminal offense" is, and what should be considered a res judicata (a completed trial/prosecution) in different member states. To solve these problems between two jurisdictions a third legislative authority has to settle what counts as a prosecution, and establish *subsumption relations* between crime descriptions in multiple jurisdictions – and usually multiple languages.

The RDF concept repository distinguishes the identities of expressions, concepts, and

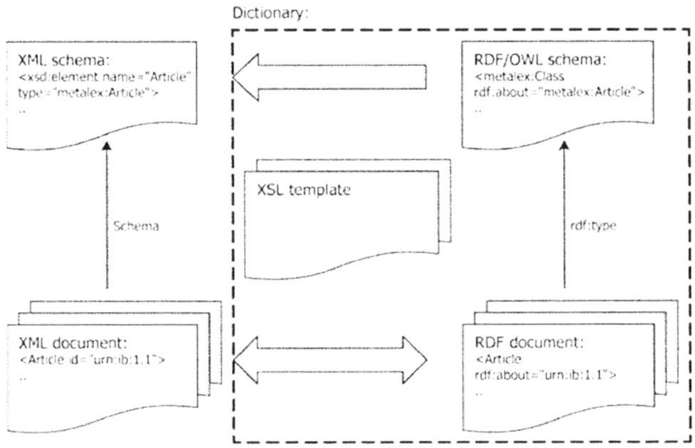

Figure 1: Hierarchical XML and relational RDF representation of Legislation

$[identity, expression, concept]$ triples relative to a perspective. In addition to synonyms and homonyms, there are cases the same legal expression defined equivalently in different sources (e.g. 'wages' in wage tax and social insurance co-ordination laws in the Netherlands; LB64 art. 10, CSV art. 4): the reason to do this is that, although the definitions are equivalent now, they may diverge in the future[4].

Our tests with multiple language versions of one contract (French and Dutch) in the E-POWER project shows that a reliable concept-to-concept correspondence between languages is not always achievable [2]: sometimes a word must be translated to one or more sentences. A lexical-concept-centered way of linking multilingual regulations is therefore not sufficient, and a "dictionary-style" browser is insufficient. The English concept of "Theft", for instance, falls in a different ontological category than its dictionary synonyms "Diefstal" (Dutch) and "Diebstahl" (German) since "theft" is an act of appropriation, and "diefstal" an act of taking (and both jurisdictions do separate these notions). Pragmatically the British and Dutch legal evaluative perspectives on this crime are very similar compared to for instance the "common-sense" evaluative perspective of a libertarian who maintains that taxation is theft. The words are synonyms relative to the many contexts in which they can be interchanged, but synonyms are not equivalent.

We may be believe that selected representative case positions will be classified as both "diefstal" and "theft", but they are not in a logical subsumption relation to each other. The adjudicated case description must be a prime implicant of theft (cf. [14] and generally [10]; i.e. no "substantial" fact can be omitted without changing the judgment) or else principles like *Lex Superior*, *Stare Decisis*, and *Ne Bis in Idem* loose their logical meaning. The modeler and the judge must come to the same decomposition of case positions into "substantial" facts. Looking at the definitions only, it does seem possible to prosecute someone for theft and then for "diefstal": each requires a substantive fact that the other does not.

For managing subsumption between norms and concepts we use two, complementary solutions: Firstly, the legislative drafter is given the opportunity to add explicit subsumption relations. Secondly, the system can try to find subsumption automatically based on detailed models of descriptive and normative content as we have demonstrated in the CLIME project (cf. [15]). The observations we made in that project about calculating descriptive subsumption and normative exceptions will be integrated into a petri-net based formalism for expressing procedures and norms (cf. generally [11]).

[4]In contracts this is a normal phenomenon: definitions are re-used instead of referred to.

4.3 Evaluation Models

Substantive criteria in regulations for legislative drafting – the ones that cannot be operationalized as restrictions on (XML) form – serve as source material for the decision support functionality. Substantive criteria work as norms of analysis – they serve to choose between alternatives. Norms of analysis are also found in other higher legislation, whether in the same jurisdiction or in the international arena, that the proposed legislation must comply with. Finally there are also important political goals – translated to norms of analysis – to be realized by the proposed legislation. All of these together make up the evaluative perspective of the legislative drafter, that forms the content of an RDF evaluation model about legislation, as described below:

Evaluation Model Some outcome is a reason to choose for or against an alternative from an evaluative perspective. The evaluative perspective is described in the evaluation model, which consists of:

Identity commitments With whose interests does the evaluator identify for the purpose of drafting. This may for instance be the communal interest of the people of the Netherlands, or those of particular vulnerable groups. Different stakeholders have different evaluative perspectives for the same legislation, but the evaluative perspective does not merely represent someone's interests: Presumably the authors serve the communal interests of the Netherlands, and those of academics, because that is part of their identity commitments. At the same time, their evaluation of the communal interests of the Netherlands is not necessarily identical because of differences in assumptions and political outlook.

Norms The metrics that make it possible to identify what alternative serves relevant interests better. These are often relative to the identities committed to: economic growth may be good in general, but the legislative drafter may only be interested in economic growth in the Netherlands – not somewhere else. In other cases they are universal.

Evaluative Concepts The norms of analysis will usually be defined in terms of evaluative concepts; Theft is a typical example – descriptive and prescriptive. The application of the concept is guided by descriptive restrictions and it is an argument against the facts described by it. A label such as "illegal" can be applied to anything, whereas a label like "appropriation" is not an argument against the thing described by it.

Descriptive Concepts Evaluative concepts are defined in terms of descriptive concepts that are understood well enough to recognize their instances.

Causal Assumptions Since evaluative concepts often evaluate situations that cannot be directly controlled, they are often accompanied by certain causal assumptions about how the situations judged undesirable are brought about about. Regularities of behavior are the most important class of these assumptions.

Descriptive and evaluative concepts are imported from RDF models that contain fragments of ontology. A comparison between two regulations involved three evaluation models: Two evaluation models that describe the norms expressed in the regulation that serve as *comparatum* and *comparandum*, and a third that serves as *tertium comparationis*. Norms can be considered as a motivator of (my) behavior, or as descriptions of regularities in behavior – a norm that "works" causes a regularity in behavior. Lets take a very simple case. The *tertium comparationis* expresses $[\neg\, smoking] \prec [smoking \wedge \neg\, inside] \prec [smoking \wedge inside]$, the *comparatum* expresses $[smoking \wedge \neg\, inside] \prec [smoking \wedge inside]$ and the *comparandum* is silent on the issue. The norm in the *comparatum* can be assumed to work as a behavior regularity $smoking \Rightarrow \neg\, inside$, in which case the comparatum is better, or not, in which case we are indifferent. Alternatively, there may be a known probability that people will comply with the norm, or there may be categories of people that do, and categories that don't comply. The norms of the comparatum and comparandum become a basis for assumptions about behavior in the *tertium comparationis*.

Because legislation is essentially a tool for evaluating behavior, it is not surprising that it can be represented itself as an evaluation model. In addition to the basic deontic binary distinction *allowed* $\prec$ *disallowed* attached to a situation description, there are explicit evaluative distinctions such as *reasonable* $\prec$ *unreasonable* for behavior, *admissible* $\prec$ *inadmissible* for evidence, and implicit evaluative distinctions such as *status offense* $\prec$ *delinquent act* $\prec$ *crime*, or *verified by evidence* $\prec$ *verified by oath*. Some of the rare cases where the legislator explicitly uses (almost) continuous evaluative scales occur in criminal law (days in prison or amount of fine) and consumption taxes (percentage added) where such taxes are intended to cause evasive behavior.

4.4 Decision Support

Theory construction about law can be treated as an enormously complex system of assumptions about the likelihood of, and preferences for outcomes. Decision support systems (DSS) help us to manage the complicated interactions between our preferences for outcomes and the likelihood that those outcomes come about. Sometimes we choose if we want one thing *or* another, establishing preferences. Sometimes we choose if we want one thing *before* another, establishing priorities. Preference and priority rankings can always be established by comparison of pairs of alternatives. DSS technologies formalizes the problem to be solved in terms of possible choices, likelihood of choices, possible outcomes of choices, likelihood of outcomes of choices, and preference for outcomes.

Legislation expresses norms, and norms express a preference of the legislator, ceteris paribus, of case P over Q as long as the legislation exists, given that description P is ceteris paribus preferable ([6]) to description Q if all alternative situations $p_1, p_2, .., p_n$ are preferable to alternatives $q_1, q_2, .., q_n$ and one is otherwise indifferent between those alternatives. This expression of preference is limited to situations that can be caused by a group of people addressed by the legislator and is optionally accompanied by a threat of punishment for disobedience. The punishment is effected by norms that instruct others (police, etc.) to react.

The norms aim to change existing preferences between choices displayed by that group – sometimes by adding a new cost or benefit to a choice. The value of the legislation is primarily based on its results on behavior. The expected desirable effect of legislation on behavior is based on beliefs about people's preferences between alternatives without the legislation, and beliefs about how the new legislation will affect people's preferences (through mechanisms such as mimesis and conditioning). The field of taxation is a shining example of people's ability to adapt their choices in unforeseen and undesirable ways to new legislation.

When multiple, incompatible norms have to be applied to a case, we can choose between the norms, or weigh the relative importance of the norms. The standard criteria for choosing between norms in a norm application context are the authority of the source of the norm (Lex Superior) and the cognitively valid rules of belief revision (Lex Specialis, Lex Posterior).

Since norms, as expressed, are often indicative of underlying preference dimensions that meet criteria such as decomposability, mutual preferential independence, or even mutual utility independence, there is often a standard method (additive value function, multiplicative utility function) for weighing their importance. There are also a number of procedures to reconcile incompatibilities between preferences of different decision-makers (one of the simplest ones being being the "anonymous voter" procedure of representative democracy). Using such methods and procedures is usually not acceptable in an application context, but they can, and do, play a role in the context of drafting and evaluation.

A very well-known and standard method assigns utilities and probabilities to outcomes and evaluates alternative choices as alternative "lotteries". Assigning probabilities gives the whole exercise a sense of exactness that is often undeserved: the real problem is one of coming up with the alternatives and foreseeing the possible outcomes. For this purpose an ontology of the problem domain, like the criminal ontology of our department ([3]), is useful. In the context of law – or almost anywhere outside lotteries – the actual outcome of your choice usually depends on other people's choices. This can be approached with statistics or, better, with assumptions about the evaluative perspective of others. Legislators typically assume that the norms of analysis of its subjects are largely the same, and the identity commitments are different in that they are selfish. This assumption underlies the simple approaches to game theory that dominate political argument. Civil servants are on the contrary expected to adopt the norms of analysis of legislation, and the identity of the community they serve.

5 Discussion and Conclusions

We have expressed the need for knowledge management support for legislative drafting. Such a support environment should at least provide the following functionalities: Management of references, version management, management of subsumption structures, access to other (similar) legal documents ('best practices'), and access to guidelines or norms about drafting. Prerequisite for such support is a standard way for describing legal sources. Since legislative drafters are more and more working in an international setting, this standard should be independent of language and jurisdiction. With METALex we have proposed such a standard in XML.

Since an important subtask of legislative drafting is the comparison of normative systems, we have explored the usability of METALex models of structure and RDF models of content for this purpose. Even in the trivial case of theft a reliable concept-to-concept correspondence is not achievable on purely logical grounds. The feasibility of 'legal dictionary' attempts like the ones in the LeXML (cf. [9]) and Legal XML communities is doubtful for more than the most trivial applications. Looking for correspondence at the level of 'norms' appears to be more promising.

In a comparison context, civil servants are usually expected to adopt the norms of analysis of legislation, and the identity of the community they serve, unless the comparison concerns civil servant integrity policy. In economic analysis of taxation the rule-following behavior of civil servants is usually abstracted away completely (see e.g. [8, 7]), and the tax administration is described as a machine. Computer-assistance of administrative procedures – expert systems for instance – on the contrary usually coerces the civil servant (internal perspective on obligations), and passively monitors the actions of actors on the outside (external perspective on obligations). This shows that different contexts lead to different assumptions about the norms as motivators of behavior. Often different assumptions in different analyses are reasonable, but it easily leads to confusing intentions with expectations, for example if we assume in one context that a tax on diesel intended to generate income generates income, and in another that a tax on diesel intended to cause evasive behavior causes evasion to another fuel.

An obvious criticism of our focus on codified legislation is that we must assume that the surrounding legal systems are the same for the results to be meaningful. The same can of course be said of the legal theorist who compares legal systems with the intention of a so-called "legal transplant" of interesting (foreign) concepts to another situation: it is another jurisdiction with another culture, another vocabulary, even another role of codified legislation, etc. The freedom of expression granted by the Soviet constitution and the U.S. constitution are for instance clearly not equivalent. In Comparative Law the results are equally restricted by simplifying assumptions.

References

[1] A. Boer, R. Hoekstra, R. Winkels, T. van Engers, and F. Willaert. ^{META}lex: Legislation in XML. In T. Bench-Capon, A. Daskalopulu, and R. Winkels, editors, *Legal Knowledge and Information Systems (Jurix 2002)*, pages 1–10, Amsterdam, 2002. IOS Press.

[2] A. Boer, T. van Engers, and R. Winkels. Using Ontologies for Comparing and Harmonizing Legislation. In *Proceedings of the International Conference on Artificial Intelligence and Law (ICAIL)*, Edinburgh (UK), 2003. ACM Press.

[3] J. Breuker, L. Elhag, E. Petkov, and R. Winkels. Ontologies for legal information serving and knowledge management. In T. Bench-Capon, A. Daskalopulu, and R. Winkels, editors, *Legal Knowledge and Information Systems (Jurix 2002)*, pages 73–82, Amsterdam, 2002. IOS Press.

[4] I. Brightwell and R. D. Hughes. Computerised Legislative Drafting and Access to Statutes. *The Journal of Information, Law and Technology (JILT)*, 1, 2000.

[5] S. Debaene and B. van Buggenhout. *Informatietechnologie & de kwaliteit van wetgeving, Intersentia Rechtswetenschappen*. Antwerpen, 2000. In Dutch.

[6] J. Doyle and M. P. Wellman. Representing preferences as ceteris paribus comparatives. In *Decision-Theoretic Planning: Papers from the 1994 Spring AAAI Symposium*, pages 69–75. AAAI Press, Menlo Park, California, 1994.

[7] W. Hettich and S. L. Winer. Economic and political foundations of tax structure. *American Economic Review*, 78(4):701–712, 1988.

[8] W. Hettich and S. L. Winer. Rules, Politics, and the Normative Analysis of Taxation. Carleton Economic Papers 00-12, Carleton University, 2000.

[9] M. Muller. The RDF Dictionary and the standardisation process in the legal domain. In *Proceedings of XML Europe*, 2002.

[10] L. Pallipoli, F. Pirri, and C. Pizzuti. Algorithms for Selective Enumeration of Prime Implicants. *Artificial Intelligence*, 111:41–72, 1999.

[11] J. Raskin, Y. Tan, and L. van der Torre. How to model normative behavior in Petri nets. In *Proceedings of Modelage '96, Sesimbra*, 1996.

[12] C. van Laer. The Applicability of Comparative Concepts. *European Journal of Comparative Law*, 2.2, 1998.

[13] W. Voermans and E. Verharen. Leda: a semi-intelligent legislative drafting-support system. In B. v. B. J.S. Svensson, J.G.J. Wassink, editor, *Legal knowledge based systems JURIX 95: Intelligent Tools for Drafting Legislation, Computer – Supported Comparison of Law*, Lelystad, 1995. Koninklijke Vermande.

[14] R. Winkels, A. Boer, and R. Hoekstra. CLIME: Lessons learned in Legal Information Serving. In F. van Harmelen, editor, *Proceedings of the European Conference on Artificial Intelligence 2002, Lyon*, Amsterdam, 2002. IOS-Press.

[15] R. Winkels, D. Bosscher, A. Boer, and J. Breuker. Generating Exception Structures for Legal Information Serving. In T. Gordon, editor, *Proceedings of the Seventh International Conference on Artificial Intelligence and Law (ICAIL-99)*, pages 182–195, New York (NY), 1999. ACM.

Substitution of Legal Statement and Identification of Law

Juan José Iniesta Delgado
Facultad de Derecho, Universidad de Murcia
Murcia, España
jiniesta@um.es

Abstract. Substitution is a type of normative changes produced by legal statements named substituting statement. However, this form of modification is not only a combination of derogation and incorporation of legal statement. Temporal affects grant difficulties to determine the effects of this type of legal modification.

1 Introduction

My interest in studying legislative changes a study which I have been involved with through the development of a research project at the University of Murcia in the area of philosophy of law– is due to the need to establish a theoretical base in order to elaborate and improve computer tools which are useful in enabling the identification of Law.

It needs to be said at the outset that one of the main difficulties an investigator finds when he tries to identify the entities which make up part of a specific legal system is precisely their dynamic nature[1]; these legal entities find themselves subjected to constant changes and the new provisions affect the previously elaborated ones. In this way the identification of Law converts itself into a problem of temporal delimitation: what was at one time Law, may no longer be so at later moment in time.

We can define legislative change as the production of a legal corpus which includes a statement which modifies another legal statement or other legal corpus; this modification may consist either in the suppression of one or several legal statements or the inclusion of one or several legal statements.

It's easy to understand the specific problems this type of legal production represents when it comes to the identification of law. Firstly, it's important to determine what these *modifications* consist of, only so is it possible to state explicitly how a computer programme can help to identify Law. It is equally important to differentiate it from other cases where there is no real alteration, although these may be presented by teaching as cases of changes, with the consequent dysfunction when the time comes to identifying the true identity of Law.

Before beginning an analysis of normative change, it needs to be made clear and in order to avoid future confusion that what some authors have referred to in their works as the *addition* and *subtraction* of legal norms may in principle be similar to the arguments set out here. Concretely, Carlos ALCHOURRON and Eugenio BULYGIN speak of the sum of norms which correspond to an act of normative production[2] and go on to state that the whole or sum of the resulting norms after the normative production is not equal to the sum of the whole of the previous norms before production. But this has little to do with the hypothesis that I am analyzing here. Among other reasons, because these authors talk of *norms* while I refer to

Juan José Iniesta Delgado, 'Substitution of Legal Statement and Identification of Law' in D. Bourcier (ed.), *Legal Knowledge and Information Systems. Jurix 2003: The Sixteenth Annual Conference*. Amsterdam: IOS Press, 2003, pp. 101-110.

statements. They understand norms in the sense of propositions or meanings of statements[1], like combinations of meanings or as logical consequences of these meanings and combinations of meanings. So that each time there is normative production and new meanings are incorporated to the system of meanings, the number of norms turns out to be altered in an uneven proportion to the number of norms furnished.

But I am not talking about meanings or of meaning-norms, but rather I'm speaking of statements, since I consider that it is these which effectively form part of Law.

Up to now we have indicated that change is produced when one of the statements which is incorporated in Law through the produced legal corpus alters the set of statements which belong to Law up to that moment –without taking into account its own inclusion.

This change may be due to the fact that the *modifying statement* does away with one or several legal statements, either because the modifying statement adds one or various legal statements (distinct in themselves), or else, at the same time does away with and adds one or several statements[2] . Each one of these operations has been assigned a specific name: *derogation*, *incorporation* and *substitution*.

It is precisely the aim of this paper to report on the peculiarities the last operation displays, fundamentally with a view to it simplifying the computerized process of identifying Law. In this way it could be considered that even though it is more appropriate to express it as a combination of operations of repeal and incorporation, there exist some aspects which go beyond the simple conjunction of these operations.

2 Substitution

Substitution is produced when modifying intervention means the replacement, in the core of a specific set of laws, of a statement, which we shall call the *substituted statement*, for another which we shall call the *substitute statement*. The said change is produced by means of the issue of a *substituting statement*, which in this case operates as a modifying statement.

For example:

(N1): article 6 of legal corpus X: "Those who purchase an imported car shall be liable to pay a 10 % tax on the purchase price".

(N2): "Article 6 of legal corpus X is drafted with the following text: 'Those who purchase an imported car shall be liable to pay a 5 % tax on the purchase price'".

In this example (N2) would be the *substituting* statement, (N1) would be the *substituted* statement, while the statement 'Those who purchase an imported car shall be liable to pay a 5 % tax on the purchase price' will be the *substitute* statement.

2.1 Types of Substitution

Depending on the structure of the *substituting* statement we can distinguish two classes of substitution which we shall respectively call *complete substitution* and *partial substitution*.

Complete substitution is produced when the substituting statement mentions and contains the substitute statement which occupies the place of the substituted statement, which was only mentioned. Complete substitution can be *symmetric* or *asymmetric*.

[1] Meaning-norms are abstract entities and their existence (if it is possible to talk of such a thing, as it is pretty unusual to talk of the existence of propositions) is timeless. [2], ibid. p. 61.

[2] Which corresponds to the three ways in which a normative system may be changed according to Bulygin: 1) the introduction of new norms; 2) the derogation of existing norms (through new norms) and 3) the substitution of existing norms for others; [4]

Complete symmetric substitution is produced when there is the same number of substituted statements as substitute statements. An example can be found in the first section of the final provision number 18 of LO 1/1996 of 15th June, one of whose statements modifies article 1330 of the Civil Code, substituting one statement for another.

Complete asymmetric substitution is produced when there are either more substituted statements than substitute statements, or there are less substituted statements than substitutes. An example of the first case can be found in another statement of the same section of the above mentioned final provision, which modifies article 996 of the Civil Code, substituting the two statements of the previous draft for only one statement in the new draft. An example of the second case constitutes the first paragraph of the final disposition of L 7/2003, which modifies article 1056, paragraph two of the Civil Code, substituting the only statement which formed part of the said paragraph for five new statements.

Partial substitution occurs when the substituting statement mentions the substituted statement and identifies certain changes in the expressions or the punctuation marks contained in the said statement. Depending on the nature of the changes partial substitution can be *by elimination* of an expression or punctuation mark, *by integration* of an expression or punctuation mark or *by replacement* of an expression or punctuation mark. The substituting statement does not contain, in this case, the substitute statement, in contrast to what happens in complete substitution. Instead it either contains certain expressions of the substituted statement, or of the substitute statement, or both of them.

Partial substitution by elimination is produced when the substituting statement does away with or eliminates words, expressions or punctuation marks of the substituted statement. Partial substitution by integration consists of including words, expressions or punctuation marks in the substituted statement. Partial substitution by replacement occurs when words, expressions or punctuation marks of the substituted statement are changed for other different ones.

Examples of all these types of partial substitution can be found in the second section of the final provision number 18 of the quoted L 1/1996. So there is partial substitution by elimination when it is noted "at the end of the final paragraph of the same article 171 the phrase 'or Guardianship, according to whichever applies' is included"; there is partial substitution by replacement when it states that "in articles 323 and 324, the words 'tutor' and 'tutors' will be substituted respectively for those of 'guardian' and 'guardians'".

It needs to be pointed out that partial substitution may be produced by two types of substituting statements depending on the way through which the substituted statement is identified:

1) If the substituted statement is designated individually by the substitutingstatements, this is called the *nominative substituting statements*. This is the most common case.

2) If the substituting statement does not individually designate the substituted statement but rather this is identifiable due to its belonging to a set of statements that possess certain specific characteristics, it is called a *nameless substituting statement*. For example, when the substituting statement refers to the replacement of a term for another in all clauses which make reference to it.

2.2 *The Interpretation of the Substituting Statement*

2.2.1 Forms of Substituting Statement

As and how we have just seen, the substituting statement can adopt diverse forms which give rise to the diverse forms of substitution previously mentioned; and even within each one of these types different expressions are used to indicate the production of the indicated effect. When we are dealing with complete substitution, the substituting statement usually begins with expressions such as "the articles... shall be drafted in the following way..." or "the law... shall be modified in the following terms...". When it's the case of partial substitution, the terminology is much more varied; for example partial substitution by replacemen is often expressed by "this word '...' shall be substituted for the word '...'; partial substitution by elimination through "the words '...' shall be eliminated" or "the words '...' shall be removed', even, the expression "they are derogated' has come to be used, quite unsuitably, to refer exclusively to specific expressions of a legal statement.

2.2.2 Legal Theory of Substitution

Any of these statements can give rise to a normative modification, in so far as it affects in some form the substituted statement. As regards the basic modifying operations –eliminate and include– only abolishment changes the other legal statements (inclusion only alters other legal corpus). We can, then, state that the alteration which a substituted statement suffers consists in its derogation.

In so far as the substituted statement is concerned, it can, therefore, be said that substitution is the equivalent of derogation. This explains why the substituting statement has to meet the following necessary requirements as part of a legal theory of derogation, in order that the elimination of the substituted statement can be produced:

1. There is a substituting statement which mentions the substituted statement.
2. The substituting statement is powered to derogate the substituted statements.

The situation of a statement substantial enough to "is powered to derogate" is linked to the possible relationship between the modifying and modified statements in so far as they are integrals of the same system. The relations that can give rise to a situation "is powered to derogate" are:

a When the derogate provision is higher in hierarchical rank than the statement which is going to be derogated.

b When the derogate provision is of the same hierarchical rank to the statement which is going to be derogated, providing the following condition is met: the derogate provision must have been produced by an authority which is powered to produce legal statements which come under its territorial and material terms of reference corresponding to the legal corpus to which the statement, which it is intended to derogate, belongs.

c When the derogate provision is of inferior or equal hierarchical rank to the statement it is intended to derogate, providing the following conditions are met:

- there is, at the moment in which the derogation takes place, a legal statement that meets one of the conditions that gives power to derogate the statement which it intends to derogate.
- this statement grants to the derogate provision power to derogate.

d The substituting statement is a legal statement at the time substitution should occur.

e The substituted statement is a legal statement at a moment prior to the production of the substitution.

As regards the substitute statement, it is finally incorporated into the set of laws belonging to the same legal corpus to which the substituted statement belonged. That is, as regards the substitute statement, substitution is the equivalent to incorporation. It is necessary, therefore, that certain necessary requirements need to produce themselves for the incorporation of the substitute statement:

1. There is a substituting statement which mentions substitute statement.
2. The substituting statement is powered to incorporate statements to the receiving legal corpus.
3. The substituting statement is a legal statement at the time when substitution should take place.
4. The receiving legal corpus is a legal statement just prior to substitution taking place.

If the substituting statement meets the requirements in order to be able to derogate the substituted statement, it will also necessarily meet the requirements to incorporate the substitute statement. Given the receiving legal corpus is the same as where the substitute statement can be found, we can say that if the substituting statement is powered to derogate a statement of this legal corpus of laws, it will also have it to incorporate statements. On the other hand, if the substituting statement is a legal statement at the time of derogation, it will also be so at the time of incorporation. If the substituted statement is a legal statement just before its substitution, the set of laws to which it belongs will necessarily also be a legal corpus.

It needs to be pointed out that the derogation of a statement which has to be substituted, it is essential for the incorporation of the substitute statement is produced, hence the effects of derogation and incorporation are necessarily linked. The incorporated legal statement enters to form a part of the legal system under the condition that it occupies the place of the substituted statement in such a way that if the said statement does not abandon the legal system, the substitute statement does not meet the conditions to belong to Law.

In this way, the substituting statement has two joint meanings: on the one hand, it qualifies a statement (the substituted one) as not legal, and on the other, it qualifies another statement (the substitute one) as legal. Put another way, the substituting statement jointly has the meanings of derogate provisions and of incorporating statements[3].

2.2.3 Another Interpretation of the Substituting Statement

Interpreting substitution without attending to the composition of the basic modifications, although this may appear attractive, is all the same flawed. In this case, the aim is not to see substitution as the sum of derogation and incorporation, but instead as a normative modification with its own substantiveness. Substitution would be the change to the text of the substituted legal statement. The substituted statement, according to this interpretation, is not derogated but rather only a part of its text is altered. There is, therefore, no substitute statement. The word substitution (an expression which suggests the exchange of one element for another) does not refer here to the affected statement (which it would be incorrect to call the substituted statement) but rather to the elements of this statement (words or even punctuation marks).

[3][5] p. 96.- considers that substitution consists in the end of belonging to the Law of one norm, which differs from derogation, because at the same another norm begins to belong to the law. I believe that this interpretation is not correct, because the derogation of a legal statement may or may not coincide with the inclusion of another norm in a legal system and no necesarily, we are before a case of substitution.

This explanatory model is essentially devised for the case of partial substitution. In fact, in complete substitution the scheme of the substituting statement reflects exactly the elements of substitution which form a part of the initial explanation: both the substituted statement and the substitute statement appear mentioned in it, in such a way that it is clear to appreciate the change whereby one element abandons the legal system and the entrance of a new one. On the other hand, in partial substitution the substituting statement seems to only expressly mention the substituted statement, and hence apparently confirms the thesis that in this case there is no substitute statement. It would, therefore, appear easy to conclude that the substituting statement does not derogate the substituted statement, but only alters its text.

However, I believe that beneath this form of understanding substitution there lies a confused concept about language. Two different entities can both have the same name and despite this still remain two separate entities, even in the case where one of them occupies –to a certain extent- the place of the other[4] . Let's think of a couple who have a son whose name is Peter; but which dies only a few months after birth. Time passes and they have another son who they also call Peter. Obviously, the usual way to express this situation is that the second son has the same name as the first deceased son; nobody would seriously try to explain this situation in the following way: Peter has been modified.

Two distinct statement are also two distinct entities. The statement 'those who purchase an imported car must pay a tax levy of 5% on the purchase price' is a distinct statement to the statement 'those who purchase an imported car must pay a tax levy of 5% on the purchase price', although both are denominated article 6 of legal corpus X. No matter how we formulate the second statement, we could mention the first one and say that we change it for the second, or rather we could mention the first and indicate that where it says 5% it should read 10%; we will have two different statements, although each with the same denomination.

On the other hand, we run the risk of finding incongruent situations. Let us consider what would occur if a derogate provision indicated the derogation of a statement at a specific time and before that moment arrived, in which the corresponding derogate effect should come into action, the statement which is going to be derogated is substituted. If we understand that the substituted statement continues to belong to the legal system, that is, the previous statement continues to be the same but with a distinct text, we will have to admit that the said statement must be derogated when the time for the derogative effect arrives, even though the said statement has been substituted during this time. And even taking into account that the intention to substitute were a legislative will, after the intention of derogate. On the other hand, if we admit that the substituted statement is no longer a legal statement, the derogative effect of the provision could no longer take place, as one of the conditions which dashes the expectation of derogation will have been produced: the statement which is going to be derogated would not be a legal statement at the time of its derogation.

We can also observe that it is incorrect to state that in partial substitution the substituting statement only mentions the substituted statement; the substitute statement is also mentioned. Let us look carefully at, according to the basis of this presentation, a substituting statement of the type 'in article 6 of legal corpus x the expression 5% shall be substituted for the expression 10%' could be interpreted with the following meaning: 'article 6 of legal corpus x is substituted by an enunciative statement with the text of article 6 of legal corpus x changing the expression 5% for the expression 10%'. It is therefore clear that the substitute statement is not contained within the substituting statement, but is mentioned in it. If it were not even mentioned, then the first requisite needed for the completion of the normative incorporation

[4]Waismann has paid particular attention to this problem and has assembled a series of examples from pathological psychiatry. Nonetheless, for our purposes the following example will serve our needs even though it isn't as showy. [6]

theory essential for incorporation to produce itself would not be met; just think it would be impossible for the substituting statement to declare it legal, because for a statement to qualify another in some way it is necessary for it to be metalinguistic with respect to the other, and to do so it is absolutely necessary that it mentions it.

Anyway, it is at this point when semantics and logic come in to play with respect to an analysis of identity and the conditions for this, in which a profound debate about how far it is possible to consider that an entity continues to be the same despite its changes and when does it convert into a different entity[7]. Nevertheless, in linguistic terms, none of the notions of identity admitted is able to support the idea that there has not been substitution of one statement for another distinct one. Identity is either syntactical or semantic. Neither of these identities can be found among the substituted statement or the substitute statement, if there is no identity, then there is necessarily diversity of entities.

None the less, it needs to be stressed that the lack of formulation in the substitute statement produces more than a certain degree of difficulty. In which ever of the other hypothetical cases of normative incorporation (incorporation properly said or complete substitution), the text of the statement which is classified as legal is contained in the incorporating or substituting statements. Instead, with partial substitution, the substituting statement does not contain the text of the statement which establish it as belonging to Law; its own formation is left to the work of interpretation through a type of guesswork, a fact which reveals not only terrible legislative technique, but also its lack of responsibility. There are already quite enough problems in their own right when it comes to identification of Law without having to complicate it with absolutely unnecessary guesswork and crossword puzzles, especially as it is always possible in cases where partial substitution is employed to fall back on, at least, complete substitution, which although not exempt of complications, is not as disastrous as the other.

The vices of partial substitution are not in the least unknown to the legislator. Tax law, a field noted for its extreme sensibility towards the exact identification of law, has produced a number of rules about how to articulate normative modifications. In so far as it concerns us here, special mention needs to be made of the second paragraph of article 4 of L.1/1998, of 26th February, concerning the Rights and Guarantees of the taxpayer: 'the laws and regulations which modify tax laws shall contain a complete list of all the derogated norms and the new wording of the resulting modified norms'. In the said provision we can find two diverse orders, one referring to the derogative process and the other to substitution. The second of them, serves to prescribe that all substitutions which are made to laws and regulations concerning tax law shall be complete substitutions. It aims to repeal ill-fated partial substitutions, "sparing the taxpayer the time consuming and absurd task of recomposing texts interlining the modified line, word or paragraph"[8].

Nevertheless, the said prescription still only remains a recommendation for legislative technique, just as the situation had been up to then -article 16 of L. 230/1963, 28th December, at least in so far as the legislator is concerned[9].

3 Conclusion

The understanding of legislative substitution together with other modifications is important in any technological system whose function it is to provide information (both to judicial workers and to the general public) about the Law in force at any specific moment in time. The importance of the said understanding is maintained whether the changes introduced into the system are made by humans or articulated through semi or automatic management models of legislative change.

In this sense, it should be pointed out the appropriateness of normative change is guided by a series of theoretical concepts which jurists use and concretely form an integral part of the definition of what Law is. On some occasions the said concepts are reflected in Law, (for example, in Spanish Law, the indication that the laws are amended by others), but in other cases they continue to operate as definable criteria in the mind of the jurist (for example, the consideration that derogation puts an end the legal existence of a norm).

Modifications to the computerized information system must be carried out in such a way as to make sure that the results achieved at the end concur as near as possible with those expected according to the theoretical concepts operational at the time.

When normative changes are introduced by humans, it is necessary and sufficient for the person to be aware of the criteria provided by the said concepts and that they use them to reach appropriate decisions. However, when changes are introduced through an automatic process, criteria based on theoretical concepts are not enough in themselves.They need to be transformed into formal algorithmic criteria.

In this sense, the project which we are developing within the sphere of the University of Murcia and which encompasses the process of substitution has a similar objective to that of the Norma–System project which was pursued in the CIRSFID at the University of Bolonia[10]. The task is to make explicit the said theoretical concepts in the most suitable way possible in order to convert them into criteria of a formal nature.

Our own approach differs form that of Norma-System in that the processing of modification is not done with respect to complete normative texts, but rather by taking the statement as the basic unit of the process of modifications, which can be defined as a textual unit with complete meaning.

The statement is a portion of text . Nowadays legal statements are portions of written text from which copies are made. Data bases collect and store copies of the said statements in a computerized medium. The main difficulty with this type of processing can be found when it comes down to delimiting and identifying the statements, as nowadays not all the statements are identified in statutes. Normally under the same identifiable sign (paragraph or article) a number of statements can be found.

The advantage , on the other hand , is obvious with regard to the processing of temporary effects. It allows the statute's temporals aspects to be processed separately, as well as advising of the vicissitudes regarding its application (indications concerning its temporal sphere of reference).

Anyhow, it is essential the identification of each statement, with respect to which a markup language is applied, such as XML in such a way that this enables identification through the use of a modifying statement.

What follows is an attempt to show explicitly how to understand one of the phenomena of normative change, substitution. This can be seen to be the integration of the other two normative modification phenomena, derogation and incorporation. As has been shown, it is necessary to set out explicitly these criteria in order to elaborate the formal criteria by which the computer system operates.

References

[1] Bulygin,E., 'Teoría y técnica de legislación' in *Analysis logico y Derecho*, Centro de Estudios Constitutionales, Madrid 1991, pp. 419 ss.

[2] Alchourron, C.E., Bulygin, E., *Sobre la existencia de las normas jurídicas*, Distribuciones Fontamara, Mexico 1997 , pp. 73 ss.

[3] Bulygin, E., 'Dogmática jurídica y sistematización del Derecho', ibid. p. 477.

[4] Guastini –*Distinguendo. Studi di teoria e metateoria del diritto,* ibid. p. 96.

[5] Waismann, F., *Los principios de la filosofía lingüística* translation by José Antonio Robles, Instituto de Investigaciones Filosóficas, Universidad Autónoma de México 1970, pp. 237.

[6] Waismann, F., *Los principios de la filosofía lingüística,* Ibid., pp. 227.

[7] Paso Bengoa, J.M. Del Jiménenz Jiménez, C., *Derechos y Garantías del Contribuyente. Comentarios a la Ley 1/1998*, CISS, Valencia 1998.

[8] FERREIRO LAPATZA, J.J., "Fuentes de Derecho tributario. Disposiciones derogatorias" en *Comentarios a la Ley General Tributaria y líneas para su reforma,* volume I , Instituto de Estudios Fiscales, Madrid 1991, pp. 275.

[9] PALMIRANI, M., *Norma-System*, Clueb, Bologna 2000, p. 137.

IPROnto: An Ontology for Digital Rights Management

Jaime Delgado Isabel Gallego Silvia Llorente Roberto García
Universitat Pompeu Fabra (UPF), Departament de Tecnologia
Pg. Circumval·lació 8, E-08003 Barcelona, Spain

Abstract. Ontologies are a way to express semantics of concepts in a formal way. IPROnto is an ontology of the Digital Rights Management (DRM) domain. It has been specified to facilitate the development of e-commerce applications that need to be aware of rights associated to specific multimedia content. The paper describes the ontology and its possible uses. Since we started this work in the context of MPEG21 standardisation, we are currently progressing in the development of applications that follow the DRM MPEG-21 standards, such as a REL (Rights Expression Language) and a RDD (Rights Data Dictionary), and aligning our ontology to those specifications.[1]

1 Introduction

The main objective of this paper is to describe a specific ontology we have developed in our group. It is an attempt to specify in a semantic way the domain of Intellectual Property Rights (IPR). Since we are working in the area of e-commerce of multimedia content, we often talk about Digital Rights Management (DRM), that better express the scope, instead of IPR, that is a broader term.

The paper puts the ontology (IPROnto) into context by establishing the basis on which we have made our developments. We have been always trying to not *re-invent the wheel* by basing our work on existing activities, models and specifications.

IPROnto has two basic views: A static and a dynamic one. We start, in section 3 with the description of the static view. Since the ontology is rather complex and complete, we concentrate in the paper only on some aspects of it. In particular, we describe the concepts of IPR Agreement, including Contract and License (section 4), and some specific rights, such as Explotation or Moral rights (section 5). The IPROnto LegalEntity element is then described in section 6, before briefly entering into the dynamic view, that defines a content life cycle for DRM and an example of sub-ontology.

The paper finalises with the identification of the next steps and some conclusions.

2 Development of an IPR ontology: IPROnto

There are many initiatives trying to build an IPR framework for Internet-wide management of intellectual property. For instance, MPEG-21 [1] or, in the W3C (World Wide Web Consortium) initiatives framework, the ODRL (Open Digital Rights Language) proposal [2].

[1]This work has been partly supported by the Spanish Ministry of Science and Technology (AgentWeb, TIC2002-01336)

Jaime Delgado, Isabel Gallego, Silvia Llorente, and Roberto García, 'IPROnto: An Ontology for Digital Rights Management' in D. Bourcier (ed.), *Legal Knowledge and Information Systems. Jurix 2003: The Sixteenth Annual Conference*. Amsterdam: IOS Press, 2003, pp. 111-120.

Most of these initiatives have one thing in common: they work at the syntactic level. Their approach is to make a formalisation of some XML DTDs and Schemas that define a rights expression language (REL), such as the MPEG-21 REL [3].

In some cases, the semantics of these languages, i.e. the meaning of the expressions, are also provided but formalised separately as rights data dictionaries (RDD), for instance MPEG-21 RDD [4]. Rights dictionaries define terms in natural language, solely for human consumption; for this reason it is not easy to make an automatic processing of those terms.

However, the syntactic approach does not scale well in really wide and open domains like the Internet. An automatic processing of a huge amount of metadata coming from many different sources requires machine understandable semantics. The syntax is not enough when unforeseen expressions are met. Here is where semantics come to help their interpretation to achieve interoperation.

Our idea is to facilitate the automation and interoperability of IPR frameworks integrating both parts, the Rights Expression Language and the Rights Data Dictionary. These objectives can be accomplished using ontologies, which provide the required definitions of the rights expression language terms in a machine-readable form. Thus, from the automatic processing point of view, a more complete vision of the application domain is available and more sophisticated processing can be carried out.

We have taken the Semantic Web approach [5] because it is naturally prepared for the Internet domain and thus we use web ontologies. The modularity of web ontologies allows their easy extension and adaptation.

Since a lot of work has been done in the area of IPR representation and definition, we started the development of our ontology, that we have named IPROnto, from selected specifications. The results from <indecs> [6] and Imprimatur [7] projects were a suitable starting point because of their coverage in describing the IPR domain, so the terms definitions and their structure were adopted and formalised using web-ontology tools. This was complemented with previous work in our research group DMAG [8].

Furthermore, in order to provide a robust ontology basis for interoperability we rooted all our work in an upper ontology. We selected SUMO, a result of the SUO IEEE WG [9] attempt to establish a standard upper ontology. We are also considering other recent upper level alternatives like DOLCE [10] and LRI-core [11]. Finally, since the World Intellectual Property Organisation (WIPO) [12] is defining a common legal framework for IPR, we have used it to complete the legal aspects of the ontology.

These knowledge sources, identified in the IPROnto analysis phase, have been arranged as shown in Figure 1. Finally, during implementation phase, knowledge was acquired from the different sources and formalised using a Semantic Web ontology language, DAML+OIL [13].

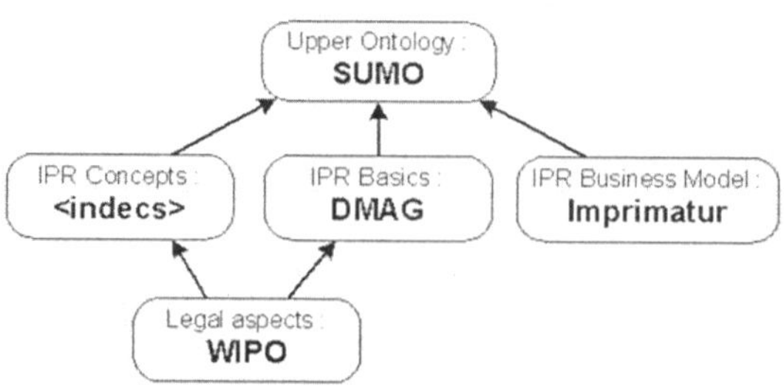

Figure 1: IPROnto knowledge sources design diagram

3 Static View of IPROnto

We can see the static view of IPROnto as a tree where elements are related from the bottom to the top. In Figure 2 we introduce a skeleton of the tree where only core elements, for simplicity, are presented. In the following subsections, some of the key elements are detailed to give a more complete view of the ontology. The root of the tree is an Entity, which may be Physical or Abstract. In turn, a Physical entity may be an Object or a Process, being this one more interesting, which might be an Event or a Situation. The only elements below Event that we will detail concern the concept of Agreement, including contract or license for the distribution of copyright protected electronic material.

In the other side of the tree, although several elements may belong to an Abstract entity, only the LegalConcept is presented in the skeleton. Nevertheless, other options, not sketched here, are possible, such as Relation or Quantity. While the LegalConcept might come from a few elements, only details are given for two cases: IntellectualPropertyRight and LegalEntity. The presence of dots in the tree means that other *brother* elements exist, but have not been included in the skeleton.

The most interesting part of the IPROnto related to legal aspects is that related to the LegalConcept and the Transaction elements. In the first case, the IntellectualPropertyRight IPROnto tree element and their derived rights specifically. These rights are associated to multimedia digital content for automatic ecommerce in the Internet. In the case of the Transaction element, it is specially interesting the Agreement tree element related to the conditions that define to whom to commerce with multimedia content and their associated rights. All elements of the tree below LegalConcept and Agreement, together with some leaves, are detailed in the following subsections. For a global graphical view of how IPROnto looks like, see [14].

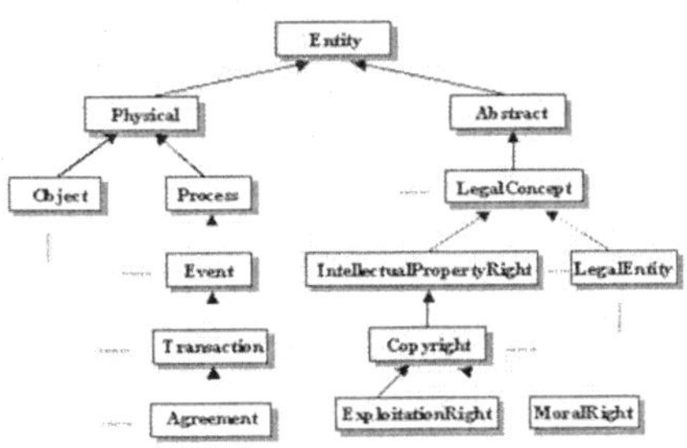

Figure 2: Core elements of the IPROnto skeleton

4 IPROnto Agreement

When a consumer wants to purchase, to a content distributor, audiovisual material subject to copyright, the content distributor presents an initial offer to the consumer. The process might finalise by accepting or not this offer. However, after the initial proposal, the negotiating entities might elaborate the contract, using a negotiation protocol, through a sequence of proposals and counter-proposals until a final agreement is reached, forming then the final electronic contract, which is signed by all the entities involved in the agreement. We have been previously working on implement this kind of IPR negotiation and contract development [15][16]. Figure 3 shows the Agreement tree element together with its dependent elements, IPRContract and IPRLicense. The dots in the tree mean that other kind of contract and licenses exist, but we only detail some examples.

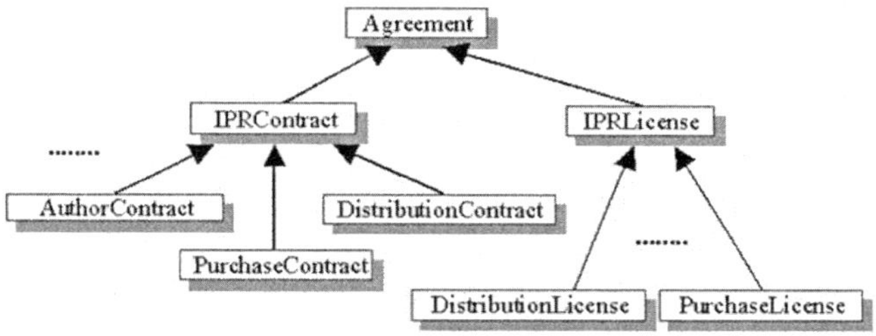

Figure 3: IPROnto Agreement

With IPRContract, we are grouping different kinds of contracts. One of them is *author's contract*, which represents the following scenario. Initially, the creator (writer, composer, actor, software programmer, etc.) of an intellectual work is holder of all the rights over it. Authors may not have the economic power to exploit their creations in an effective way, in such case, exploitation rights can be transferred to publishers/producers specialised on this task (a Rights Holder). Through *author's contract*, a publisher/producer becomes the exploitation rights holder of the work. As a counterpart, the original creator will receive royalties for the benefits derived from the exploitation of the work, or/and an initial fix revenue.

Another scenario represented by IPRContract is the one related with publishers/producers. They do not usually have direct contact with end-users. They commercialise works through distributors, entities specialised in acquiring part of the rights of copyrighted works to allow them to satisfy final users demand of these works (a Media Distributor). Formalisation of these agreements is made through *distribution contracts*, that may transfer some constrained exploitation rights or be mere licenses allowing the required actions to complete the commercialisation to end-users.

An IPRLicense represents the legal instrument by which a rights holder conveys usage rights associated to a resource to certain conditions to a consumer. Generally speaking, a license contains the following information:

- Entity that issued it. Typically, this entity has an associated authentication mechanism by which can prove its identity.
- Rights: Specifies an action or activity that an entity may perform using a resource.
- Resource: Identifies the object with associated rights to be used in a license.
- Conditions: Specifies the terms, conditions and obligations under which rights can be exercised, i.e. a time interval within which a right can be exercised, a limit to the number of times a right can be exercised, a fee that must be paid, etc.

For example, a *distribution license* is a kind of license in which a RightsHolder authorises a MediaDistributor the dissemination of a certain creation in a determined set of conditions. Copyrighted works arrive to their consumers through distributors. End-users acquire the right to access and use them by *purchase licenses*.

5 IPROnto IntellectualPropertyRight

Intellectual Property Rights (IPR) are legal instruments that provide a limited monopolistic right to the owner of things such as patents, trademarks or copyrighted works. They provide an incentive for the creation of and investment in new works (music, films, print media, software, performances, broadcasts, etc.) and their exploitation, thereby contributing to improved competitiveness, employment and innovation.

Some of the Intellectual Property Rights considered in IPROnto are shown in Fig. 4. This description is based on the Berne Convention [17] and the WIPO Copyright Treaty [12]. It is, as the sources state, broaden enough to ensure international applicability. There are local initiatives to implement these recommendations, as the EC Directive on Copyright 2001/29/EC [18] or the US Digital Millennium Copyright Act [19].

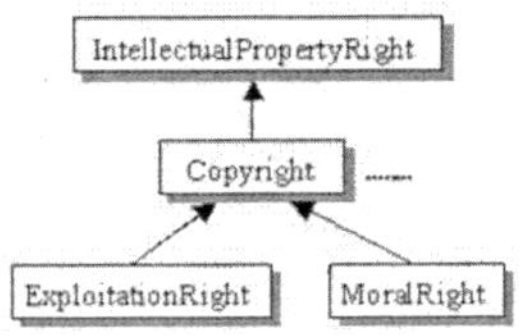

Figure 4: IPROnto IntellectualPropertyRight

All intellectual property rights are automatically given to originators of works (creators) by the simple fact of their authorship. They include moral rights that are independent of the author's economic rights and even after their transfer and exploitation right (economic rights), which are oriented to guarantee financial profit to originators of works. Figure 4 shows the relationship between Copyright, ExploitationRight and MoralRight.

Exploitation rights (so called economic rights) are oriented to guarantee financial profit to originators of works. The ExploitationRight includes:

- ReproductionRight: Exclusive right to authorize the reproduction, direct and indirect, permanent or temporary, in any manner or form.
- Communication to the Public Right (CommunicationRight): Exclusive right for the authorisation of any communication to the public of their works. These includes that members of the public may access them from a place and at a time individually chosen by them. Examples are: public performance, broadcasting, interactive on-demand transmission, etc.
- DistributionRight: Exclusive right to authorize the making available to the public of the original or copies of the work by sale or other transfer of ownership. Relevant only to tangible objects.
- TransformationRight: Exclusive right to authorize the manipulation of their works in any manner or form.

6 IPROnto LegalEntity

A LegalEntity relates to a LegalConcept, that is a concept defined by law, statute or international convention. Its terms are generally understood and defined in a series of international conventions and treaties and under national laws. An entity possessing capacity in law to exercise or enjoy an intellectual property right is a LegalEntity. It can be divided into two categories, CorporateLegalEntity, which refers to a legal entity inside a corporation and a NaturalLegalEntity, which could also be seen as a person in the real world.

Different business models, such as the IMPRIMATUR one [7], identify a series of entities that may take different roles, such as Creator, Provider, Rights Holder or Distributor. The relationships we have specified in IPROnto are sketched in Figure 5. Figure 6 shows a DAML+OIL serialisation of the LegalEntity shown in Figure 5. They include the following elements:

- Creator: Owner of the copyright in a work. He/She holds the exclusive right to use or authorize others to use the work on agreed terms.
- Rights Holder: Provides a license to exploit the creation on terms, which may be either predefined subject to negotiation.
- Content Provider: It acts in name of the Rights Holder, compiles and packs creations to provide to the distributors with multimedia content.
- Media Distributors: Apply to a Rights Holder for a license to exploit the creation.
- Customer: Person who wants to make use of a creation.

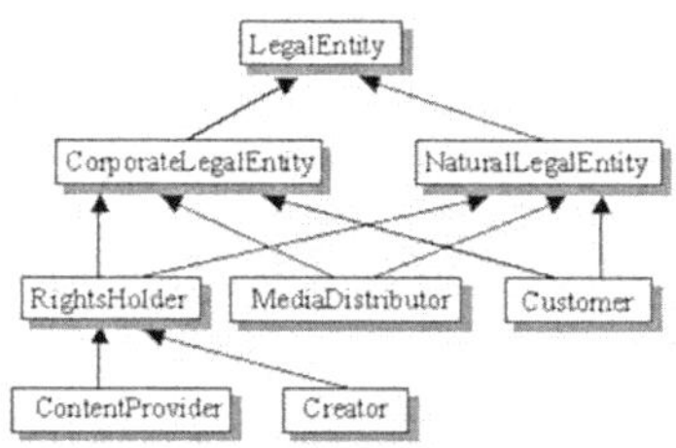

Figure 5: IPROnto LegalEntity

```
...
<daml:Class rdf:about="#CorporateLegalEntity">
   <rdfs:subClassOf rdf:resource="#LegalEntity" />
   <daml:disjointWith> <daml:Class rdf:about="# NaturalLegalEntity " /> </daml:disjointWith>
</daml:Class>
<daml:Class rdf:about="#NaturalLegalEntity">
   <rdfs:subClassOf rdf:resource="#LegalEntity" />
   <daml:disjointWith> <daml:Class rdf:about="# CorporateLegalEntity " /> </daml:disjointWith>
</daml:Class>
...
```

Figure 6: DAML+OIL fragment for IPROnto LegalEntity

7 Dynamic View of the IPR Ontology

The dynamic view of IPROnto allows the construction of IPR business models for its use in electronic commerce. This includes the possibility of defining events in the IPR domain. Some examples of events inside this context are Create or IPRContract. The description of these events and some other can be found in [20].

In the following subsections, we describe in more detail the creation process life cycle and the creation process subontology, a subontology derived from IPROnto.

7.1 Content Life Cycle

Concepts and relationships defined in IPROnto can be used to represent typical processes inside the IPR domain, together with the agents and resources they involve. These representations can be automatically tested to check semantic consistency, thanks to the explicit semantics that emerge from the ontology structure of concepts and relationships.

To show the expressive power of this semantic IPR approach, we present a detailed view of the creation life cycle in Figure 7.

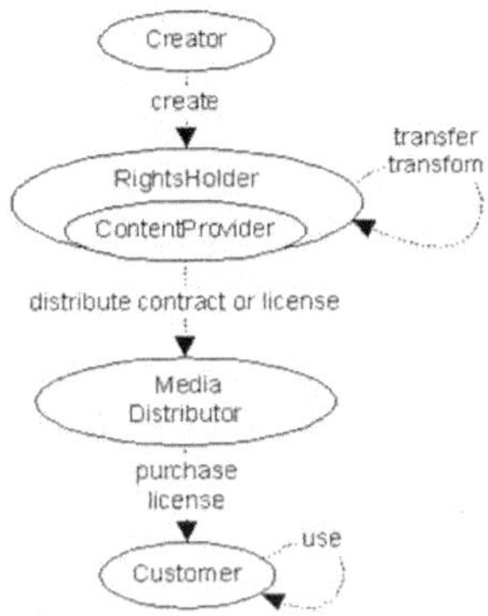

Figure 7: Content life cycle

The creation life cycle shown in Figure 7 involves roles (the ellipses) and actions (the arrows between ellipses). This generic business model has been inspired in the one defined by the IMPRIMATUR Project [7]. In the following paragraph, the content life cycle explanation, we are using italics to indicate that a concept appears in Figure 7.

The life cycle starts when someone with the role *Creator* originates a creation. This is the first role performing an action, *create*. Automatically, someone becomes the *RightsHolder* of the rights over this creation. The *RightsHolder* can be either the *Creator* or another legal entity with which the *Creator* has a contractual liaison.

At this point, the creation can be transferred (*transfer* action), changing the rights owner, or transformed (*transform* action), e.g. edited as a book. Also at this point, a *ContentProvider*, a kind of *RightsHolder* specialised in managing creations, may initiate its distribution. This is done through a *MediaDistributor*, who can hold rights or not depending on the contract agreed with the *ContentProvider*. We have considered two ways of allowing the distribution of the creation, through a contract or through a license. Finally, the last role involved is the *Customer* who receives the permission to *use* the content purchasing a license from the *MediaDistributor*.

7.2 Subontologies

The hierarchy of concepts and relations from the static view of the ontology, plus some of their interrelation constraints, has to be translated to a machine aware form. This leads to situations in which the relationship between concepts is difficult to explain in a tree, so we need a more complex graph. An example is shown in Figure 8.

Figure 8 shows the special relationship among the Manifestation, Abstraction and Expression elements of the IPROnto tree, being a Creation the union among the three elements.

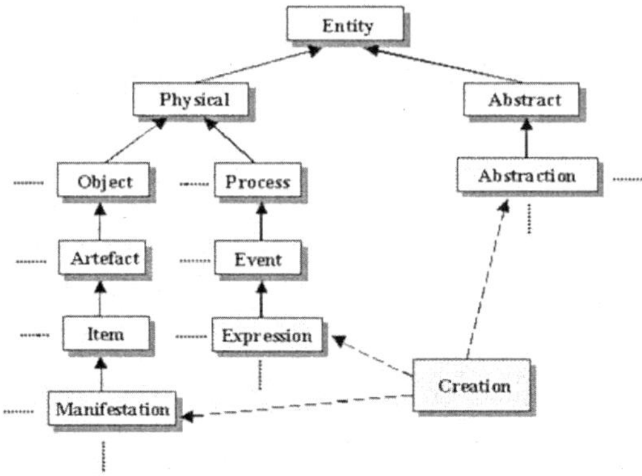

Figure 8: IPROnto Creation graph

The broken line arrows in Figure 8 represent this special relationship, a union. The rest of arrows represent an is-a relationship among elements.

Apart from relating the Creation with some other elements of the IPROnto tree, we have developed a new subontology derived from IPROnto, shown in Figure 9, that goes one step further from the static view.

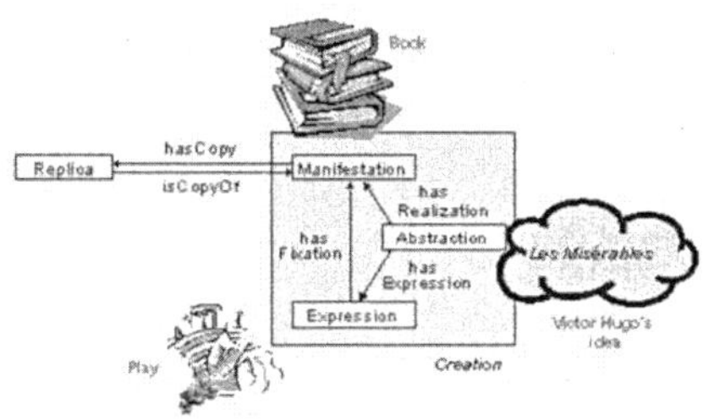

Figure 9: Creation subontology

Figure 9 shows the Creation subontology (the union of its abstract, material and temporal forms). These are the three points of view of a creation, the abstract, object and event perspectives that relate it to the upper level ontology from SUMO. For instance, if we take the creation *Les Misérables*, we observe its object view in a script, a book, etc. At the same time, its film projection would be the event part and all (script, book, film...) have in common an abstraction that comes from the original Victor Hugo's idea.

8 Implementation

IPROnto has been put into practise in the NewMARS project [21]. This project implements a broker-based application for digital content management. NewMARS supports a content life cycle based on the IPROnto one presented in Figure 7. The web interface of the application offers two IPR roles: Customer and Content Provider.

The customer can search the IPR database where IPROnto based metadata is stored. The first step is to locate an interesting digital content. Currently, this can be done using the Dublin Core and MPEG-7 metadata attached to the digital contents managed by NewMARS. Once a digital content has been selected, we enter the IPR related area. The customer can look for available offers for that content. The offers can be accepted or negotiated.

On the other hand, content providers can register digital contents in the NewMARS IPR database. The registration is performed uploading IPROnto based descriptions that model the life cycle of the contents they are offering. These descriptions can model all the digital content life cycle events except the purchase license, which is created when a customer accepts an offer. The events the content distributor can register are creations, rights transfers, transforms and distribution contracts and licenses. Moreover, distributors can register offers for the content they manage in order to meet their customers.

The distributor methods have not been integrated in the web interface yet and IPR information is only available for video contents. However, all IPR events information can be viewed through the administrator's free search web interface.

9 Next Steps

Since IPROnto tries to cover as much as possible of the IPR or DRM domain, it is open by definition. Although we have a stable version, different approaches or deeper details of some covered aspects could lead to an extension or modification of the ontology.

Many possible uses of IPROnto exist. We have explained one, NewMARS, an ecommerce application where we use IPROnto for negotiating digital rights.

However, we have new plans of work in the area, coming from our experience in MPEG-21. This standard is a multimedia framework that complements the previous MPEG standards that specify coding mechanisms for audiovisual material (such as MPEG-1, MPEG-2 and MPEG-4), and metadata schemas for content retrieval (MPEG-7). A few new parts of the MPEG-21 under-development standard deal with DRM aspects. The most relevant ones to this paper are a REL (Rights Expression Language) and a RDD (Rights Data Dictionary). These two standards, currently in the ISO/IEC FDIS (Final Draft International Standard) status since July 2003, specify how conformant applications interchange digital rights information, such as licenses.

One of our activities here is the development of the REL Reference Software [22], but we are also specifying a new DRM ontology that strictly follows the MPEG-21 RDD standard, so we have a clearly delimited scope.

10 Conclusions

We have introduced IPROnto, an ontology for the domain of Intellectual Property Rights (IPR). However, we are focussing on e-commerce applications in which multimedia content subject to rights is distributed, so we rather talk about Digital Rights Management (DRM).

IPROnto has a static and a dynamic view. The static view could be partly seen as a tree, where the different concepts are related. The paper gives some details on Agreements (Contracts and Licenses), Rigths (Exploitation, Moral, ...) and the LegalEntity concept.

Furthermore, a content life cycle helps putting actors, events and rights into context.

The ontology helps developing DRM applications, like NewMARS, by changing the current syntactic approach of standards such as MPEG, to a more semantic-oriented approach.

We started IPROnto a few years ago at the same time that current REL (Rights Expression Language) and RDD (Rights Data Dictionary) MPEG-21 standards, but the current scope of IPROnto is wider. We are currently working in a subset of IPROnto that strictly follows these new standards so we can guarantee compatibility of applications.

References

[1] MPEG-21 Overview, ISO/IEC JTC1/SC29/WG11/N5231. http://www.chiariglione.org/mpeg/standards/mpeg-21/mpeg-21.htm

[2] R. Iannella, Open Digital Rights Language (ODRL) Version 1.1, W3C Note 19 September 2002. http://www.w3.org/TR/odrl

[3] ISO/IEC FDIS 21000-5, MPEG-21 Rights Expression Language (REL), ISO/IEC JTC 1/SC 29/WG 11/N5839, July 2003

[4] ISO/IEC FDIS 21000-6, MPEG-21 Rights Data Dictionary (RDD), ISO/IEC JTC 1/SC 29/WG 11/N5842, July 2003

[5] The Semantic Web. http://www.semanticweb.org

[6] G. Rust and M. Bide, The <indecs> metadata framework, principles, model and data dictionary. In: <indecs>TM Framework Ltd, WP1a-006-2.0, 2000. http://www.indecs.org/pdf/framework.pdf

[7] The IMPRIMATUR Business Model, Version 2.1. In: IMPRIMATUR Project (Esprit 20676) http://www.imprimatur.net/IMP_FTP/BMv2.pdf

[8] DMAG (Distributed Multimedia Applications Group). http://dmag.upf.es

[9] Standard Upper Ontology (SUO) IEEE Working Group. http://suo.ieee.org

[10] DOLCE: a Descriptive Ontology for Linguistic and Cognitive Engineering. http://www.loa-cnr.it/DOLCE.html

[11] J. Breuker and R. Winkels, Use and reuse of legal ontologies in knowledge engineering and information management. In: ICAIL Workshop on Legal Ontologies and Web Based Legal Information Management, 2003

[12] World Intellectual Property Organization. http://www.wipo.org

[13] I. Horrocks, F. van Harmelen and P. Patel-Schneider, DAML+OIL (March 2001), Joint US/EU ad hoc Agent Markup Language Committee, 2001. http://www.daml.org/2001/03/daml+oil-index.html

[14] J. Delgado, I. Gallego, R. García and R. Gil, An ontology for Intellectual Property Rights: IPROnto. In: International Semantic Web Conference, 2002. http://dmag.upf.es/ontologies/ipronto/PosterISWC.pdf

[15] J. Delgado, I. Gallego and X. Perramon, Broker-Based Secure Negotiation of Intellectual Property Rights. In: Information Security, 4th International Conference (ISC2001), LNCS 2200, SpringerVerlag, 2001

[16] J. Delgado, I. Gallego, R. García and R. Gil, An architecture for negotiation with mobile agents. In: IFIP IEEE International Workshop on Mobile Agents for Telecommunication Applications (MATA'02), LNCS 2521, Springer-Verlag, 2002

[17] Berne Convention for the Protection of Literary and Artistic Works. http://www.wipo.int/treaties/ip/berne/index.html

[18] Directive 2001/29/EC of the European Parliament and of the Council of 22 May 2001 on the harmonisation of certain aspects of copyright and related rights in the information society. http://europa.eu.int/eur-lex/en/consleg/pdf/2001/en_2001L0029_do_001.pdf

[19] US Digital Millennium Copyright Act. http://www.loc.gov/copyright/legislation/hr2281.pdf

[20] J. Delgado, I. Gallego, S. Llorente and R García, Regulatory Ontologies: An Intellectual Property Rights approach. In: Workshop on Regulatory ontologies and the modeling of complaint regulations (WORM CoRe 2003).

[21] NewMARS research project. http://hayek.upf.es/newmars

[22] J. Delgado, I. Gallego and E. Rodríguez, Use of the MPEG-21 Rights Expression Language for music distribution. In: IEEE International Conference on Web Delivering of Music (WEDELMUSIC'03).

Cognitive Interfaces for Legal Expressions Description – Application to Copyrighted Works Online Sharing and Transactions

Melanie Dulong de Rosnay
Research Centre for Administrative Science (CERSA)
Information Technology, Law and Linguistic Laboratory
CNRS - Law University Paris II, Paris, France
melanie.dulong-de-rosnay@medialive.fr

Abstract. Legal and technical means regulate the digital dissemination of creative works. Technological protection measures and rights management information implementing copyright licenses or contracts are based on Rights Expression Languages, i.e. machine-readable ontologies that link copyright concepts and terms to events occurring on digital networks. While developing such devices, specific attention shall be dedicated users' expectations in terms of problem description and legal situations expression. In order to be interoperable and fair, Digital Rights Management systems need a common vocabulary describing legal use cases and supporting opposing interests, as well as architectural conditions enabling to describe contexts and express questions, toward a dialog between users. After a presentation of the domain legal framework and an evaluation of current standardization initiatives, we will apply the concept of cognitive interface to the conception of copyright regulation applications.

1 Introduction

The combination of compression, network capabilities and digital rights management technologies offers a great opportunity for a wide, quick and low cost public dissemination of creative and information works. Copyrighted works management is getting highly automated and IPMP systems are becoming Information Technologies regulators. Rights holders expect DRM systems to express and enforce legal conditions under which they decide to disseminate their works. Intermediate and end-users with no legal education expect to access to works through user-friendly and interoperable interfaces.

These interfaces are intended to describe contractual and legal situations. Both the vocabulary and the structure of these interfaces shall be compatible with accurate legal expression within copyright legislation requirements, enabling use context description by keywords or metadata simple to understand for all users, from legal professionals to non legal-experts.

Cognitive interfaces are defined as modes of questioning based on dynamic shape of users requests rather than on problem domain static knowledge. Decision making models including IPMP architectures and DRM applications can be build upon a representation of legal concepts and procedures. We therefore propose to develop a cognitive interface, which will allow the communication between various software resources and agents, "taking into account a meta-knowledge implied in the situation of dialog with a view to adapting it to types of specific requests in a domain" [2].

Melanie Dulong de Rosnay, 'Cognitive Interfaces for Legal Expressions Description – Application to Copyrighted Works Online Sharing and Transactions' in D. Bourcier (ed.), *Legal Knowledge and Information Systems. Jurix 2003: The Sixteenth Annual Conference.* Amsterdam: IOS Press, 2003, pp. 121-130.

2 Users Expectations about Digital Copyright Management Systems

The term 'user' is understood as all groups of actors of the dissemination chain interacting with copyrighted works: authors, creators, producers, distributors, intermediate and end-users (private, corporate and institutional), broadcasters...

Authors, original creators of works distributed on networks, have the exclusive right to authorize the reproduction and the communication of their works, within certain limits. They might license these rights to producers or mandate collective societies for the commercial exploitation of their works.

Authors benefit from technological innovations at several levels. They will find a large audience for their works in an environment where several barriers are removed. Audiences are no longer restricted to national markets and linguistic areas; authors can benefit from distribution platforms, providing a large visibility, metadata for an enriched access to content according to end-user's preferences; authors can also publish and distribute directly their works through personal websites or community portals.

They expect IPMP systems to express and enforce the rights they decided to attach to their works. Their expectations can be financial but also related to the moral control of works' destination, initiatives close to open source philosophy being "devoted to expanding the use of creative work available for others to build upon and share" [25]. Identification, marking and watermarking systems ensure a persistent protection of their moral rights, at first attribution rights i.e. paternity recognition. Authors also expect to enjoy an easy access to other authors' works as source of inspiration, or as reusable material to be integrated to their own works, according to new creation techniques (sampling, VJ, cut-up, tributes, covers...). Information Technologies can provide interfaces facilitating contacts between creative communities; and DRM are expected, if not to support, at least not to restrict those exchanges.

End-users expect a user-friendly and easy access to culture, education, heritage and entertainment while preserving their privacy. Producers and distributors are looking for a return on investment, reliable event reporting, and cost-effective management. Producer's representatives are afraid of peer-to-peer file sharing consequences on their sales. They express publicly their disapproval by asking for Internet service technical providers and Courts support. Public institutions, open source communities and academics fear that DRM systems, acting as electronic fences, replace legal public mediation and restrict exceptions to exclusive rights and therefore legitimate access to works.

3 Technical Standardisation and Metadata Interoperability

Electronic commerce is faced to obstacles that prevent the full development of digital media and services. Digital media creation, sharing and distribution has to be supported by intelligent DRM systems, able to adapt to new use models and to cope with contradictory interests of all stakeholders. DRM solutions should therefore be able to process dialog, arbitration, mediation between those expectations expressions. It should also allow easy update of content rights management policy, according to expectations and time-to-market strategies evolution.

From Consumer Electronics manufacturers and industry point of view, bits shall be delivered at low cost, technical standardization of delivery formats enabling interoperability between systems and devices. The Moving Picture Expert Group [17] develops ISO technical standards for coded representation of digital audio and video, and enabled the development of multimedia standards such as mp3 format, digital television, DVD, multimedia information retrieval and description... Launched in June 2000, MPEG-21 standard [18] plans to define a global framework to enable transparent and augmented use of multimedia resources across networks, equipments and communities through an architecture structuring identification, management and protection of multimedia works. Software tools shall provide interoperability enabling to use the content "without being bugged by incompatible formats, codecs, metadata" [19].

The framework foresees therefore to include the definition of legal metadata identifying works and describing rights, users and conditions. MPEG-21 is expected to make interaction with content more transparent, and to define the relationships between the normative technologies needed to regulate the multimedia delivery chain. These elements are elaborated by defining the syntax and semantics of their characteristics, such as interfaces to the elements.

The integration of those modules is not only faced to technical requirements, but also to emerging uses and business models. A machine-readable language able to express rights, which are getting more and more complex in the digital world, is supposed to define algorithms enforcing electronic content governance within a trusted environment. "Code is Law", and software developers shall be aware of the values they embed inside their code and architectural design [9], [10]. Computed access control may indeed stand for legal code. Current DRM systems are based on interoperable languages describing terms and conditions for digital resources manipulation, transport and usage. Such languages shall be able to express simple and complex rights expressions, based on standardized Rights Data Dictionaries. An IPMP language and dictionary will be used on IPMP interface to describe use context, users, actions, rights, works, conditions...

4 Rights Expression Languages State of the Art

Grounded on Imprimatur European project results [21], <indecs> and <indecs>2rdd [20] provide a methodology for the interoperability of metadata's supporting electronic commerce. Rights and permissions basic structures are expressed by a Context Model defining the relationships between entities, organized around the notion of Action on a Resource.

ODRL (Open Digital Rights Language) [22] developed another semantic on XML standard. Rights governing Assets are including Permissions characterized by Constraints, Requirements and Conditions. Rights are expressed by Parties through Offers, Agreements and Revoking Rights.

XrML, Extensible Rights Markup Language [23] is organized around Authorization Context fundamental notion: a Right can be performed by a Principal on a Resource under specific Conditions.

IPROnto [24] formalized on a semantic web approach, structures IPR information at a higher level of abstraction. This ontological domain representation expresses IPR roles and events capturing the various steps of the content lifecycle: creation, rights transfer, distribution, use, reproduction, and transformation, providing a broad framework for Automatic Negotiation. Two consenters are involved, the Requester and the Licensing Agent, representing the rights holders. Offers and Counteroffers expressed with IPROnto help to reach an Agreement for a defined time period, compensation and action [4].

5 Legal Requirements for IPMP Architectures

Our position elaborated in context of MPEG-21 requirements [19] claims that in order to be agnostic and not to preclude non-static legislations and favour specific business models, only a minimum core of compulsory features (the lowest common denominator of worldwide copyright legislation and contractual practices) should be specified within a standard that aims at defining an interoperable framework for future DRM applications.

Legal knowledge has to be embedded in an interface expressing copyright law context and questions related to content distribution: licensing, infringement, and exception.

We will first present legal requirements with regards to the hierarchical relationship between international conventions and national legislations. Legal norms provide their own exceptions: prior rights holder's authorization is requested before use, but a work unauthorized use do not always constitute a copyright infringement. We will then describe the consequences of those legal requirements on IPMP architecture, and propose several architectural features. The exclusive right of authorizing can be materialized within an automated dialog through an 'Event Request' made by the client to the rights holder or its representative. Communication between users is made possible through the implementation of a Rights Expression 'bi-directional dialog', formalizing contractual conditions.

5.1 National Copyright Expressions

National copyright expressions allocate different rights to entities, and these entities are defined differently. For instance, works categorization has implications on work's legal qualification (audiovisual or multimedia work, database or software, are handled differently) and similar works will receive different treatments and induce different remunerations according to the jurisdiction they depend. These local differences have consequences on rights expressions representation. Negotiation conditions will vary from one case to another and jurisdiction is not always simple to determine in case of international sales and international law conflicts. Reasoning automated systems (e.g. authorization, compulsory licences and royalties sharing, fair use scope) shall be adapted, as embedded concepts may have different interpretation and deserve different processing.

5.2 International Legal Principles: the Authorization/Exception Pattern

An analysis of legislative texts and situations allowed the retrieval of copyright situations patterns. The model of prior authorization for limited rights granting is associated to the principle of exception to exclusive rights, applying in certain cases determined differently in each jurisdiction according to the use context

Some principles or pieces of legislation are internationally recognized. At the top of copyright norms international hierarchy, WIPO Berne Convention [13] is enforceable in most countries. Its minimum common legal principles are translated in national copyright laws and shall therefore be embedded into copyright management systems. 'Exclusive rights' means that rights holders are, if no other provision is applying, sole actors allowed to fulfil or authorize the accomplishment of specific acts related to their works. Even if it is not always desirable [11], prior authorization from the rights holder shall usually be requested before any analogue or digital action, such as digital display, reproduction, communication to the public, performance, distribution, rental, translation, adaptation... Authorization is then granted for a defined use context in exchange of remuneration.

Nevertheless, this general principle presents several exceptions within international and national legislations that avoid the user to have to ask rights holders' prior authorization every time before s/he wishes to perform an action on a protected content. Before XVIII th century legislations limiting uses by a temporary monopoly, creative works natural state was full availability. Public domain was the general rule, not the exception. Current prior authorization legal paradigm could be reversed: some use might be freed and exclusive or reserved rights would become the exception.

Limitations on exclusive rights have various explanations (technique, privacy, fair use...) and restrict the obligation to request an authorization before performing an action. Temporary acts of reproduction part of a network transmission technological process are exempted from prior authorization in Europe, but not in USA. Favourable translation licensing conditions can be granted to developing countries [13]. Compulsory licenses avoid asking prior authorization before any act, because it is burdensome, materially impossible (radio broadcasting...), or mandatory (cable distribution in Europe) to proceed through collective management. Authors can also restrict their exclusive rights on a voluntary basis and place their creations into the public domain, or voluntarily restrict their exclusive rights to commercial uses [25]. Fair uses are generally admitted if they do not affect normal exploitation or rights holders' legitimate interests, but it is up to national states to precise their scope and implementation.

If an exception to exclusive rights applies, an action that would deserve prior authorization is not considered as an infringement and rights holders shall on no account restrict content access or usage through DRM. But an exception can be enforced, meaning an event will not require prior authorization, only once the use case context has been defined and qualified, and not previously according to content nature or user affiliation. At a first glance, it looks impossible to formally represent a priori fair use cases. Nevertheless, it is important to distinguish legal authorization concept from client-server automated processing authorization requests. Legal concepts or rights and their implementation in a computer system belong to different knowledge levels and do not necessarily match point-to-point.

6 A Cognitive Interface for Problems Expression and Solving

6.1 Expression of Events, Requests and Computed Actions Based on Rights Granting Dialog

Notwithstanding limitations on exclusive rights prerogatives, we can assume that all DRM applications and REL systems will translate prior authorization requirement for commercial licensing. After an authorization request, rights holders will answer by a minimal Boolean operation: refuse or allow the requested act under previously stated conditions. The agreement is typically materialized through a temporary licence agreement sent back from the rights holder to the client and activating rights processing on the end-user terminal, i.e. reproduction right will be materialized by the operation 'print' or 'copy'. Of course, there are valid models and practices that work differently from this general way, and architecture requirements shall, rather than limit choices, try to satisfy the broadest scope of requirements. If proposed licensing terms do not fulfil user expectations, s/he should have the opportunity and the tools to express her/his own particular conditions and confront them online to the rights holder disputed licensing terms.

6.2 Adaptation to Use Profiles through Scalability and Subsidiarity

Most client-server architectures allow a dialog between users and the added value of a cognitive interface is to provide the terms to express both rights and processing of actions on digital works files. Not only rights holders shall be allowed to express and propose use conditions, leaving end-users with no other choice than approving all the licensing terms or refusing them all and ending the transaction. The end-user shall be made able to propose alternative Rights Expressions and confront them to rights holder's Rights Expressions.

A cognitive interface will not propose the whole set of terms and rules, burdening the system and the user, but only the knowledge needed for the problem. The knowledge database shall therefore be scalable and propose different sets according to use cases or users profiles. The situation can be described with many criteria. The categorization of the action (referring to the Right) and of the place (human-readable definition for applicable law) can be expressed easily in simple cases. On the contrary, the categorization of the user him/herself may request the interaction of a trusted third-party to validate the user legal qualification, i.e. if identity and location have legal consequences.

The range of implicated criteria determining the set of expressions and terms proposed to the user is dynamic, such as the level of control and trust. Sometimes, decisions shall be taken at a high level whereas in other cases, they can or even need to be taken at a lower level. Subsidiarity concept might help to determine the ad hoc level where a policy will receive the best management, and to distribute competences between decisional architecture levels, deduced from an efficiency assessment. Subsidiarity principle was first expressed in XIIIth century by Thomas Aquinas and recalled by constitutional federalists (Germany, Swiss, Italy, European Community…). High-level entities' action is legitimated only and as long as their added value enhances the inadequate capacity of lesser entities. Subsidiarity can be vertical and regulate governance levels. It can also have horizontal applications and help to share competences between regulating actors (public/private, law, standard, market, individuals, and even elements of an abstract architecture). As far as and DRM architectural and interface design are concerned, this concept might also help to choose the right level of management and decision.

6.3 An Architecture for Rights Expressions Local Adaptation

The mass of Rights Expressions combinations makes it impossible, regarding networks and users congestion, to associate all possible legal national requirements to a single request or piece of content. Therefore, it is advisable to delegate Rights Expression local governance at a lesser level than worldwide content provider. We consider here the possibility for a central content server to delegate legal questions to specialized trusted servers. A local server contacted by a central server will process Rights Expression Adaptation to non-static local legal requirements.

A first central server would send the resource and its Rights Expression to many other decentralized servers, which would adapt it to local requirements. Such a second level server can be a specialized network or a national platform. If it is dedicated to private documents sharing within a family, it will offer the broadest scope of Rights Expressions: all actions being allowed, and no authorization or reporting mechanisms between registered members preventing access to content. On the contrary, if the second level server is a commercial application, it will request a fee for a determined event, all other events being forbidden. Providing a scalable range of applicable terms and licenses would permit to handle every situation with the adequate level of control. Any user and right holder would choose the set corresponding to its needs and expressed situation. Each level would define its own rules and desired level of control on actions according to legal, business, social norms and uses.

A first Rights Expression is requesting a prior authorization (1), to be applied if nothing else indicates a fair use or public domain context. Local servers adapt (4), the first Rights Expression to national laws e.g. mandatory levy or classification update and local business model. Prior authorization condition will be skipped if the Rights Expressions from the top meets a Rights Expressions from a lower level that exempts the specific action from prior authorization (public domain, compulsory licence, fair use national provision…).

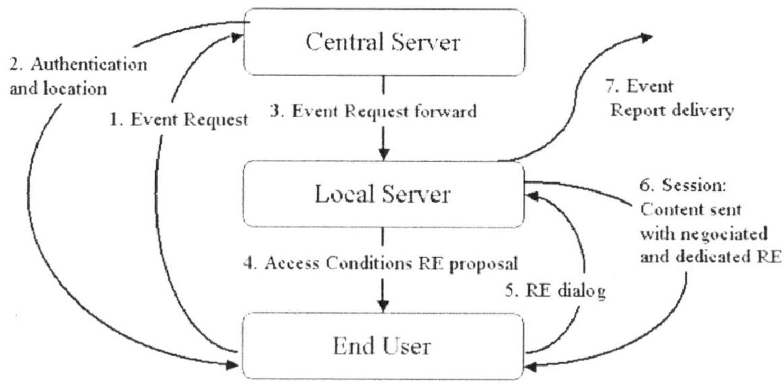

Figure 1: Proposed IPMP architecture enabling Rights Expressions (RE) dialog.

7 Current and Future Work: a Knowledge Database for Copyright Online Problems Description

A knowledge database gathering possible terms and concepts for Rights Expressions is being elaborated. According to intended use, and in order to allow a dialog between users and levels, Rights Expressions have to be formally represented by an ontology to express questions relevant to the context and propose answers corresponding to users' needs. Rights Expressions have to support confrontation, negotiation, decision and solution enforcement (licence agreement, copyright exception, nothing) between Rights Expressions set up by rights holders and use conditions adapted by a local server. The benefit of including a dialog allows real world dialog conditions between users. Communication is allowed in both directions (i.e. with a return path) and not only reduced to an offer from the rights holder representative to the end-user with no further choice than block acceptance or refusal. If the Rights Expressions issued by the right holder do not foresee to grant printing permission, the end-user might well communicate his request to the server.

7.1 A Methodology to Build a Legal Ontology

Even if efforts have been made by 1996 international treaties [15], [16] and 2001 European Directive [14], copyright national terms are not harmonized. Their interpretation is subject to changes and uncertainties, which are unfavourable to investment and commerce development. Legal concepts are open textured concepts [8] as their understanding is related to external conditions such as the context. This diversity generates difficulties for the implementation of DRM systems. Indeed, it is important to express the conditions attached to a work's use with accuracy and flexibility.

Ontologies can be defined as referential abstractions providing notions and concepts of a domain with a formalization of the links between those concepts [7]. This modelling is useful for knowledge representation and computed exploitation. Our work-in-progress research is based on the development of a legal ontology that will allow expressing rights and use situations attached to a context and a work. As it is possible to build several ontologies for a single legal domain, the composition of our ontology will be deduced from the task it is designed for [1], i.e. expression of questions and decisions about copyright and use context description by all users, balancing stakeholders interests within creative content electronic delivery. The cognitive interface and its knowledge database should be reusable by other IPMP and DRM systems.

The preliminary phase of our work was to study previous results of other Rights Expression Languages (RELs) and dictionaries, most relevant being XrML, ODRL, <indecs> and IPROnto. Except the latter one, all projects started from use cases and not from legal texts in order to define a core set of semantics.

The added value of the proposed methodology is to start from an expertise of the legal knowledge domain, defined as the intersection between copyright law, law for Information Technology and media law. This expertise aims at avoiding texts partial understanding or misinterpretations, as legal doctrine and case law knowledge enable to throw light on texts interpretation. Our reasoning process aims at modelling the core of all use cases and especially re-use cases, the latter aspect being outside other projects' scope. We also include public institutions requirements instead of limiting our representation to business interests. Archival or re-use of protected content in a library, a museum or within teaching and research materials are definitively part of content electronic delivery targets and shall be taken into account [6], [12]. Other REL give priority to commercial uses and hardly tackle fair use because it is technically easier to close than to open access. Making a work available for specific uses may cause security wholes for unauthorized persons. REL are deemed to be agnostic and able to express all uses and legislations, at least indirectly or by default. However, a statistical study of the vocabulary captured by existing terminologies allowed to detect an important under-representation of terms and concepts attached to end-users and copyright exceptions, in comparison with expressions describing rights holders, collective management, contractual conditions and remuneration sharing.

We propose to restore copyright initial purpose and are developing a bank of terms large and representative enough to describe core situations and specificities with respect to ungoverned uses. A cognitive interface should process access requests according to context and express use cases with a simple metadata system, reducing the situation to the ad hoc level of legal information needed for the problem description and solving. Applications for a cognitive interface providing appropriate semantic (rights expressions) and syntax (computed architecture for questions fields) can be selection of relevant text to allow or turn down a request, rights holder license granting and remuneration process automation. The metadata system, based on a copyright ontology, is supposed to enable non-lawyer users to describe their status and requested use conditions.

7.2 *First Classes and Concepts*

An ontology dedicated to copyright situations description and expression shall be able to describe at a meta level national copyright legislations and case law subtleties. Classes shall be intuitive enough for a self-categorization by non-lawyer users. Links between classes (users, rights, attributes, decisions...) are representing digital content life-cycle steps from creation to ungoverned and non-copyrightable uses (public domain, fair use...) to licensing and re-use management.

Here is an excerpt presenting terms categorization. Terms have been extracted from legal texts and existing Rights Expression Languages with the objective of reflecting use cases and user profiles. Subsequent intensive work is dedicated to the completion of the domain ontology, including concepts definition in national legal systems and links design between **classes**, concepts and associated *attributes* in order to implement it within a DRM system.

Domain conceptualisation within an ontology can help users to express a situation and an action, but also to appreciate an existing DRM system and evaluate its completeness and embedded values, control, trust or privacy level. This aspect can be helpful when a user has

Table 1: Excerpt of terms classification prior to ontological domain representation

USER	WORK	RIGHT-ACT	*CONDITION*	DECISION
Licensor	**Non copy-**	**Economic**	*Fee*	**Fair use** case identifi-
Right	**righted**	**Rights**	*Quantity*	cation
Holder	Public domain	Communicate	*Levy*	*Berne Convention*
Author	Ideas	Copy	*Time*	*three-step test*
Producer	Personal data	Distribute	*Format*	*Quotation scope crite-*
Distributor	**Copyrighted**	Derivate	*Quality*	*ria*
Collective so-	Book	Aggregate	*Resolution*	**License** agreement for-
ciety	Translation	Quote	*Location*	malisation
Licensee	**Joint work**	Rent	*Public*	*Exploitation domain*
End-user	Phonogram	Lend	**Moral rights**	Copyright infringe-
Private user	Motion picture	**Moral rights**	Attribution	ment
Teacher	**Collective**	Withdrawal	Integrity/Respect	Access refusal
Journalist	**work**	Divulgation	Open source	
	Videogame		Copyleft	
	Software			
	Database			

to choose between different applications reflecting an IPMP policy.

Acknowledgments

We would like to acknowledge CERSA and MEDIALIVE for supervising and funding our research within MPEG-21 stimulating framework.

References

[1] Trevor Bench-Capon, Task Neutral Ontologies, Common Sense Ontologies and Legal Information Systems. Second International Workshop on Legal Ontologies, JURIX 2001, Amsterdam.

[2] Filipe Borges, Danièle Bourcier, Evelyne Andreewsky, Raoul Borges, Conception of cognitive Interfaces for legal knowledge – Evolution of the JURISQUE project on the risks of avalanches, ICAIL 2001 The Eighth International Conference on Artificial Intelligence and Law, May 21-25, 2001 St. Louis.

[3] Jaime Delgado, Isabel Gallero, Standardisation of the management of Intellectual Property Rights in multimedia content, Proceedings of the Second International Conference on Web Delivery of Music, IEEE Computer Society, 2002, p. 125-132.

[4] Séverine Dussolier, Fair use by design in the European Directive of 2001: an empty promise, 12th Conference on Computers, Freedom and Privacy, 2002. http://www.cfp2002.org/fairuse/dusollier.pdf

[5] Tom Gruber, A Translation Approach to Portable Ontology Specification, Knowledge Acquisition, 5/1993, p. 199-220.

[6] Guiraude Lame, Using text analysis techniques to identify legal ontologies components, ICAIL 2003, Workshop on Legal Ontologies & Web Based Legal Information Management.

[7] Lawrence Lessig, Code and Other Laws of Cyberspace, Basic Books, 1999.

[8] Lawrence Lessig, The future of Ideas, The Fate of Commons in a Connected World, Random House, 2001.

[9] Jessica Litman, Revising Copyright Law for the Information Age, 75 Oregon Law Review 19, 1996. http://www.law.cornell.edu/commentary/intelpro/litrvtxt.htm

[10] Deirdre Mulligan, Aaron Burstein, Implementing Copyright Limitations in Rights Expression Languages, 2002 ACM Workshop on Digital Rights Management.

[11] Berne Convention for the Protection of Literary and Artistic Works http://www.wipo.int/clea/docs/en/wo/wo001fr.htm

[12] Directive, 2001. Directive 2001/29/EC of the European Parliament and of the Council of 22 May 2001 on the harmonisation of certain aspects of copyright and related rights in the information society, OJ L 167 22.06.2001 p. 10. http://www.europa.eu.int/eur-lex/en/index.html

[13] WIPO Copyright Treaty, World Intellectual Property Organization, 20/12/1996 http://www.wipo.org/eng/diplconf/distrib/94dc.htm

[14] WIPO Performances and Phonograms Treaty, World Intellectual Property Organization, 20/12/1996. http://www.wipo.org/eng/diplconf/distrib/95dc.htm

[15] MPEG, http://www.mpeg.telecomitalia.com

[16] MPEG-21 http://www.chiariglione.org/mpeg/index.htm

[17] MPEG-21 N4518. ISO/IEC JTC 1/SC 29/WG 11 N4518, From MPEG-1 to MPEG-21: creating an interoperable multimedia infrastructure http://mpeg.nist.gov/

[18] Indecs http://www.indecs.org/pdf/framework.pdf

[19] Imprimatur project http://www.imprimatur.net

[20] ODRL http://odrl.net/

[21] XrML http://www.xrml.org/

[22] IPROnto http://dmag.upf.es/ontologies/ipronto/index.html

[23] Creative Commons http://www.creativecommons.org/

MIRIS Unleashed

Paolo Dongilli Johann Gamper*

Faculty of Computer Science
Free University of Bozen/Bolzano
Dominikanerplatz 3, 39100 Bozen, Italy
{paolo.dongilli, johann.gamper}@unibz.it

Abstract. Documentation and easy accessibility of data on matters relating to national and ethnic minorities is becoming increasingly significant. Even over the last couple of years, legal standardisation in Europe, the enlargement of the European Union and the establishment of international instruments such as the Framework Convention for the Protection of National Minorities and the European Charter for Regional and Minority Languages of the Council of Europe have contributed to a greater awareness of minority issues. However, the rapid growth of the Web makes it increasingly difficult to locate, organize, and integrate the available information. We herein present the research project MIRIS which for the very first time offers a web portal to all relevant information on minorities of all member states of the Council of Europe. MIRIS contains both legal as well as non-legal documents and provides a coherent presentation with powerful query capabilities including an ontology-driven search.

1 Introduction

Due to a new sensibility towards minority questions, the documentation and easy availability of data on ethnic, national, and linguistic minorities is increasingly significant. While international treaties and documents of international organizations are mostly available on the Web, the gathering of extensive information on the legal standards in different countries, such as national legislation or case-law, is still a difficult task. The existing databases about ethnic/linguistic minorities are either limited to a few countries (e.g. MINELRES and CEDIME-SE, which are focusing on south-eastern European Countries only) or they only cover a few topics (e.g. Mercator, which focuses on linguistic rights only). Furthermore, those databases are mostly unstructured. Often, documents are simply listed without being organized by keywords or topics. From a content and technical point of view, the users search is not supported/backed up. Thus, a quick search or a comparison between different countries is often a difficult task.

Taking into account these problems, the ongoing research project MIRIS (Minority Rights Information System) aims to develop a comprehensive information system about ethnic minorities and autonomies in Europe. MIRIS offers for the very first time a Web portal to all relevant information on minorities of all countries which are member states of the Council of Europe. It will become a major consultation center for minority questions in Eastern and Western Europe. MIRIS is a project led by the European Academy of Bozen/Bolzano in cooperation with the Faculty of Computer Science of the Free University of Bozen/Bolzano (Italy).

*In cooperation with the European Academy of Bozen/Bolzano. Project funded by Propter Homines, Liechtenstein.

Paolo Dongilli and Johann Gamper, 'MIRIS Unleashed' in D. Bourcier (ed.), *Legal Knowledge and Information Systems. Jurix 2003: The Sixteenth Annual Conference*, Amsterdam: IOS Press, 2003, pp. 131-140.

In the present article we will explore in detail the architecture of MIRIS and in particular its main components: the user interface, the ontology-driven search and the authoring tool as front ends of the whole MIRIS architecture.

2 The MIRIS Technical Architecture

The MIRIS system can be seen as a three-layered architecture (see figure 1) consisting of the following blocks:

- Applications and Services,
- Middleware,
- Remote and data services,

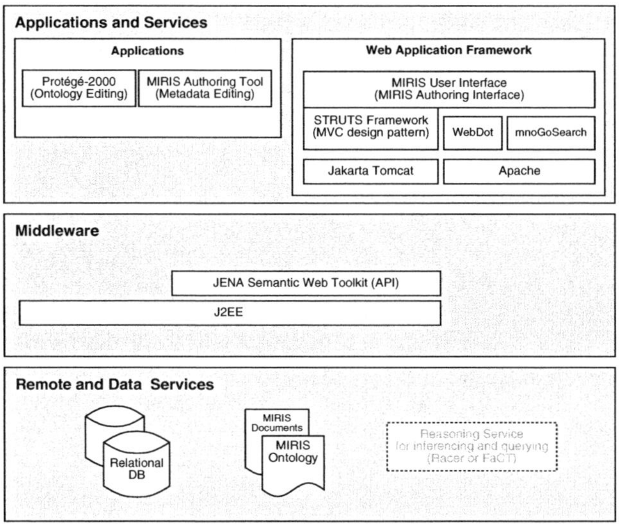

Figure 1: MIRIS system architecture.

In the following sections we will explain in detail, meaning and functionalities of the single layers building up MIRIS.

3 Applications and Services

This layer represents the interface to the two categories of users of the system: *active* and *passive users*. The team of jurists working for MIRIS are the active users who are responsible for the information-gathering process which began in 2001 and is focusing on some twenty-eight countries in Western and Eastern Europe. On the other hand the passive users are all the people interested in the implementation of minority rights: not only experts, public officials, NGO's (Non-governmental Organizations) and minority representatives but also researchers and students.

The applications will be presented first, and followed by a description of the underlying services.

Table 1: Overview of MIRIS documents (September 2003)

Document types	Internal	External	Total
Case Laws	223	25	*248*
Country Information	119	76	*195*
International Organization Documents	39	52	*91*
Info about International Organization Documents	23	25	*48*
Minority Information	105	78	*183*
National Laws	1376	612	*1988*
Reports	284	269	*553*
Treaties	84	48	*132*
Total	2253	1185	***3438***

3.1 MIRIS Authoring Tool

The active users are currently eight jurists (out of a total of sixteen experts who have been working for the project). Their main task is to create and store for all candidate documents a set of metadata which include administrative information as well as content information. These pieces of information are important for organizing, accessing, and presenting the documents. When properly implemented, metadata can crisply and unambiguously describe information resources, enhancing information retrieval and enabling accurate matches to be done, while being totally transparent and invisible to the user. Search specificity is increased (noise reduction — only good matches) and search sensitivity is boosted (i.e. silence or missed matches are decreased and signal-to-noise ratio increased — all good matches) [6].

Table 1 represents a snapshot of the documents we collected to date (September 2003). We distinguish between internal documents, which are physically stored in our database, and external documents, for which we only store a URL.

The MIRIS Authoring Tool (MAT) is the application used by the jurists to edit the metadata related to the documents they process. In particular with the MAT the active users can view, create, edit and delete the metadata which are stored in the database.

The first version of the MAT was a web application which has been dismissed and reprogrammed into a pure Java program. Figure 2 shows two screenshots of the metadata-editing phase of a Greek case law and a Bulgarian national law.

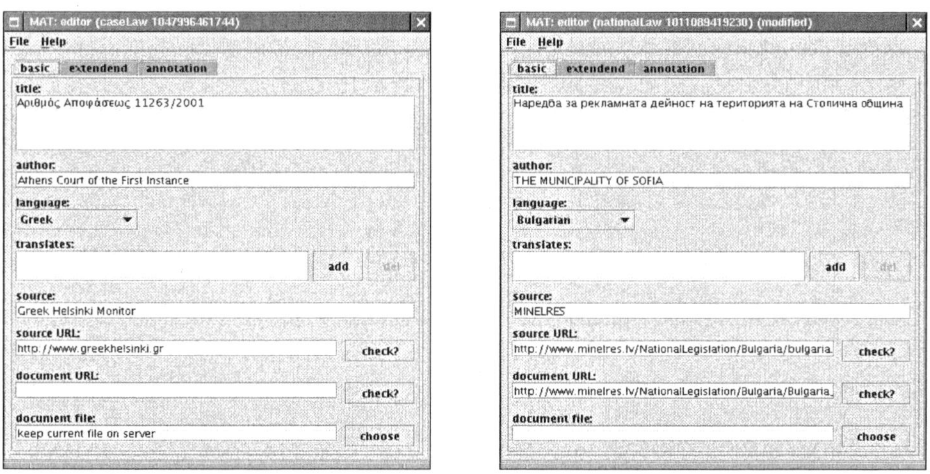

Figure 2: MIRIS Authoring Tool: metadata editing.

The items shown in the *basic* tab are only a part of the metadata fields accompanying each document; the hidden *extended* tab contains other fields such as *date of judgment*, *date of entry into force*, *guiding principle*, *document number*, *related minorities*, etc. These fields vary according to the document type chosen. The third tab (*annotation*) is used to annotate the documents with topics. The editors can navigate the ontology and they can assign one or more topics referring to each document as a whole or to the single sections of it.

3.2 Ontology Editor

We put a particular emphasis on the extension of our metadata with topics, which explicitly describe the content of the documents. We allow content annotation not only at the document level, but down to the level of law articles. The topics are organized in a domain ontology which represents common knowledge about ethnic minorities and provides the vocabulary required for describing the content of the documents. An excerpt of our relatively simple topics ontology is shown in figure 3. The ontology consists of a taxonomy built on the *isa*-relation and a *relatedTo*-relation which connects related topics.

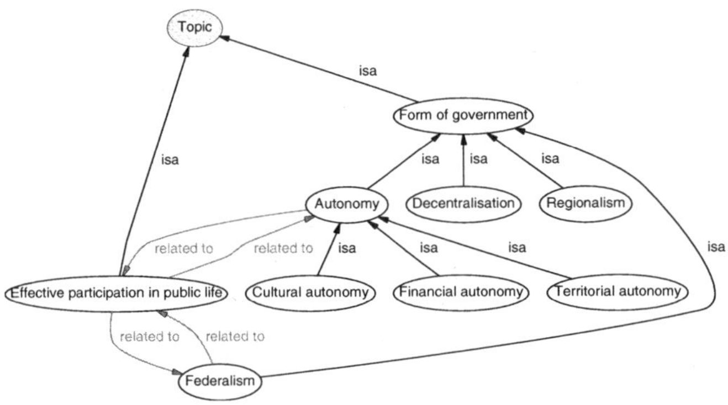

Figure 3: Extract of the topics ontology.

The ontology is currently being created by our lawyers using Protégé-2000, a powerful knowledge-base-editing environment developed at the Stanford University [7, 8]. It allows us by means of its flexible metaclass architecture to use configurable templates for the classes we include in our knowledge base.

We generate content annotation at different levels for internal and external documents. This allows fine-grained, content-based search in a uniform way independent of the location of the actual document. Additionally, for local documents MIRIS guides the user directly to relevant parts of the document. For external documents, only the entire document can be accessed and the user has to scroll to the indicated part.

3.3 MIRIS User Interface

An important aspect of the MIRIS system is to provide a coherent presentation and powerful query capabilities to information about minority rights. The following functionalities and interactions are offered:

- full-text search,
- metadata-based search, and
- ontology-driven search.

Full-text Search About 40% of the documents available in MIRIS are stored in a keyword index available for full text searching. For each document found, the title, a short text sample, as well as type and size of the document are indicated (see figure 4). For implementing the full-text search we use a slightly modified version of *mnoGoSearch*[1], a full-featured SQL-based web search engine; for UNIX it is free software covered by the GNU General Public License (GPL). *mnoGoSearch* consists of two parts. The first part is the indexing mechanism (indexer). The indexer walks over html hypertext references and stores found words and new references into the database. The second part is a web CGI front-end which provides search using data collected by the indexer.

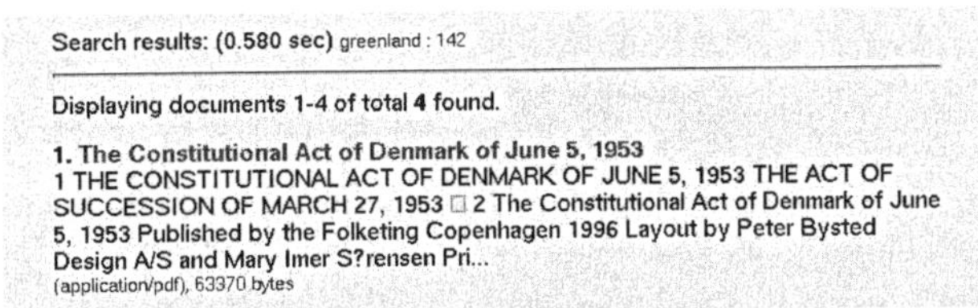

Figure 4: Screenshot of the MIRIS full-text search.

Metadata-based Search Figure 5 shows instead a screenshot with the components of the MIRIS interface for the *metadata-based search mode*.

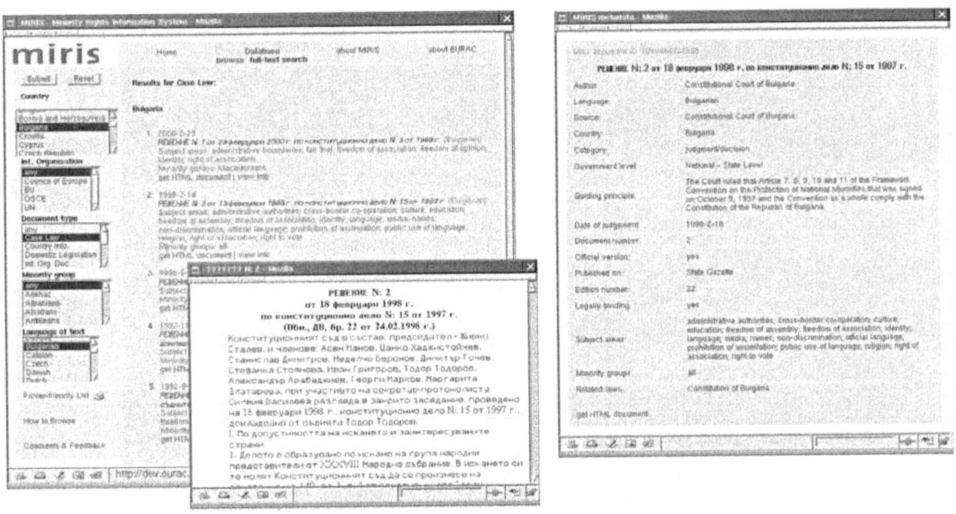

Figure 5: Screenshot of the MIRIS metadata-based search interface.

On the left-hand side of the main window (left), the user can specify up to five query parameters by choosing values from several select boxes. In the example shown, we are interested in all case laws of Bulgaria in Bulgarian language. The right-hand side of the same window reports the result of the query ordered by country (only one in this case) and by date. The result list contains for each hit some important metadata including the date of the document, the topics which are regulated in the document (related subjects), and the minorities

[1]http://search.mnogo.ru/

for which this document applies. The user can choose then to visualize the document in the proposed format (window in the middle) along with a full version of the pertaining metadata (window on the right).

Ontology-driven Search The last component of the MIRIS user interface is the newly developed prototypical web application for the ontology-driven search. The user can navigate the nodes of the topics ontology following the existing relations: *broader term*, *narrower term* and *related term*. Whenever a node is clicked, the term (topic) is shown along with its description, possible synonyms, comments and the relations to other terms. A navigation graph is generated and the user can see the selected term, its immediate super-topics and sub-topics. The system displays also the number of documents which are tagged with the chosen topic and the user can decide to finally see the list of texts found (see figure 6).

There are some extensions we want to implement in the user interface of this component. First it would be useful to additionally show the number of documents pertaining not only to the selected topic but also to the broader, narrower and related terms. Second, the result set, for performance reasons, should only be an overview of the documents, organized in a table e.g. by document type and country (to name just two search criteria). Then it's up to the user to refine the search selecting a specific country and/or one of the document types getting the complete set of information about the documents found. Third, we could let the users choose more than one topic. This requires though a more sophisticated query input mechanism, which will be part of our future work (see section 6).

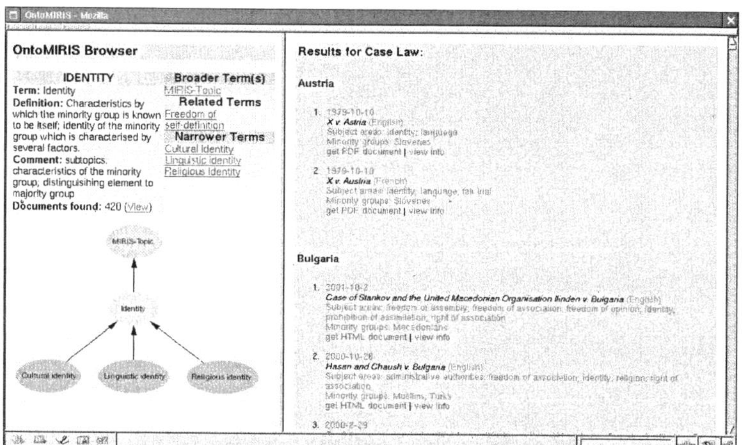

Figure 6: MIRIS ontology-driven search

3.4 Underlying Tools and Services

The MIRIS User Interface is a web application built using the Jakarta Struts Framework[2]. Struts combines two of the most popular server-side technologies – JSPs and servlets – into a server-side implementation of the Model-View-Controller (MVC) design pattern. Struts is currently supported by all the major application servers including BEA, SUN, HP, and (of course) Apache Jakarta-Tomcat, the JSP/servlet container which runs on the MIRIS server.

[2]http://jakarta.apache.org/struts/

The web server Apache is also installed to execute among others the CGI-scripts WebDot[3], and mnoGoSearch (see paragraph *Full-text Search* in section 3.3).

In our system we use WebDot to create the navigation graph for the ontology-driven search (see section 3.3). WebDot is a graph layout engine (based on the Graphviz[4] package from AT&T Research) that converts a graph description from a `.dot` file into an image. A graph can contain URLs so that the nodes and edges are clickable. To respond to user mouse events, a map must be provided. This mapping information is generated dynamically from the same graph source file as the image itself (see figure 7).

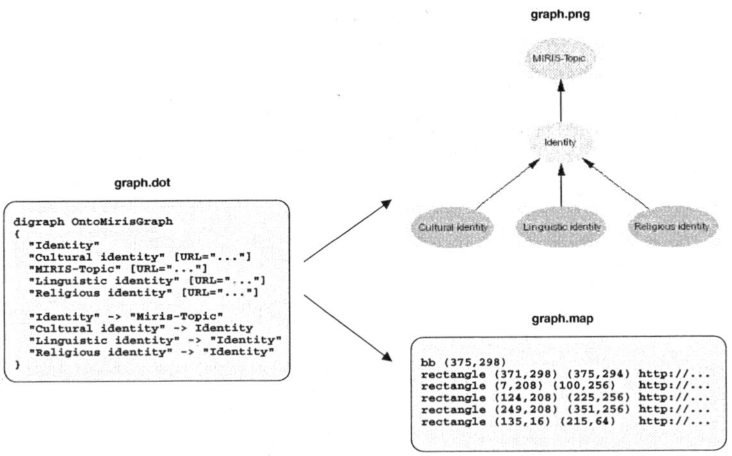

Figure 7: Conversion of a `.dot` file into an image and a map.

In MIRIS a Java class creates first the `.dot` file on the fly, depending on the current topic that the user is exploring. As soon as the `.dot` file is saved on the system, WebDot can retrieve it to generate the image and the map for the requesting browser.

4 Middleware

All the applications we developed (the Miris Authoring Tool, the Miris User Interface and some other unmentioned routines for our jurists) are platform-independent programs built upon J2EE. The same applies for the application server we use (Apache Jakarta Tomcat) and the ontology editor Protégé-2000 which are pure Java applications.

For the ontology-driven search we also use the JENA semantic Web Toolkit[5], a Java API for manipulating RDF graphs. We use it for accessing our ontology of topics which is exported from Protégé-2000 in RDF format.

Finally we have WebDot which is not based on Java: it is written in Tcl language and requires the Tcldot package from Graphviz.

5 Remote and Data Services

The central repository of the MIRIS metadata set is stored in an Oracle 9i database. Whenever a piece of metadata is requested, it is retrieved from the database as XML file and rendered

[3]http://www.graphviz.org/webdot/
[4]http://www.research.att.com/sw/tools/graphviz/
[5]http://www.hpl.hp.com/semweb/

to HTML via an XSL stylesheet for being displayed to the requesting user.

As far as the documents are concerned, rather than storing them in the database, we decided to save them directly on the MIRIS server for a faster access. The MIRIS ontology is also stored on the server. It is possible for our jurists to change it uploading a new one in case some corrections need to be made. An ontology change is automatically detected and the new uploaded ontology is reread and deployed by the MIRIS Authoring Tool and by the ontology-driven search application.

Nearly all of the relevant information is stored in human-readable documents, such as the state reports to which the member states are committed, minority reports, international law contracts, national laws, etc. The most important documents though, are encoded for structural information using XML, which not only allows a coherent visualization of the documents but also a more specific and fine-grained search. We decided to use the DocBook XML document type definition (DTD) because of its general nature. DocBook has been adopted by a large and growing community of authors writing documents of all kinds, it is easy to understand and there is a rapidly expanding support for it in a number of open source environments. Since structural encoding is a very time-consuming task, as stated above only the most important documents and documents which rarely change can be stored locally.

6 Conclusions and Future Work

In this paper we have presented MIRIS, an information system about minority rights and autonomies in Europe. Using the tools provided by the MIRIS system, the jurists working for the project have cataloged to-date 3438 documents from Eastern and Western Europe, providing metadata descriptions for each resource (document) found. The content of the documents has also been described using topics picked from an ontology built by our domain experts. All the information collected are made available to the public through the MIRIS user interface including a metadata-based search and an ontology-driven search.

For the future, our main efforts will converge towards three main points.

First of all we want to map (part of) our metadata fields onto the Dublin Core metadata element set (DCMS) which consists of the following 15 elements: *title*, *creator*, *subject* (our topics), *description*, *publisher*, *contributor*, *date*, *type*, *format*, *identifier*, *source*, *language*, *relation*, *coverage* and *rights*. The reason is that the DCMS is now an international standard (ISO 15836:2003(E)) for cross-domain information resource description and we want to conform to it. For further details about the Dublin Core Metadata Initiative see [3].

Second, we want to extend our topics ontology to a broader ontology including most of the concepts and relations which are related to our project. Our final aim is to build a good-quality ontology where our domain experts make a full use of the chosen language (DAML+OIL [2], OWL [9] or ODL_{I^3} [1]), in a way that the ontology can capture the author's rich knowledge of the domain.

Third and last point, we will interface the ontology editing phase and the MIRIS Ontology-driven Search application with one of the free Description Logics reasoners available (FaCT [5] or RACER [4]). Description logics (DLs) are knowledge representation languages tailored for expressing knowledge about concepts and concept hierarchies. DLs models a domain in terms of *individuals* (modelled objects), *concepts* (descriptions of groups of objects sharing common characteristics) and *roles* (the relationships between concepts and individuals). The abovementioned languages (DAML+OIL, OWL, and ODL_{I^3}) can be viewed as dialects of DLs. The presence of a DLs reasoner in the background of MIRIS will be a great help for our jurists who will be able to automatically classify the ontology concepts and check them for satisfiability. On the other hand our passive users will be presented a richer interface where they will have the opportunity to incrementally build a query choosing concepts and properties (relations or attributes) via an ontology-driven diagrammatic support.

References

[1] S. Bergamaschi, S. Castano, and M. Vincini. Semantic integration of semistructured and structured data sources. *SIGMOD Record (ACM Special Interest Group on Management of Data)*, 28(1):54–??, 1999. Special section on semantic interoperability in global information systems.

[2] The DAML+OIL web site. http://www.w3.org/TR/daml+oil-reference, 2003.

[3] Dublin Core Metadata Initiative. http://dublincore.org, 2003.

[4] Volker Haarslev and Ralf Möller. Description of the RACER System and its Applications. In *Proceedings of the International Workshop on Description Logics (DL-2001)*, Stanford, USA, August 2001.

[5] Ian Horrocks. FaCT and iFaCT. In P. Lambrix, A. Borgida, M. Lenzerini, R. Möller, and P. Patel-Schneider, editors, *In Lambrix et al.*, pages 133–135, Stanford, USA, August 1999.

[6] Boulos M., Roudsari A., and E. Carson. Towards a semantic medical Web: HealthCyberMap's tool for building an RDF metadata base of health information resources based on the Qualified Dublin Core Metadata Set. *Medical Science Monitor*, 8(7):124–136, 2002.

[7] N. F. Noy, R. W. Fergerson, and M. A. Musen. The knowledge model of Protégé-2000: Combining interoperability and flexibility. In *Proceedings of the 12th International Conference on Knowledge Engineering and Knowledge Management (EKAW'2000)*, pages 12–32, October 2000.

[8] N. F. Noy, M. Sintek, S. Decker, M. Crubezy, R. W. Fergerson, and M. A. Musen. Creating semantic web contents with Protégé-2000. *IEEE Intelligent Systems Journal*, 16(2):60–71, 2001.

[9] Web Ontology Language (OWL). http://www.w3.org/2001/sw/WebOnt/, 2003.

An Interactive Form for Customer Complaints: Matching the Cases

Boris Galitsky*
School of Computer Science and Information Systems
Birkbeck College, University of London
London, United Kingdom
galitsky@dcs.bbk.ac.uk

In the last two decades, the interest to formal modeling of various forms of human reasoning and mental behavior has strongly risen, particularly in connection with legal reasoning. A series of phenomena in human reasoning have been reflected in such approaches as reasoning about action and knowledge, space and time, nonmonotonic and counterfactual reasoning, etc. Also, algorithms of information extraction from legal documents that is expected to form an initial knowledge base for further reasoning have undergone dramatic improvement. However, extraction of information about conflicting agents from a plain text (a written complaint) is still hard and unreliable.

We suggest a novel legal application area for machine learning and reasoning – the interactive forms for representation of multiagent conflicts (customer complaints). In this research abstract we explore the role of *mental component* in a natural language legal document, written by a person who is not a legal professional. We call mental component of a text its formal semantic representation that consists from the entities for mental states including *knowledge, belief, intention, desire, dissatisfaction*, as well as entities for mental actions such as *inform, check, reject, appeal, ask*, etc. In this respect we follow along the lines of what is called BDI model, subject to our development in a series of studies.

We choose such a domain as customer complaints because they are primarily descriptions of multiagent conflict, where the mental states and actions of the participating agents are essential. Also, our choice is motivated by a high logical complexity of textual complaints on one hand and availability of a large relatively uniform dataset of complaints on the other hand. In the domain of customer complaints, the general task of understanding a natural language legal document allows a specific and feasible formulation. We pose the task of understanding a customer complaint as determining whether it is valid (justified) or invalid (non-justified). It is then necessary to obtain an accurate description of agent's problems, intentions and opinions from text and to suggest possible ways of its resolution. In our studies [1-3] we have explored a series of logical means to process customer complaints, assuming the ideal natural language information extraction.

Analyzing the experience of previously designed systems for understanding multiagent interaction, one can easily come to conclusion that the performance limitation is caused by the natural language processing unit, because the vocabulary the plaintiffs express their problems is rather extensive and their emotional writing is rather hard to understand (even for humans). Therefore, in this study we focus on the way to efficiently extract information about multiagent interaction, based on the division of the domain knowledge into domain-specific and mental components.

---

*http://www.dcs.bbk.ac.uk/~galitsky/complaints.htm

Boris Galitsky, 'An Interactive Form for Customer Complaints: Matching the Cases' in D. Bourcier (ed.), *Legal Knowledge and Information Systems. Jurix 2003: The Sixteenth Annual Conference*. Amsterdam: IOS Press, 2003, pp. 141-142.

The back end of the interactive complaint forms includes the following reasoning components:

- Machine learning logic programming-based system Jasmine, capable of predicting the mental action, given the dataset of mental states and actions of a given opponent agent, http://www.dcs.bbk.ac.uk/~galitsky/JaSMine/JaSMine.htm;
- Logic programming implementation of reasoning about mental actions, predicting the opponent actions given the explicitly coded pre-conditions and effect axioms;
- Multiagent mental simulator NL_MAMS, which yields the consecutive mental states given the initial one, simulating the decision-making process of agents, http://www.dcs.bbk.ac.uk/~galitsky/Nl_mams/NL_MAMS.htm

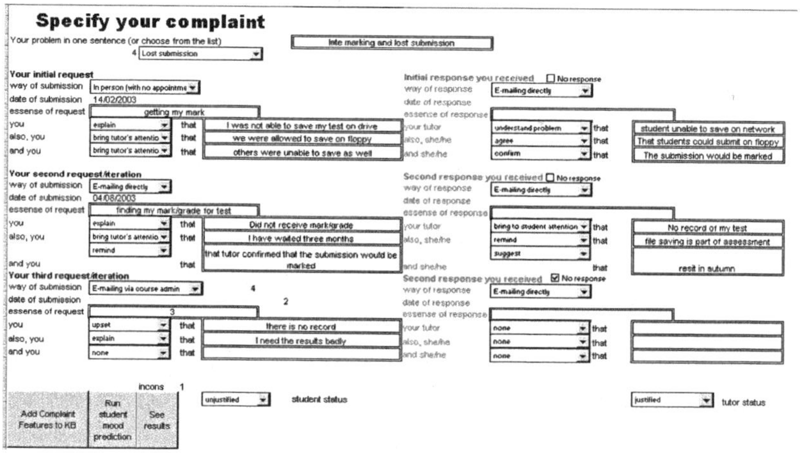

Figure 1: A front end of the interactive form.

The interactive form for filing the students' complaints is shown at Fig.1. It is suggested instead of plain text to present a conflict between a student and a tutor. On the left, the student plots her attempts to resolve the conflict, and on the right side the tutor's responses (from the student's viewpoint) are specified. The soundness of a given complaint is determined, using analysis of agents' mental states and experience with previous complaints: the system obtains the complaint status (justified, unjustified).

The deployment of the complaint justification system ComplaintEngine with interactive form has lead to a significant improvement of complaint handling procedure. ComplaintEngine accelerates the complaint response time, increases the objectivity and efficiency in the complaint resolution strategy and decreases the stress and emotional load of the participating parties.

References

[1] Galitsky, B. and Vinogradov, D. Using inductive reasoning and reasoning about dynamic domains for automatic processing of claims. DIMACS Tech Report #2002-42, 2002, Rutgers University NJ.

[2] Galitsky, B. and Pampapathi, R. Deductive and inductive reasoning for processing the complaints of unsatisfied customers 16th *IEA/AIE Conference*, LNAI 2718 Loughborough University, UK 2003.

[3] Galitsky, B. and Mirkin, B. Building interactive forms to input the scenarios of multiagent conflicts *Proceedings of the 2003 UK Workshop on Computational Intelligence*, 2003.

Mission Impossible?: Automated Norm Analysis of Legal Texts

Emile de Maat Tom M. van Engers
Leibniz Center for Law
Faculty of Law, Universiteit van Amsterdam
Amsterdam, The Netherlands
{demaat, vanengers}@lri.jur.uva.nl

1 Introduction

Although many legal experts thought this would be impossible we are very close in creating an algorithm for automated norm analysis from legal texts. This algorithm makes use of invariant linguistic structures at the syntactical level that characterises specific normative expressions in natural language. Since the algorithm has not been realised and tested completely jet, we will limit ourselves in this article to explaining the invariances in the natural language representations in which norms in legal texts are expressed.

As part of the POWER research program [1], the Dutch Tax and Customs Administration has created a method to formalise normative expressions in legal texts in UML/OCL models. These UML/OCL representations of the legal texts have showed to be quite suitable. To support knowledge analysts in creating these UML/OCL-models, an automated concept extractor was created, which allows a computer to identify the different concepts that exist in a given legal text [2]. This automated concept extractor reduces the amount of work of the knowledge analysts and results in more uniform models as well. The research described here is aimed at further automating the translation of a legal text to a model.

Automated generation of models would not only lead to a reduction in the amount of work needed, it would also increase inter-analyst independency. Normally, models created by different analysts could differ in various small details. Removing those difference would lead to more uniform models, which can more easily be understood, and are also easier to process when creating applications based on these models.

This article discusses the first results of this research into automated analysis of legal texts.

2 Main Sentences in Legal Texts

Research within the POWER project has lead to the conclusion that the sentences that occur in legal texts can be grouped in few categories. These main categories are: *definitions and type extensions*, *deeming provisions*, *application provisions*, *value assignments and changes*, *norms*. For each category (with the exception of norms), there is a limited set of possible language constructs used in the sentence. A sentence can be classified by studying the construct used.

The main sentences can be extended by adding a subordinate clause. Just like the main sentences, these extensions can also be identified by the language constructs used in the subordinate clauses.

Emile de Maat and Tom M. van Engers, 'Mission Impossible?: Automated Norm Analysis of Legal Texts' in D. Bourcier (ed.), *Legal Knowledge and Information Systems. Jurix 2003: The Sixteenth Annual Conference*, Amsterdam: IOS Press, 2003, pp. 143-144.

3 Applying Sentence Categories: Parsing

An important advantage of the sentence types defined above is that they make it possible for a computer to classify the different sentences. Because all but one of the categories can be identified by the language constructs that are used, a computer can test for the presence of these constructs.

In order to be able to parse sentences, we will need to formalise the patterns that can occur. In order to identify the sentence types, this could be done by building a context-free grammar. Normally, context-free grammars are not the most successful tool to model natural languages. This is because natural languages are highly ambiguous and context-sensitive [3]. Normally, a problem arises when we try to parse a sentence like "The man walked to the woman with a limp." This sentence is ambiguous, since there are two different interpretations: the man has a limp, or the woman has a limp. It is not possible to distinguish between the two different interpretations, unless we have got more information.

However, we will be able to use the context-free grammars to parse and translate legal sources. Syntactical ambiguity should not be a problem here: the text should be syntactical unambiguous[1], since this is a legal text, a law. We do not want any lawyers arguing that the sentence "You are not allowed to shoot anyone with a gun." means that you can shoot anyone who doesn't carry a gun. Thus that problem is not present here. Of course, although a legal source should be syntactical unambiguous, there can still be ambiguity in a given legal source, which cannot be handled correctly. However, since it is an error in the legal source (it should be unambiguous), it is not a problem if it is not translated correctly.

Finally, it is not necessary to recognize the entire sentence; it is sufficient to parse the top levels. This is because (in the POWER project) great parts of the sentences are kept in one piece. For example, a deeming statement has the following pattern: "*noun-phrase* [wordt geacht] *fiction*". When building a model of this text, the entire fiction (the largest part of the sentence) is often kept in one piece.

4 Conclusion

Legal texts, although expressed in natural language, provide us with enough clues to identify norms merely by looking at the syntactical structure. This allows us to develop an algorithm for automated norm extraction. We hope to have the first prototype ready in the beginning of 2004. Although we don't claim 100% recognition, a significant reduction of knowledge analysis effort (and improvements realised in inter-coder independencies) will mean a small revolution in the AI& Law world.

References

[1] Van Engers, T.M., Boekenoogen, 2003, Improving Legal Quality - an application report, in Proceedings of ICAIL2003, ISBN 1-58113-747-8, ACM Press.

[2] R. van Gog and T.M. van Engers, Modelling Legislation Using Natural Language, *Proceedings of the 2001 IEEE Systems, Man and Cybernetics Conference.*

[3] H. Alblas and A.Nymeyer. Practices and Principles of Compiler Building with C. Prentice Hall, London, 1996.

[1]Note that the legal text should only be syntactical unambiguous. This does not mean that the legal text should be entirely unambiguous. It will always retain a certain degree of vagueness. However, this ambiguity is semantically, and lies in the interpretation of the words, not in the interpretation of the structure of the sentence. This does not affect the translation process, since the words are retained in the model.

On the Structure and Soundness of AI & Law Objects

Clara Smith
Facultad de Informática, Universidad Nacional de La Plata, Argentina
csmith@info.unlp.edu.ar

1 Introduction

We present a (meta)theory that serves as a framework where case-based or statute-based models and systems can be understood, compared and prototyped. Central to our approach is the organization of theories under a notion of covering. This view helps to identify a disposition of elements based on a well-recognized underlying algebraic structure where theory definitions are reified and included in the same set together with their extensions and practical implementations.

2 The Nature of AI & Law Objects and a Logic for their Construction

We believe AI & Law objects of study are not legal intelligent systems or models for legal systems *alone*: they are the *relation* established between a legal domain or system of concepts and a corresponding computational specification (a "translation" where a given system of concepts is somehow transformed in another one), relation we call reduction.

The set of possible reductions can be defined as the cartesian product $Law \times AI_{\perp}$. Law is a compound domain (i.e. it can be a cartesian product itself) encompassing a wide variety of denotable values referring to ideal, factual, prescriptive and descriptive phenomena: legislation, facts, cases, court decisions, *et cetera*. $AI_{\perp}$ is a domain holding formal specifications [1] e.g. well-formed constructions established mainly at symbolic levels ($AI_{\perp}$means AI holds an "undefined" element). Stated as denotable values, elements in Law can be organized under a notion of *covering*, a relation organizing knowledge with respect to their "definedness", i.e. with respect to their "knowledge content" [2] (for example: $< name, age, course >$ has less content than $< ``Bob", 24, Logics >$). $AI_{\perp}$ specifications can also be ordered under their "definedness" [1] (e.g. a many-sorted signature with respect to a single-sorted signature holding just one of those sorts.) Provided this, we define

Def. 1. *Covering relation for reductions: Let* $r =< l, a >\in Law \times AI_{\perp}$. *Let* $r', r'' \in Law \times AI_{\perp}$. *Let* $(Law, \leq), (AI_{\perp}, \leq)$ *be covering relations based on the notion of "definedness" of denotational semantics over both* Law *and* $AI_{\perp}$. *Then* $(Law \times AI_{\perp}, \leq)$ *is a covering relation over reductions if and only if* $< l, a >\leq< l', a' >$ *implies* $l \leq l'$ *or* $a \leq a'$ *(or both) for every* $< l, a >, < l', a' >\in Law \times AI_{\perp}$.

Definition 1 says "more abstract" AI & Law objects (e.g. theories) are placed above their extensions, instantiations and practical implementations. Therefore under this denotational semantics view the same object is an instance of the object(s) above and a class of all objects located below (figure 1.) The $\leq$ relation is an induced *partial order* over reductions as it verifies [3]: reflexivity ($< l, a >\leq< l, a >$), antisymmetry ($< l, a >\leq< l', a' >$ and $< l', a' >\leq< l, a >$ imply $< l, a >=< l', a' >$) and transitivity ($< l, a >\leq< l', a' >$ and $< l', a' >\leq< l'', a'' >$ imply $< l, a >\leq< l'', a'' >$). Now let $\wedge$ denote a generalization operation over denotational definitions (i.e. some knowledge is *removed*) and let $\vee$ be a specialization operation over definitions (i.e. knowledge is *joint together* and/or *added*):

Clara Smith, 'On the Structure and Soundness of AI & Law Objects' in D. Bourcier (ed.), *Legal Knowledge and Information Systems, Jurix. 2003: The Sixteenth Annual Conference*, Amsterdam: IOS Press, 2003, pp. 145-146.

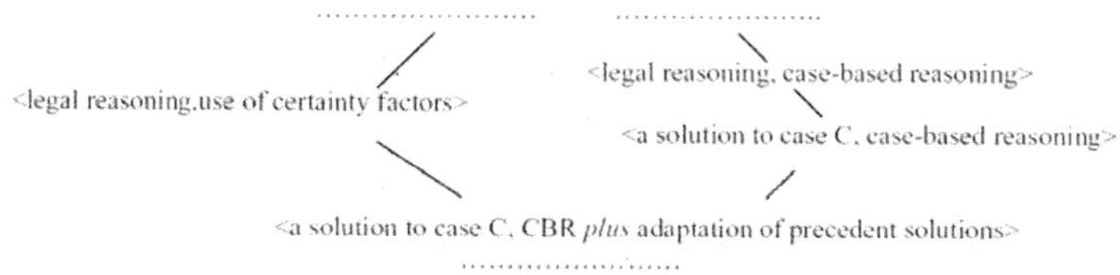

Figure 1: A sketch of a *Hasse diagram* for the reductions' poset.

then the following properties are easily verifiable on $(Law \times AI_{\perp}, \leq)$: conmutativity $(< l,a > \vee < l',a' >=< l',a' > \vee < l,a >$ and $< l,a > \wedge < l',a' >=< l',a' > \wedge < l,a >)$, associativity $(< l,a > \vee(< l',a' > \vee < l'',a'' >) = (< l,a > \vee < l',a' >)\vee < l'',a'' >$ and $< l,a > \wedge(< l',a' > \wedge < l'',a'' >) = (< l,a > \wedge < l',a' >)\wedge < l'',a'' >)$, idempotence $(< l,a > \vee(< l',a' > \vee < l'',a'' >) = (< l,a > \vee < l',a' >)\vee < l'',a'' >$ and $< l,a > \wedge(< l',a' > \wedge < l'',a'' >) = (< l,a > \wedge < l',a' >)\wedge < l'',a'' >)$ and absorption $(< l,a >=< l,a > \vee(< l,a > \wedge < l',a' >)$ and $< l,a >=< l,a > \wedge(< l,a > \vee < l',a' >))$. This way we identify an algebra for AI & Law objects in its own right. It can be seen as a logic of construction of AI & Law objects. The theory proposal method in [4] is an example of $\wedge$-use.

Comparisons among objects can be performed by analysing their relative positions in the poset. *Is-a* relationships can be discovered following paths in the poset.

3 The Interdisciplinary Validity Problem (IVP)

We are interested in AI outcomes to be accepted as *legal* answers, that is: *"outcomes must not only be checked for (specification) correctness but also confronted to expected legal results"* Stated this way, IVP establishes a relation connecting a "low level" AI interpreter and a "high level" legal interpreter. Given a reduction $< l,a >$, given $vm(Law), vm(AI_{\perp})$ available validation methods for Law and $AI_{\perp}$ elements respectively, and being $eval$ an evaluation relation, we have the following IVP schema

Def. 2. $IVP(< l,a >, vm(l), vm(a)) : eval(vm(l), l)) \approx eval(vm(a)a); eval(vm(l), a))$

In IVP the relation among l and a through $vm(l)$ is what counts. Def. 2. holds when the evaluation of l through legal methods agrees (under some criteria abstractly denoted $\approx$) with outcomes obtained when evaluating a using the same methods used for l, given a correct.

4 Definition of a Reduction (meta)Theory

Def. 3. *A Reduction Theory is a tuple:* $< (Law \times AI_{\perp}, \leq), vm(Law), vm(AI_{\perp}), IVP >$

The Reduction Theory models AI & Law objects as relations among legal phenomena and specifications; models generalization/specialization relationships among reductions through an induced notion of covering, and it includes an IVP axiom schema (which we believe is a truly AI & Law-sensitive feature) that works as a tool for legal accuracy measurement.

References

[1] D. Schmidt. Denotational Semantics. A Methodology for Language Development. Allyn and Bacon, 1986, MA.

[2] M. Kifer, G. Lausen. F-Logic: A Higher-Order Language for Reasoning about Objects, Inheritance and Scheme. ACM 1989.

[3] S. Burris, H. Sankappanavar. A Course in Universal Algebra. Graduate Texts in Mathematics, Springer 1981.

[4] T. Bench-Capon, G. Sartor. A Model of Legal Reasoning with Cases Incorporating Theories and Values. Artificial Intelligence. Kluwer, 2003.

Electronic Notification of Block Exempted State Aid

Erich Schweighofer* Doris Liebwald Mathias Drachsler
University of Vienna, Department of International Law, Center for Legal Informatics
A-1090 Vienna, Universitätsstraße 2, Austria
{erich.schweighofer,doris.liebwald}@univie.ac.at

1 Introduction

EU law provides that state aids have to be notified and approved by the Commission according to Article 87 and 88 of the EC Treaty. The high number of cases - about 1000 per year - and the complexity of information make this area a good candidate for new methods of knowledge handling. Electronic communication and analysis of summary information that has to be submitted for block excepted state aids seems to be a first good start.

The aims of this project are to develop a sufficient XML structure for electronic communications of state aids in agriculture based on electronic forms, a Web interface for filling in the forms and the reuse of the data for electronic publication or further analysis by the Commission. A very important part of the project consists in the semi-automatic assessment of the electronic notifications by heuristic rules.

2 Legal Environment

Council Regulation (EC) No 994/98 empowers the Commission to exempt aid granted by Member States to small and medium-sized enterprises from the notification requirement of Article 88(3) of the EC Treaty. In the area of agriculture, the Commission has recently published a Draft Commission Regulation on the application of Article 87 and 88 of the EC Treaty to state aid to small and medium-sized enterprises active in the production, processing and marketing of agricultural products (OJ C 194 of 15.8.2003, hereinafter: Draft Block Exemption Regulation).

Member States have special information obligations. They shall forward to the Commission, with a view to publication in the Official Journal, summaries of the information regarding exempted state aids granted. The form of this report is defined in Annex I of the Draft Block Exemption Regulation. The Draft Block Exemption Regulation provides a block exemption system for certain types of state aid up to certain ceilings granted to farmers or companies processing and marketing agricultural products. The Commission intends to adopt the final text by the end of 2003. At the beginning of our project, some work has also been based on Commission Regulation (EC) No 69/2001 on *de minimis* aid.

*Presently on leave; working for the European Commission. The expressed views are those of the author.

Erich Schweighofer, Doris Liebwald, and Mathias Drachsler, 'Electronic Notification of Block Exempted State Aid' in D. Bourcier (ed.), *Legal Knowledge and Information Systems. Jurix 2003: The Sixteenth Annual Conference*. Amsterdam: IOS Press, 2003, pp. 147-148.

3 Project Description

Presently, the information communicated by Member States is usually sent in paper and additionally as an electronic document (e.g. Winword file). In our project, this information is provided electronically using XML tagging. As users may not be sufficiently familiar with XML, an Internet portal has been developed for data input. Some checks guarantee a complete and coherent notification. Then, this structured information is reused in various forms by the Commission: data administration, publication in the Official Journal, statistical analysis and examination of the submitted data concerning compliance with the Block Exemption Regulation.

The project consists of five independent modules: login module, state aid module, module XML output, check text module and database access module.

As database we have used MySQL. Server side scripting was done in PHP. Additionally, JavaScript is utilised for field and text checking and XML style sheets for visualisation. This concept allows the use of any common Internet browser running on any operating system for the data input, e.g. notifications given by Member States.

The most interesting module is the *check text module*, developed for a more sophisticated examination of the notifications. Text is put under scrutiny using various heuristic rules for linguistic analysis. The basis of this analysis are legal ontologies defining the various concepts. Simple heuristic rules define words and word combinations which have to or must not occur in the text. Presently, the field *objective of aid* is the primary target of analysis of this module. Word sets are put into the database for defining concepts, e.g. investment aid (actually three tables: condition_AND, condition_OR, neg_condition_AND). This allows an easy add-on of further elements of definitions without changes in the programme. Existing notifications and the requirements of the Draft Block Exemption Regulation were the basis of the development of such rules. For the first tests we used Article 4 (investment in agricultural holdings) of the Draft Block Exemption Regulation and checked successfully for the fulfilment of the rule that investment aid for the purchase of animals is prohibited.

The *module XML output* will allow an easy change of layout for different purposes like comparison, localisation or statistical means, sorting functions, the presentation of requested subsets and an automatic linking between different presentations.

4 Conclusions and Future Work

The advantages of using electronic forms allowing reuse and recycling of information are obvious. The main difficulty is the definition of the XML structure as well as the following processing of this information. State aids are in particular well suited because a highly developed structure has been developed over the years. But future work may show that the structure has to be adapted for more sophisticated analysis.

Linguistic analysis by heuristic rules has been proven as quite powerful although the reliability is limited. For a more complete analysis, a deeper linguistic model has to be developed. As the output should only provide help for further analysis by an expert, the achieved results are satisfactory for this purpose.

An electronic communication of summary information for publication in the official journal for aid schemes and individual aid fulfilling the conditions of the Draft Block Exemption Regulation provides some advantages in comparison with the paper communication. The developed prototype of an application for the electronic communication procedure about the aid has shown that important gains of efficiency can be obtained by reusing the recycling the data for publication and further analysis.

Intelligent Electronic Inter-Systemic Contracting - Issues on Contract Formation

Francisco C.P. Andrade
Law School, Minho University, Portugal
franc.andrade@netcabo.pt

Electronic Contracting as an object of legal studies is getting more and more complex. Computers are currently being used not only as a way of searching and processing information, but also as communication tools, as automatic operators and already as a way of developing and accessing new forms of intelligent behaviour through the use of intelligent devices. New ways of electronic communicating and contracting have appeared and with them different kinds of interactions that must be analysed in electronic contracting: human interaction through electronic devices, human interaction with electronic devices, automated computer interaction and intelligent computer interaction. This led Brazilian legal doctrine to establish a specific way of classifying electronic contracts: Interpersonal Electronic Contracting, when computer is used as a mere communication tool, allowing both simultaneous (through Chat, Video-Conference) and non-simultaneous (through electronic mail, mobile phone written messages) contracting; Interactive Electronic Contracting, when interaction is effected between a human party and an informatics system, either through means of semi-automatic interactive connection (a natural person interacting with a previously programmed device automatically "declaring the will of its owner") or through means of human communication with an "intelligent device"; and Inter-systemic Electronic Contracting, when offer and acceptance derive from an electronic dialogue (and acting) between electronic systems or devices which are able to act on their own, without any human intervention. As far as Inter-systemic Electronic Contracting is concerned we can also distinguish two important sub-groups: "automatic inter-systemic electronic contracting", as the informatics systems on their own execute in an automatic way the instructions previously incorporated in the programme (EDI), and "intelligent inter-systemic electronic contracting", for the special case of electronic devices contracting through the only intervention and interaction of autonomous intelligent systems, capable of acting, learning, reasoning, modifying program instructions and taking decisions.

Inter-systemic Electronic Contracting is most challenging for legal theory, especially in what declaration of will and consent are concerned. In all the other above mentioned kinds of contracts the parties can still totally control the process of contract formation, either when both parties actually perform the acts embodying offer and acceptance, or at least when one party electronically "adhere" to contractual clauses predisposed and offered to the public by the other party. But in Inter-systemic Electronic Contracting, the whole process of communication is "between applications" without any human intervention.

As far as "automatic inter-systemic contracting" is concerned, there are two main ways of facing the problem of consent: either by requiring an expression of will for each message exchanged, which lead us to the question of the electronic or digital signature (however, these transactions require full automated process, which means that it would be completely useless to require a personally digitised signature for each message); or by having a single expression

Francisco C.P. Andrade, 'Intelligent Electronic Inter-Systemic Contracting - Issues on Contract Formation' in D. Bourcier (ed.), *Legal Knowledge and Information Systems. Jurix 2003: The Sixteenth Annual Conference.* Amsterdam: IOS Press, 2003, pp. 149-150.

of will displayed when the system is set up or initialized, that's to say through an Interchange Agreement, stating the will of the parties to a fully acceptance of the contents and effects of the legal transactions to be concluded. Anyway, the interconnection of the systems by itself already reveals this full acceptance of contents and effects. The behaviour of the parties, keeping the system functioning, is totally conclusive.

Yet, Intelligent Electronic Inter-systemic contracting requires a different analysis. Because intelligent artefacts will not only act according to its in-built knowledge and rules, but they will also be able to learn from experience, modify its own behaviour, according to cognitive, reactive and pro-active processes quite similar to human acting and reasoning. This leads us to an imperious need of analysing the question of expression of consent in inter-systemic intelligent transactions in a different way. Some possibilities must be dealt with: firstly, the possibility of considering a computer intelligent agent as a machine or tool. As Jean-Franois Lerouge puts it, "if a party create a situation in which an electronic agent is to act on his behalf, then a party is bound by the actions of the "agents"". The assent of the electronic agent would be inferred from the assent of the (human) user of the agent - the risks of the transactions would entirely be put on the persons who program, control or use the electronic agent. Another possibility could eventually be the application of the rules of representation, mandate or agency to electronic transactions. However this possibility faces a major difficulty, as for its full implementation we must analyse whether or not electronic agents can be considered as legal persons, in order to have legal personhood and legal capacity to undertake binding transactions. So, attribution of legal personhood to electronic agents could be a solution with some advantages. It would solve the question of consent and of contracts validity without affecting the established civil law theories. And it would reassure programmers, owners and users of the agents in what liability is concerned, by limiting their own liability while considering an "agents liability". But conferring legal personhood to electronic agents also faces some difficulties. Issues such as identification and domicile of agents, as well as the need of attributing them a patrimony, could become difficulties. Not to speak of the daring possibility of agents dividing or multiplying themselves "into undistinguished copies". A special registration procedure would be required for authorized agents, as well as a minimum patrimony and eventually a special insurance regime. Another possible solution would be, as Giovanni Sartor suggests, to create companies for on-line trading, "which would use agents in doing their business". The consent of the agents would "represent" the will of the company and counterparties would be warranted by the capital of the company. But this seems like considering agents as a tool of a "limited responsibility company".

Further possibilities must be exploited. For instance, to foresee a new legal approach of the contract itself, considering not the agreement of wills but the resulte of the acts of machines or devices predisposed by human or corporate bodies. Or even to consider informatics systems as instruments capable of creating new forms of life, maybe new germs of legal personhood.

The debate about Intelligent Inter-systemic contracting is still beginning. New developments are arising in the field of Artificial Intelligence such as the "embodying" of electronic "conversational agents". Virtual persons will get more and more identifiable. An ultimate choice must bc made between the fiction of considering agents acts as deriving from human's will and the endeavour of finding new ways of considering the electronic devices own will and responsibility.

A Computational Framework for Non-Monotonic Agency, Institutionalised Power and Multi-Agent Systems

Guido Governatori* Antonino Rotolo†
* *School of Information Technology and Electrical Engineering*
The University of Queensland, Brisbane, Australia
guido@itee.uq.edu.au
† *CIRSFID, University of Bologna, Bologna, Italy*
rotolo@cirfid.unibo.it

In [3, 4] the present authors and colleagues have provided a model of organisations of agents in terms of policy-based normative systems. An organisation is thus characterised by specifying the normative positions relevant to design its structure. This abstract summarises further results in this direction[1]. In particular, the research provides a computational framework based on Defeasible Logic to capture some theoretical intuitions developed in [3, 4]. The focus is on the idea of institutionalised power, as represented by the counts-as link, and on two aspects of agency: the notions of attempt and of personal and direct action to realise states of affairs. For the first issue, we adopted the approach of [3, 4], inspired, with some differences, by [5, 6]. For the second aspect, the reference is to recent developments of the Kanger-Lindahl-Pörn theory of action [7, 8, 6]. The model embeds also the modal operator *proc*, which represents the act of proclaiming to capture some minimal properties of all speech acts that are intended to modify the institutional world [3, 4]. The goal of the research is computational insofar as it proposes an efficient and flexible formalism to deal with counts-as conditionals and their interplay with agency. In fact, [4, 3], but also [5, 6], can hardly be used directly for implementation since they are based on conditional logics. On the other hand, this research aims also to provide some hints to define a non-monotonic theory of agency.

Our logic of institutional agency is based on the framework for Defeasible Logic developed in [1, 2]. The idea is to extend this framework to account for: (1) the underlying logical structure of any propositional base describing an institution; (2) the logic behavior of the modal operators of institutional agency; and (3) the relationships among such operators. The logic of agency should specify how modalities can be introduced and manipulated. To comply with this, in the setting provided by Defeasible Logic we have to set 1) the rules describing the logical inferences within the institution and 2) the rules to introduce the modal operators of agency E_i (*the agent i brings it about*), and H_i (*the agent i attempts*). Accordingly, two types of rules (strict, defeasible, and defeaters) are considered: rules for the notion

*This research was partially supported by the University of Queensland under the grant UQRSF ITEE-03/2002001335.

[1]Motivation and details of the research are provided in the full version of this paper, which is available at `http://www.itee.uq.edu.au/~guido/Papers/deontic/Defeasible-jurix03.pdf`.

Guido Governatori and Antonino Rotolo, 'A Computational Framework for Non-Monotonic Agency, Institutionalised Power and Multi-Agent Systems' in D. Bourcier (ed.), *Legal Knowledge and Information Systems. Jurix 2003: The Sixteenth Annual Conference*. Amsterdam: IOS Press, 2003, pp. 151-152.

of *counts-as* and rules for the notion of *results-in*. The language of Defeasible Logic is extended with a set of action symbols; $\alpha_i, \beta_i, \gamma_i$, which denote atomic actions, may occur in the rules. The meaning of an action symbol α_i is that the action corresponding to it has been performed by the agent i. In this perspective, a defeasible institutional action theory is a structure $I = (A, F, R^c, \{R^i\}_{i\in A}, >)$ where, A is a finite set of agents, F is a set of facts, R^c is a set of counts-as rules (i.e., $\rightarrow_c, \Rightarrow_c, \rightsquigarrow_c$), $\{R^i\}_{i\in A}$ is a family of sets of results-in rules (i.e., $\rightarrow^i, \Rightarrow^i, \rightsquigarrow^i$ for each agent $i \in A$), and $>$, the superiority relation, is a binary relation over the set of rules (i.e., $> \subseteq (R^c \cup R^A)^2$), where $R^A = \bigcup_{i\in A} R^i$. The intuition is that, given an institution I, F consists of the description of the raw institutional facts, either in form of states of affairs and actions that have been performed. R^c describes the basic inference mechanism internal to an institution, while R^A encodes the transitions from state to state occurring as the results of actions performed by agents within the organisation. The crucial notion in this model is that of derivability. Counts-as rules and conditions for derivation involving them produce the institutional facts that hold within the institution. However, the machinery requires also to account for action transitions that are recognised by the organisation. Accordingly, the introduction of the modalities of agency within the institution is obtained as the output of the general definition of derivability that involves counts-as as well as results-in rules. Suppose the agent i is acting in the context of an auction[2]:

$$r_1 : \mathbf{raises\_hand}_i,\ \mathit{auction\_begun} \Rightarrow_c \mathbf{bids}_i \qquad\qquad r_2 : \mathbf{bids}_i \Rightarrow^i \mathit{offer}$$

If no attack is possible, i's fulfilment of the conditions of r_1 produces *offer*: i's action of raising one hand has the result that i has made an offer, and so the derivation of *offer* permits to introduce $E_i(\mathit{offer})$. But the framework can deal with more complex scenarios where, e.g., i acts on behalf of the agent j. In this perspective, we may have rules such as the following:

$$r_3 : \mathbf{bids}_i,\ \mathit{proc}_i(E_j\mathit{offer}) \Rightarrow^j \mathit{offer} \qquad r_4 : \mathit{proc}_i(E_j\mathit{offer}), \mathbf{raises\_hand}_i \Rightarrow_c \mathbf{bids}_j$$

Rule r_3 means that the fact that i makes a bid and proclaims that j makes the offer may permit to introduce $E_j\mathit{offer}$, while r_4 expresses that i's proclamation that j makes an offer counts as j's action of bidding.

References

[1] G. Antoniou, D. Billington, G. Governatori, and M. J. Maher. A Flexible Framework for Defeasible Logics. In *AAAI-2000*, pages 401–405. AAAI Press, Menlo Park, 2000.

[2] G. Antoniou, D. Billington, G. Governatori, and M. J. Maher. Representation Results for Defeasible Logic. *ACM Transactions on Computational Logic*, 2(2):255–287, 2001.

[3] J. Gelati, G. Governatori, A. Rotolo, and G. Sartor. Declarative Power, Representation, and Mandate: A Formal Analysis. In *Proceedings of Jurix'02*, pages 41–52. IOS Press, Amsterdam, 2002.

[4] G. Governatori, J. Gelati, A. Rotolo, and G. Sartor. Actions, Institutions, Powers. Preliminary Notes. In *Proceedings of RASTA'02*, pages 131–147. University of Hamburg, Hamburg, 2002.

[5] A. Jones and M. Sergot. A Formal Characterisation of Institutionalised Power. *Journal of IGPL*, 3:427–443, 1996.

[6] A. Jones. A Logical Framework. In J. Pitt, editor, *Open Agent Societies: Normative Specifications in Multi-Agent Systems*. Wiley, Chichester, 2003.

[7] F. Santos and J. Carmo. Indirect Action, Influence and Responsibility. In M. Brown and J. Carmo, editors, *Deontic Logic, Agency and Normative Systems*. Springer, Berlin, 1996.

[8] F. Santos, A. Jones, and J. Carmo. Action Concepts for Describing Organised Interaction. In *13th HICSS*. IEEE Computer Society Press, Los Alamitos, 1997.

[2]Bold type expressions correspond to action symbols, the italicised ones to state of affairs.

A Predictive Role for Intermediate Legal Concepts

Kevin D. Ashley Stefanie Brüninghaus*
University of Pittsburgh - Intelligent Systems Program
Learning Research and Development Center and School of Law
Pittsburgh, PA 15260
{ashley, steffi}@pitt.edu

Abstract. Experiments described here demonstrate a role that intermediate legal concepts play in predicting the decisions of new cases. The experiments compare variations of each of an Issue-Based Prediction algorithm (IBP) and a CATO prediction algorithm in which the use of legal concepts are ablated in various ways. The results confirm those legal philosophical theories that assert that intermediate concepts in legal principles perform a guiding or extending role in deciding new cases.

1 Introduction

Legal philosophers have observed that intermediate legal concepts like "owner", "citizen", "territory", "trade secret", "breach of confidence" and others appear to serve as "vehicles of inference" between statements of legal grounds, on the one hand, and legal consequences, on the other. [11][p. 185]. According to the Scandinavian realist, Alf Ross, that was their only role [17]. In his famous example, he described a (fictional) South Seas island society with certain rules concerning *Tû-tû*, as in:

(1) If a person has eaten of the chief's food he is *tû-tû*.
(1′) If a person has killed a totem animal he is *tû-tû*. ...
(2) If a person is *tû-tû* he shall be subjected to a ceremony of purification.

According to Ross, an assertion that someone is *tû-tû*, can be verified by proving the existence of one of the factual antecedents of the rules concluding *tû-tû* or whether the purification norm is applicable as a result. This is true, Ross observed, even though the word *tû-tû* is devoid of meaning, pure superstition and nonsense. In fact, one could omit using the term altogether! "It is plain that quite apart from what '*tû-tû*' stands for, or even whether it stands for anything at all, these two pronouncements, when combined in accordance with the usual rules of logic, will amount to the same thing as the following pronouncement:

(3) If a person has eaten of the chief's food he shall be subjected to a ceremony of purification." [17][p. 814].

Similarly, Ross argued that legal concepts like " 'ownership,' 'claim,' and other words, when used in legal language, have the same function as the word "*tû-tû*"; they are words without meaning, without any semantic reference, and serve a purpose only as a technique of presentation." [17][p. 814]. That is, they serve as a vehicle of inference while affording an economy of expression. For instance, there are many facts Fi from which one may infer

*We are grateful to Vincent Aleven for sharing his code for the CATO and HYPO-based prediction methods. This allowed us to reproduce his experiments and to generate examples for this paper.
Kevin D. Ashley and Stefanie Brüninghaus, 'A Predictive Role for Intermediate Legal Concepts' in D. Bourcier (ed.), *Legal Knowledge and Information Systems. Jurix 2003: The Sixteenth Annual Conference*. Amsterdam: IOS Press, 2003, pp. 153-162.

ownership O:

(I) F1 implies O, F2 implies O,. . . ,Fp implies O,

and many consequences Ci that follow from a conclusion of ownership O:

(II) O implies C1, O implies C2,. . . , O implies Cn.

Ross argued, " 'O' (ownership) merely stands for the systematic connection that F1 as well as F2, F3 . . . Fp entail the totality of legal consequences C1, C2, C3 . . . Cn. As a technique of presentation this is expressed then by stating in one series of rules the facts that 'create ownership' and in another series the legal consequences that 'ownership' entails." [17][p. 820]. Given this function, however, since the (logical) inferences are transitive, it does not matter what O stands for or whether it stands for anything at all. One could dispense with O altogether, but it is convenient not to do so given the n $\times$ p individual legal rules it abbreviates or "presents" with n + p rules [11][p. 193]; [18].

2 Intermediate Concepts as Guiding Decision of New Cases

Some legal philosophers have criticized Ross's theory for failing to account for the role that intermediate legal concepts play in guiding decisions of new or problematic cases. Recently, Lindahl has focused on the significant role that such concepts play in legal justification and argumentation. While conceding that some legal terms serve as vehicles of inference, others satisfying general structural schemes like (I) and (II) above are also accompanied by normative justifications. That is, they are "operative conditions" or "operative grounds" of jural relations (i.e., in the Hohfeldian sense such as having the duty to pay [11][p. 190]. See also [12]). So, for instance, Lindahl says, consider two empirical facts from which X's duty to pay Y may be inferred:

F1 "X says to Y 'I promise to pay you Z dollars', thereby making Y believe that X has a duty to pay him Z dollars."

F2 "X enters a bus run by Y without paying the stipulated fare of Z dollars."

The normative justification underlying the F1 inference is, "Responsibility for inducing legitimate expectations of a claim to get payment." For F2 it is, "Taking advantage of service, given only under the condition of payment." According to Lindahl, it is a mistake to subsume both justifications under an intermediate legal concept like "promising to pay" as in "F1 implies 'promises to pay'; F2 implies 'promises to pay'; 'Promises to pay' implies has duty to pay." Beside serving as a vehicle of inference, "promises to pay" is an operative condition; the kinds of empirical factual conditions it subsumes should be homogeneous from a normative or principled viewpoint. The principles underlying F1 and F2, however, are different. F1 involves inducing expectations. F2 does not. This leads to unfortunate results when judges start to speak of "implied" or "constructive" promises.

According to Lindahl, it matters therefore which intermediate legal concepts one chooses to serve as vehicles of inference. Collecting together various legal rules that embody the same principle not only facilitates generating transparent and normatively coherent explanations but the "justificatory rationale of legal norms, in its turn, provides guidelines for the handling of new and problematic cases, in arguments *ex analogia* and *e contrario*." [11][p. 199]. Similarly, Michael S. Moore has criticized Ross's view along somewhat similar lines. "If legal principles were abbreviatory of a mass of legal rules in the way Ross's analysis suggests, then [they] . . . cannot serve the creative or extending function." He also notes, "The same holds for reductive analyses in science: being able to derive a theory from an experimental law eliminates the power of the theory to generate new predictions and laws." [14][pp. 885-6].

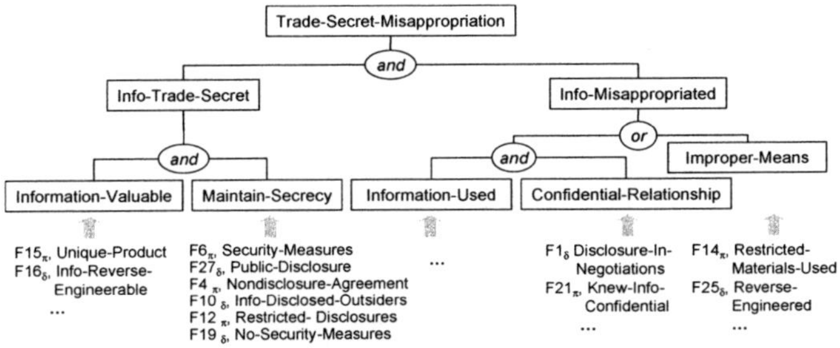

Figure 1: IBP's Domain Model

3 Using Prediction to Investigate Intermediate Legal Concepts

Some AI and Law researchers have had to grapple with the meaning of intermediate legal concepts in a very applied sense. They have developed techniques for representing such concepts and integrating them into their case-based models of legal reasoning. TaxmanII combined a template-like description of a legal concept, taxable income, and a set of possible mappings from one description into others [13]. HYPO represented case facts involving trade secret misappropriation claims in terms of Dimensions. It did not represent the claim's elements, in part because a subsequent court is free to reinterpret a prior court's holding on an issue as having been affected by other factors in the case not strictly related to that issue [3][pp. 238-241]. CABARET integrated logical reasoning with rules and dimension-guided comparisons of cases concerning the rules' terms into one legal reasoning process [16]. GREBE represented in semantic networks judges' explanations of why legal concepts, open-textured predicates extracted from statutory rules regarding workman's compensation law, applied to the facts of a case [8]. CATO's Factor Hierarchy provided legal reasons why trade secret factors mattered in terms of intermediate legal concepts, abstract factors based on the claim's issues [1]. Some complications in reasoning with factors within and across abstract factors, such as possible tradeoffs across issues, were discussed in [6]. A formal dialogue game framework has been presented that integrated cases, factors and logical reasoning with rules whose conclusions involved intermediate tax law concepts in [15].

We have investigated empirically the contribution intermediate legal concepts make to guiding, that is, predicting decisions of new cases. Originally developed for argumentation, the HYPO/CATO framework has been adapted to make predictions based on argumentation concepts [2]. The Issue-Based Prediction (IBP) algorithm [9] combines a logical representation of issues with a case-based reasoning (CBR) component for predicting and explaining case outcomes. Ablation experiments with these programs yield insights on the predictive contribution of legal concepts. An algorithm that takes legal concepts into account can be compared to a variant in which this knowledge has been turned off (i.e., ablated) with measurable results. In this way, one can begin to investigate empirically the role of intermediate legal concepts in guiding how to deal with new or problematic cases, the heart of Lindahl's and Moore's critiques.

IBP [9] uses CATO's Factor model as its case representation. A case is represented by a set of Factors, abstract fact patterns that strengthen a plaintiff's claim or a defendant's response, called pro-p or pro-d Factors, respectively. (We use subscript π and δ, as well as (p) and (d) to indicate which side is favored by a Factor.) IBP's knowledge about the intermediate legal concepts is captured in a logical structure called the Domain Model, Fig. 1. The cases all involve claims for trade secret misappropriation, and the intermediate concepts are the elements of, or issues raised by, the claim. These issues have been identified in the Restatement of Torts First, Sec. 757 and in the closely related Uniform Trade Secret Act (UTSA). In order

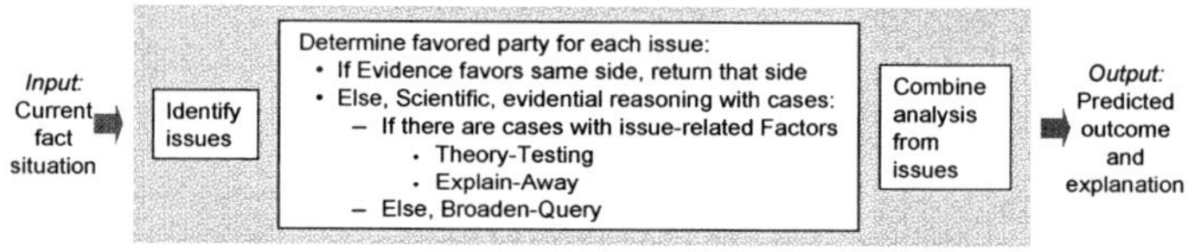

Figure 2: Overview of IBP

```
Prediction for MASON

  Factors favoring plaintiff: (F21 F15 F6)
  Factors favoring defendant: (F16 F1)

Issue raised in this case is SECURITY-MEASURES            1
  Relevant factors in case: F6(P) PLAINTIFF.

Issue raised in this case is CONFIDENTIAL-RELATIONSHIP
Relevant factors in case: F1(D) F21(P)
Theory testing has no clear outcome, try to explain away
exceptions.
Cases won by plaintiff:                                   2
  BOEING (F1 F4 F6 F10 F12 F14 F21)
  BRYCE (F1 F4 F6 F18 F21)
  DEN-TAL-EZ (F1 F4 F6 F21 F26)
  DIGITAL-DEVELOPMENT (F1 F6 F8 F15 F18 F21)
  FOREST-LABORATORIES (F1 F6 F15 F21)
  GOLDBERG (F1 F10 F21 F27)
  LASER (F1 F6 F10 F12 F21)
  LEWIS (F1 F8 F21)
  NATIONAL-INSTRUMENT (F1 F18 F21)
  VALCO-CINCINNATI (F1 F6 F15 F21 F10 F12)

Cases won by defendant:
  ECOLOGIX (F1 F19 F21 F23)                               3
Trying to explain away exceptions won by DEFENDANT
  ECOLOGIX can be explained away because of
  the unshared ko-factor(s) (F23 F19).
Therefore, PLAINTIFF is favored.

[...]

Outcome of the issue-based analysis:
   For issue CONFIDENTIAL-RELATIONSHIP, PLAINTIFF is favored.
   For issue SECURITY-MEASURES, PLAINTIFF is favored.
   For issue INFO-VALUABLE, PLAINTIFF is favored.         4
=> Predicted outcome for MASON is PLAINTIFF, which is correct.
```

Figure 3: IBP's Output for Mason

to win a claim for trade secrets misappropriation, the plaintiff has to show that the information was a trade secret (Info-Trade-Secret in Fig. 1) and that the defendant misappropriated the information (Info-Misappropriated in Fig. 1). IBP's domain model follows the UTSA and the Restatement; to be a trade secret, the information has to have value for plaintiff's business (Info-Valuable) and the plaintiff has to take measures to keep it secret (Maintain-Secrecy). The Domain Model also represents that a defendant can misappropriate the trade secret by using information (Info-Used) conveyed in confidence (Confidential-Relationship), or by using improper means (Improper-Means) to gain access to the information. IBP's Domain Model does not logically connect the issues with case facts, represented by Factors. Rather, each issue has between 5 and 7 associated Factors favoring both sides. Case-based comparisons rather than logical inferences determine whether plaintiff or defendant is favored on the issue.

In IBP, prediction is guided by its knowledge of legal issues. When IBP predicts the outcome of a new case, it combines case-based and model-based reasoning (Fig. 2). It uses the Domain Model to identify the issues related to the case facts. It then determines for each of these issues, which side is favored. In this step, IBP applies CBR if necessary [9]. The algorithm makes its final prediction by combining the analysis of the issues following the logical structure in the Domain Model.

Each of the cases in our collection is represented as a list of the factors that, after a careful reading of the opinion, were deemed to apply in the facts of the case. With respect to both IBP and CATO-Arg, it should be noted that the case representation does not include a representation of the particular issues the judge identified in the opinion, only the applicable Factors. Thus, when either algorithm asserts that an issue is relevant in the case, it is a result of an inference drawn from IBP's Domain Model or CATO's Factor Hierarchy, respectively.

4 Prediction Algorithms

The experiments described below involve comparing two sets of prediction algorithms. The first set involves the issue-based prediction in the IBP algorithm and two variations, IBP-No-Issues and IBP-Model. The second set involves the case-based prediction in CATO-Arg and a non-issue variation, HYPO-Arg.

In order to illustrate IBP, we apply it to *Mason v. Jack Daniel Distillery*. In this case, the plaintiff, a restaurant owner, had developed a mixed drink. The drink was a popular item at his restaurant. In order to keep the recipe exclusive, the plaintiff shared the recipe only with his bartenders. He also instructed them to mix the drink outside of customers' view. As a result, one could not order the drink in any other restaurant, even though skilled bartenders probably would have been able to duplicate it. When the defendant, a sales representative for Jack Daniel, visited plaintiff's restaurant, he tasted the drink. Plaintiff told defendant that the recipe was a secret and then disclosed it to defendant. Plaintiff sued for trade secret misappropriation after he learned that the Distillery marketed his drink nationwide. The court decided that the defendant was liable for trade secret misappropriation, but only awarded plaintiff symbolic damages of one dollar. In our case representation, Mason has pro-p Factors $F6_\pi$, Security-Measures; $F15_\pi$, Unique-Product and $F21_\pi$, Knew-Info-Confidential, and pro-d Factors $F1_\delta$, Disclosure-In-Negotiations; and $F16_\delta$, Info-Reverse-Engineerable.

When Mason's Factors are given as input to IBP, it first uses its Domain Model to identify the relevant issues, Security-Measures, Confidential-Relationship, and Info-Valuable. These issues have a strong impact on the rest of IBP's procedure; the program analyzes each issue in turn and focuses on the issue-related Factors, rather than the entire set of Factors.

IBP has several techniques for analyzing issues. If the issue-related Factors favor the same side, this side is returned. In *Mason*, the only Factor related to Maintain-Secrecy is $F6_\pi$, Security-Measures (Fig. 3, Nr. 1). Thus, IBP concludes that plaintiff is favored for the issue.

If there are issue-related Factors for both sides, like $F1_\delta$ and $F21_\pi$ for Confidential-Relationship in *Mason* (Fig. 3, Nr. 2), IBP uses a kind of evidential scientific reasoning with cases to resolve the conflict. In its function Theory-Testing, the program tries to find cases where these conflicting issue-related Factors apply.

If all precedents were won by the same side, there is good reason to believe that in the current problem, this side is favored on the issue. The implied hypothesis is that the conflicting issue-related factors should be resolved in favor of the same side in the problem as, apparently, in the precedents. When there are examples but no counterexamples among the cases, the hypothesis is taken as confirmed.

Theory-Testing may retrieve cases favoring both sides. In *Mason*, Theory-Testing for Confidential-Relationship retrieves 10 cases won by plaintiff and 1 case, *Ecologix*, won by defendant (Fig. 3, Nr. 3). Here, IBP does not take a vote and conclude that the same side is favored on the issue that prevailed in the majority of cases. Rather, it formulates a hypothesis that the majority side should be favored (here the plaintiff) and tests the hypothesis against the retrieved cases. When it finds *Ecologix*, it tries to salvage the hypothesis by explaining away the counterexample. The applicable Factors in *Ecologix* indicate that the plaintiff did not keep the information secret, Factor $F19_\delta$, No-Security-Measures. $F19_\delta$ applies neither in *Mason* nor in the cases that support the hypothesis. It is a very dominant Factor; (almost) all cases where it applies were won by defendant. In IBP, Factors like $F19_\delta$ that strongly dominate case outcomes are called Knockout, or KO-Factors, and are used to explain away exceptions like *Ecologix* in Theory-Testing. If all exceptions can be explained away, IBP concludes that its hypothesis was confirmed, otherwise it abstains. In *Mason*, Theory-Testing is successful in confirming hypotheses regarding issues Confidential-Relationship and Info-Valuable (not shown). When IBP has analyzed all issues, it combines the analysis for its final prediction (Fig. 3, Nr. 4).

If the fact situation is too specific, there may not be precedents that share the whole set of conflicting issue-related Factors to test a hypothesis as above. Here, IBP applies a technique called broadening a query. That function determines if cases can be found to test a more general hypothesis from which the more specific but untestable hypothesis would follow *a fortiori*. An example of broadening can be found in the output of an IBP variation called IBP-No-Issues for *Scientology*, discussed next.

For these experiments, we set up an ablated version of IBP, called IBP-No-Issues, that did not include knowledge about issues. Instead of IBP's hierarchical Domain Model (Fig. 1), IBP-No-Issues knows only one "issue," whether plaintiff should win the claim of trade secret misappropriation, an "issue" that relates to all Factors. Apart from a minor technical modification for broadening a query, all functions in IBP-No-Issues are identical to IBP, and it uses the same cases. The *Scientology* case in Fig. 5 illustrates how IBP-No-Issues works. Its initial query for Theory-Testing retrieves no cases. It is broadened to retrieve precedents for a weaker hypothesis by dropping Factors. The hypothesis is that plaintiff is favored despite the pro-d Factors even when pro-p Factors are dropped. This weaker hypothesis cannot be confirmed, however; the program finds only cases won by defendant. A similar attempt to broaden the query for defendant fails, and the program abstains.

In a second variation of IBP, called IBP-Model, access to the cases was disabled, only the Domain Model is used for predicting outcomes. IBP-Model does not reason with precedents, thus it does not carry out Theory-Testing, Explain-Away and Broaden-Query. For each issue in a new problem, IBP-Model tests whether the issue-related Factors favor the same side. If so, it infers that this side is favored for the issue; otherwise it abstains for the issue.

The HYPO/CATO-based algorithms take a different approach to prediction. Given a problem, HYPO-Arg determines whether all of the most persuasive cases to cite in an argument (i.e., the best untrumped cases or BUCs) had the same outcome. If so, it predicts that outcome; otherwise it abstains. BUCs are the most relevant cases a side can cite without fear of the opponent's responding with a more relevant (i.e., trumping) counterexample. Here, relevance is measured by the inclusiveness of the set of factors a case shares with the problem [3].

The CATO-Arg algorithm improves upon HYPO-Arg by incorporating issues. Using a more refined relevance criterion that takes Factors and issues into account, it focuses on only cases not significantly distinguishable from the problem. That is, it focuses only on relevant cases whose distinctions from the problem can be downplayed and not emphasized. Given this reduced set of cases, it applies the BUC criterion to find the best cases on which to base its prediction. CATO can downplay distinctions, unshared Factors that underlie reasons for deciding cases differently, by trying to find alternative rationales to explain the conclusion favored by the distinction. It can also emphasize distinctions by pointing out alternative rationales that would support the opposite conclusion. These alternative rationales correspond to alternate paths from a distinguishing factor to an issue in its Factor Hierarchy [2], whose top-level issues are intermediate legal concepts based on the Restatement provision.

5 Experiments and Discussion

As noted above, we ran experiments comparing the predictive accuracy of the different algorithms. We used a database of 186 trade secret misappropriation cases of which 106 were won by plaintiff, the rest by defendant. All algorithms were tested in a leave-one-out cross-validation. For details on the experiment setup see [9]. Fig. 4 summarizes the results. The best performance in our experiment was achieved by IBP's issue-based prediction. IBP correctly predicted the outcome of 169 cases, made 14 mistakes and abstained once, which corresponds to an accuracy of 91.8% (Fig. 4, Nr. 1). The observed differences with the other algorithms were statistically significant [9].

A number of two-way comparisons between methods illustrate how adding knowledge about intermediate legal issues improves prediction. Since all algorithms in our experiment use the same Factor representation, results can be compared across algorithms.

a. IBP v. IBP-No-Issues: As discussed above, IBP-No-Issues does not have knowledge of the issues, whereas IBP makes inferences about cases using its Domain Model. In our

Nr.	Algorithm	Correct	Abstain	Errors	Accuracy
1	IBP	169	1	14	91.8%
2	CATO	143	22	19	77.7%
3	IBP-No-Issues	144	30	10	78.3%
4	HYPO	125	50	9	67.9%
5	IBP-model	132	38	14	71.7%
6	Baseline	106	0	78	57.6%

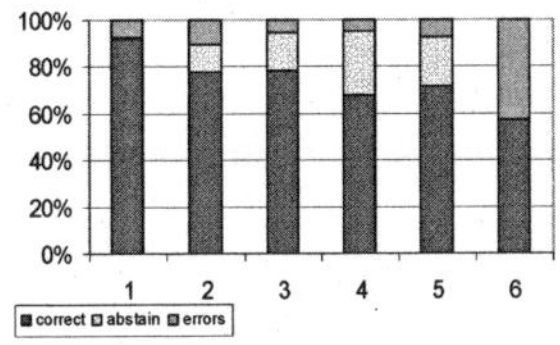

Figure 4: Experiment Results

experiments, IBP's performance is significantly better than IBP-No-Issues' (Fig. 4, Nrs. 1 and 3): accuracy is 91.8% compared to 78.3%. Because IBP abstains less frequently, it also has a much better coverage of the data set. This coverage comes at the cost of few extra errors; IBP has 4 more errors than IBP-No-Issues, but it more than compensates for this by the much higher rate of correct predictions (169 vs. 144). Both methods rely on the same set of cases, and use the same functions for reasoning with cases; the only difference is IBP's Domain Model. Thus, we conclude that adding knowledge about intermediate legal concepts leads to more accurate predictions.

```
Prediction for SCIENTOLOGY

  Factors favoring plaintiff: (F12 F6 F4)
  Factors favoring defendant: (F20 F10)

Issue raised in this case is INFO-TRADE-SECRET            1
  Relevant factors in case:
  F20(D) F4(P) F6(P) F12(P) F10(D)
Theory testing retrieved no cases, broadening query.

Query can be broadened for the plaintiff:

Dropping factor: F12
  Theory testing with Factors
  (F6 F4 F10 F20) gets the following cases:
  (MBL DEFENDANT F4 F5 F6 F10 F13 F20)
  (CMI DEFENDANT F4 F6 F10 F16 F17 F20 F27)
  In broadened query, DEFENDANT is favored.

Dropping factor: F6
  Theory testing with Factors
  (F12 F4 F10 F20) retrieves no cases.

 [...]

Trying to broaden by dropping two Pro-P-factors

Dropping F6 F4
  Theory testing with Factors (F12 F10 F20) retrieves no cases.

Broadening query for PLAINTIFF retrieves cases
won by DEFENDANT, so the algorithm abstains.              2

Query can be broadened for defendant

Dropping factor: F10
  Theory testing with Factors (F20 F12 F6 F4) retrieves no cases.

Dropping factor: F20
  Theory testing with Factors (F10 F12 F6 F4)
  gets the following cases:
  (TRANDES PLAINTIFF F1 F4 F6 F10 F12)
  (FMC PLAINTIFF F4 F6 F7 F10 F11 F12)
  (BOEING PLAINTIFF F1 F4 F6 F10 F12 F14 F21)
  In broadened query, PLAINTIFF is favored.

Broadening query for DEFENDANT only retrieves cases
won by PLAINTIFF, so the algorithm abstains.

Trying to broaden for defendant: NIL
Trying to broaden for plaintiff: NIL                      3

Outcome of the issue-based analysis:
   For issue INFO-TRADE-SECRET, NIL is favored.

=> Predicted outcome for SCIENTOLOGY is ABSTAIN
```

Figure 5: IBP-No-Issues' Output for *Scientology*

The *Scientology* case shows how IBP's knowledge about intermediate issues focuses Theory-Testing on issue-related Factors, rather than on unproductive attempts to find cases that share all Factors, as in IBP-No-Issues. IBP's processing for this case (not shown) is straight forward. It identifies four issues. For three of them, the related Factors favor one side only. For the fourth issue, Security-Measures, Theory-Testing is used. The issue analyses are combined into a correct prediction for defendant. Fig. 5 shows IBP-No-Issues' output. This time, Theory-Testing does not find any cases with all of the Factors (Fig. 5, Nr. 1). IBP-No-Issues tries to broaden the query, which is not successful: dropping pro-p Factors retrieves cases won by defendant (Fig. 5, Nr. 2), and dropping pro-d Factors retrieves cases won by plaintiff (Fig. 5, Nr. 3). The more general hypotheses can not be confirmed. In sum, knowledge of intermediate legal concepts in IBP helps formulate testable hypotheses.

b. CATO-Arg v. Hypo-Arg: As discussed in Section 4, CATO-Arg employs additional knowledge about intermediate and higher-level issues in trade secret law represented in the Factor Hierarchy. This knowledge allows CATO-Arg to perform better and make more correct predictions; its accuracy is 77.7%, compared to 67.9% for Hypo-Arg. CATO-Arg also has much better coverage. However, this performance improvement comes at the cost of more errors, about twice as many as Hypo-Arg. Although this appears to put CATO-Arg at a disadvantage, that is not necessarily so. By abstaining frequently, Hypo-Arg can limit its predictions to the easier-to-predict cases, thereby avoiding mistakes for cases with harder factual conflicts. This may be a reasonable strategy in an experiment, but it is not very acceptable in practice. Thus, CATO-Arg's better coverage and accuracy outweigh the higher error rate.

The *Chicago-Lock* case illustrates how CATO-Arg's additional knowledge about Factors and issues allows it to base its predictions on more relevant cases, those with no significant distinctions and leads to better accuracy and coverage [2]. Hypo-Arg finds four cases that satisfy its relevance criteria, two won by defendant and two by plaintiff, *K&G* and *Technicon*, and therefore abstains. By contrast, CATO-Arg uses its knowledge of intermediate legal issues to conclude that neither *Technicon* nor *K&G* are relevant precedents. Both have significant distinctions that make them much stronger for plaintiff than *Chicago Lock*. In both cases, there was evidence that defendant knew the information was confidential ($F21_\pi$) and that defendant used materials that were explicitly marked as confidential ($F14_\pi$). CATO-Arg bases its correct prediction on the two remaining BUC cases without significant distinctions, *Secure-Services* and *Flotec*, both won by defendant.

c. IBP v. CATO-Arg: Perhaps the most interesting comparison is between IBP and CATO-Arg. The algorithms have a lot in common. Both use CBR techniques related to HYPO's claim lattices (Ashley 1990). Both have a representation of intermediate legal issues in trade secret law, IBP's Domain Model and CATO's Factor Hierarchy. The algorithms, however, use this knowledge and the CBR techniques in different ways.

Our experiments show that IBP's techniques are more successful for prediction. IBP has higher accuracy, 91.3% vs. 77.7%. At the same time, IBP has better coverage and fewer errors. We think that IBP is more accurate because of how it uses its knowledge about issues. In order to illustrate this hypothesis, consider the *Mason* case. By breaking up the case into issues, IBP can focus on subsets of conflicting Factors, which facilitates finding relevant precedents. As Fig. 3 shows, the cases retrieved by Theory-Testing are related to the respective issues. CATO-Arg, on the other hand, has a complementary strategy that considers the case overall in a gestalt-like way. CATO's relevance criteria can consolidate evidence from across issues, which may sometimes lead to reasonable arguments but cause problems for prediction. For instance, in the *Mason* example, CATO-Arg retrieves seven pro-plaintiff BUCs, but let us suppose, it also retrieves a hypothetical case *c*, won by defendant with the following factors: $F1_\delta$, $F4_\pi$, $F16_\delta$, $F18_\pi$, $F19_\delta$, and $F27_\delta$. CATO-Arg does not find any significant distinctions for case *c*, even though *c* has two strong pro-d Factors, $F19_\delta$ and $F27_\delta$. These distinctions, CATO-Arg finds, can be downplayed with the following cross-issue argument: In *Mason* and *c*, since the shared Factors $F1_\delta$ and $F16_\delta$ show that the information could have been discovered by proper means, plaintiff is not significantly worse off in *c* than *Mason* even though it publicly disclosed the information ($F27_\delta$). From a normative viewpoint this is a reasonable argument and, given the overwhelming support for plaintiff's position, quite an ingenious one for defendant to make. From the viewpoint of empirical prediction, however, it causes CATO-Arg to abstain from making a prediction for *Mason*.

d. IBP v. IBP-Model: In the previous comparisons, we argued that the Domain Model makes IBP more accurate, because it guides the process of making a prediction by focusing on the relevant issues in a case. This leads to the question whether the Domain Model by itself leads to high prediction accuracy. IBP-Model took only the intermediate legal concepts into account; it did not use precedents for making predictions. Its performance, however, was significantly worse than IBP's, with an accuracy of 71.7% (Fig. 4, Nrs. 1 and 5). IBP-Model abstains for 38 cases, including *Mason* and *Scientology*. In all these cases, the Factors related to an issue favor both sides, which can not be resolved using IBP's Domain Model alone. Interestingly, IBP's prediction is correct for all cases where IBP-Model abstains. This indicates that using knowledge about issues helps focus the case-based methods, in particular framing hypotheses in Theory-Testing on the relevant Factors in a case.

6 Conclusions

To summarize, our experiments support the following conclusions about the role of knowledge of intermediate legal concepts for prediction:

1. Using knowledge about issues to focus hypothesis-testing with precedents on the issue-related conflicts leads to better prediction. (IBP vs. IBP-No-Issues)
2. Using knowledge about issues to improve case comparison leads to better prediction. (CATO-Arg vs. Hypo-Arg)
3. Using knowledge about issues to focus hypothesis-testing with precedents on the issue-related conflicts rather than to improve case comparison leads to better prediction. (IBP vs. CATO-Arg)
4. Knowledge about issues does not by itself lead to a strong predictive model; its role in guiding hypothesis-testing with precedents is important. (IBP vs. IBP-Model)

It is, perhaps, no mystery why the integration of intermediate legal concepts improves predictive accuracy. In deciding trade secret misappropriation cases, judges are aware of the legal concepts in the Restatement and UTSA provisions. While the representations of the cases used to test the prediction algorithms do not include information about which concepts were most at issue according to the judge's opinion or how conflicts were resolved, IBP's Domain Model (and CATO's Factor Hierarchy) make it possible to reconstruct reasonable rationales relating factors to intermediate concepts to outcomes. In AI terms, the background knowledge about the intermediate legal concepts provides the "right" conceptual guidance for formulating hypotheses about which party should be favored. Without this knowledge-based guidance, the hypotheses are not as successful for prediction. Often they are not specific enough nor do they correspond to the likely significance and meaning of the Factors. Given the difficulties of representing judge's rationales concerning why intermediate legal concepts apply in a case as attempted in GREBE, it is interesting that such accurate predictions can be obtained even without representing the rationales.

The empirical evidence thus appears to be consistent with Lindahl's and Moore's arguments in reaction to Ross's *Tû-tû* example: intermediate legal concepts play an important role in guiding and predicting the outcomes of new cases.

Of course, it may be objected that Lindahl and Moore were speaking about normative guidance in deciding new cases, not merely facilitating better empirical predictions. Running experiments to isolate normative guidance provided by intermediate concepts in legal principles must await new developments. Currently no AI & Law representation relates intermediate legal concepts directly to abstract legal principles. IBP and CATO represent the meanings of intermediate legal concepts only through (1) the explicit relations between legal issues and Factors represented in IBP's Domain Model or CATO's Factor Hierarchy, and (2) the database of cases whose facts are represented by Factors and whose decisions are interpretable in terms of issues using these hierarchical models. SIROCCO demonstrates how cases operationalize the meanings of abstract normative principles [5]. Sartor and Bench-Capon's recent formalizations of legal argument as theory construction involve using cases and values to derive preferences among rules expressed in terms of Factors [7]. They do not appear to deal explicitly with intermediate legal concepts, but see [10]. Once such normative representations are available, researchers will still need to do more work in reading, representing and building databases of larger numbers of real-world legal cases incorporating the normative representations.

In the meantime, the experimental results in this paper imply that the guiding or extending function that Lindahl and Moore see for intermediate legal concepts reflects not only a normative component but a cognitive one, as well. For one thing, Lindahl was concerned about heterogeneous normative justifications; we observed cross-over instances where a case's strength in one issue may compensate for or interfere with the predictive influence of weakness in another issue. For another, the observation that intermediate legal concepts provide the right conceptual guidance for framing predictive hypotheses to test against actual cases should be important for certain theories of analogical legal reasoning. As explicated in [4], Sunstein's and Brewer's theories of relevance in legal analogies focus on the defining role of lower-level legal principles abduced in the process of comparing cases, and which may be informed by or related to more abstract normative principles. Parenthetically, these accounts seem to tie in well with Lindahl's focus on operative conditions in legal principles as guiding reasoning *ex analogia*. Conceptually guiding the framing of predictive hypotheses plays an important role in that process of abduction and testing.

References

[1] Aleven, V. (1997) *Teaching Case-Based Argumentation through a Model and Examples.* PhD Dissertation, University of Pittsburgh.

[2] Aleven, V. (2003) Using Background Knowledge in Case-Based Legal Reasoning: A Computational Model and an Intelligent Learning Environment. *Artificial Intelligence* In Press.

[3] Ashley, K.D. (1990) *Modeling Legal Argument, Reasoning with Cases and Hypotheticals.* MIT-Press.

[4] Ashley, K.D. (2002) An AI Model of Case-Based Legal Argument from a Jurisprudential Viewpoint. *Artificial Intelligence and Law* 10(1-3):163-218.

[5] Ashley, K.D. and McLaren, B. (2001) An AI Investigation of Citation's Epistemological Role. In *Proc. ICAIL-01*, 32-41.

[6] Bench-Capon, T. (1999) Some Observations on Modelling Case Based Reasoning With Formal Argument Models. In *Proc. ICAIL-99*. 36-42.

[7] Bench-Capon, T. and Sartor, G. (2001) Theory based explanation of case law domains. In *Proc. ICAIL-01*. 12-21.

[8] Branting, L.K. (1991) Building Explanations from Rules and Structured Cases. *International Journal of Man-Machine Studies* 34(6):797-837.

[9] Brüninghaus, S. and Ashley, K.D. (2003) Predicting the Outcome of Case-Based Legal Arguments. In *Proc. ICAIL-03*. 234-242.

[10] Greenwood, K., Bench-Capon, T. and McBurney, P. (2003) Towards a Computational Account of Persuasion in Law. In *Proc. ICAIL-03*. 22-31.

[11] Lindahl, L. (2003) Operative and Justificatory Grounds in Legal Argumentation. *Associations* 7(1):185-200.

[12] McCarty, L.T. (2002) Ownership: A Case Study in the Representation of Legal Concepts. *Artificial Intelligence and Law* 10(1-3):135-161.

[13] McCarty, L.T. and Sridharan, N.S. (1981) The Representation of an Evolving System of Legal Concepts: II. Prototypes and Deformations. LRP-TR-11. Laboratory for Computer Science Research. Rutgers University.

[14] Moore, M.S. (1997) Legal Principles Revisited. *Iowa Law Review* 82:867.

[15] Prakken, H. and Sartor, G. (1997) Reasoning with Precedents in a Dialogue Game. In *Proc. ICAIL-97*, 1-9.

[16] Rissland, E.L. and Skalak, D.B. (1991) CABARET: Statutory Interpretation in a Hybrid Architecture. *International Journal of Man-Machine Studies* 34(6):839-887.

[17] Ross, A. (1957) *TÛ-TÛ*. *Harvard Law Review* 70(March):812-825.

[18] Wedberg, A. (1951) Some Problems in the Logical Analysis of Legal Science. *Theoria* 17:246-275.

How to model legal reasoning using dynamic logic programming: a preliminary report

Nuno Graça Paulo Quaresma
Departamento de Informática, Universidade de Évora
7000 Évora, Portugal
{ngraca,pq}@di.uevora.pt

Abstract.
Dynamic logic programming allows the representation and the inference of evolving knowledge.

Legal knowledge reasoning needs the capability to model laws that change over time and to model laws produced by distinct entities with different priorities at different time points.

In this paper we propose the use of dynamic logic programming to model these legal dynamic situations. Some examples are discussed and the implementation of a legal oracle server is described.

1 Introduction

It is well known that knowledge representation needs to take into account the dynamic nature of knowledge. As new information is acquired, new pieces of knowledge need to be dynamically added to or removed from the knowledge bases. Moreover, information may be produced from different sources having different degrees of reliability and, as a consequence, having different priorities.

In [2] dynamic logic programming was proposed as a possible solution to the problem of knowledge base updates and in [3] a new language, *LUPS – Language of UPdateS*, was described and applied to the representation of actions.

On the other hand, legal knowledge reasoning needs the capability to model laws that change over time and to model laws produced by distinct entities with different priorities at different time points. These problems have been studied by several researchers, being Prakken and Sartor's work one of the most relevant [8, 10]. In their work they have proposed an argument-based extended logic programming framework with defeasible priorities. In another work, Sartor [7] and Provetti [11] have proposed the use of Event Calculus [5] as the base formalism to model time. A complete survey about the existent approaches to the use of logic to model legal reasoning was presented in [9].

In this paper we propose the use of dynamic logic programming to model some legal dynamic situations. Specifically, we will deal with the representation of evolving rules and with the problem of having several sources of laws with possible contradictions.

In order to fully explore these situations, a legal server was implemented in Prolog and it is able to receive logic programming descriptions of laws and events and to answer queries about what is valid in specific states. Some simple examples are described and discussed.

Nuno Graça and Paulo Quaresma, 'How to Model Legal Reasoning Using Dynamic Logic Programming: A Preliminary Report' in D. Bourcier (ed.), *Legal Knowledge and Information Systems. Jurix 2003: The Sixteenth Annual Conference.* Amsterdam: IOS Press, 2003, pp. 163-172.

At this stage, it is important to point out that we do not claim that dynamic logic programming is able to deal with every legal reasoning situation. This paper is just a preliminary step in this direction.

In section 2 the logic programming framework used to model the legal server is presented. Then, in section 3, the legal server implementation is briefly described and in section 4, examples of hypothetical server interactions are presented. Finally, in section 5 some conclusions and future work are pointed out.

2 Dynamic Logic Programming

Before describing the legal server it is necessary to present the formalism used to implement it. As referred in the previous section, the basic formalism is the dynamic logic programming paradigm and the related language used to represent actions: LUPS[1].

2.1 Dynamic Knowledge Representation

One of the main requirements of the formalism used to represent legal knowledge is to be able to handle evolving knowledge. In fact, legal knowledge may be represented by specific knowledge states but, after each event, such as a law change, knowledge evolves to another state. The formalism should be able to handle these situations, allowing the inference of what properties are valid in each knowledge state.

Dynamic logic programming (DLP) was proposed [2] as a possible solution to this evolution requirement. In fact, DLP defines how a knowledge base can be updated by another knowledge base, obtaining a new knowledge base.

Specifically, given an original knowledge base KB, and an updating knowledge base KB', it is possible to obtain a new updated knowledge base $KB^* = KB \oplus KB'$ that constitutes the update of the knowledge base KB by the knowledge base KB'. In order to make the meaning of the updated knowledge base $KB \oplus KB'$ declaratively clear and easily verifiable, in [2] there is a complete semantic characterisation of the updated knowledge base $KB \oplus KB'$. In this work, knowledge bases are defined by sets of generalized logic programs and the updated knowledge base is obtained by a linear-time transformation of the knowledge bases KB and KB' into normal logic programs The basic idea is to add new logic programming rules for modeling inheritance, update, and default situations (the transformation is fully described in the referred paper). As a result, not only the update transformation can be accomplished very efficiently, but also query answering in $KB \oplus KB'$ is reduced to query answering about normal logic programs using the stable model semantics.

2.2 LUPS – Language of UPdateS

In DLP, a knowledge base evolves from one knowledge state [2] to another as a result of a knowledge update. Given the current knowledge state KS, its successor knowledge state $KS' = KS \oplus KB$ is obtained as a result of the occurrence of a non-empty set of simultaneous updates, represented by the updating knowledge base KB.

However, dynamic knowledge updates, do not provide any language allowing the specification of knowledge state changes. Accordingly, in [3] it was described a fully declarative, high-level language for knowledge updates called LUPS "Language of UPdateS") that

[1]This section is based on a previous work describing DLP and LUPS [4]

[2]In this context, a knowledge state can be viewed as a snapshot of the knowledge base at a specific point (state).

describes transitions between consecutive knowledge states KS_n. It consists of update commands, which specify what updates should be applied to any given knowledge state KS_n in order to obtain the next knowledge state KS_{n+1}. In this way, update commands allow us to implicitly determine the updating knowledge base KB_{n+1}. The language LUPS can therefore be viewed as a language for dynamic knowledge representation.

The simplest update command consists of adding a rule to the current knowledge state and has the form: $assert\ (L \leftarrow L_1, \ldots, L_k)$. For example, when a law stating that abortion is illegal is adopted, the knowledge state might be updated via the command: $assert\ (illegal \leftarrow abortion)$.

In general, the addition of a rule to a knowledge state may depend upon some preconditions being true in the current state. To allow for that, the assert command in LUPS has a more general form:

$$assert\ (L \leftarrow L_1, \ldots, L_k)\ when\ (L_{k+1}, \ldots, L_m) \tag{1}$$

The meaning of this assert command is that if the preconditions $L_{k+1}, \ldots, L_m$ are true in the current knowledge state, then the rule $L \leftarrow L_1, \ldots, L_k$ should hold true in the successor knowledge state. Normally, the so added rules are *inertial,* i.e., they remain in force from then on by inertia, until possibly defeated by some future update or until retracted.

However, in some cases the persistence of rules by inertia should not be assumed. Take, for instance, the simple action $request\ help$. This is likely to be a one-time event that should not persist by inertia after the successor state. Accordingly, the assert command allows for the keyword $event$, indicating that the added *rule* is *non-inertial.*

$$assert\ event\ (L \leftarrow L_1, \ldots, L_k)\ when\ (L_{k+1}, \ldots, L_m) \tag{2}$$

Update commands themselves (rather than the rules they assert) may either be one-time, non-persistent update commands or they may remain in force until cancelled. In order to specify such *persistent update commands* (which are called *update laws*) there is the syntax:

$$always\ [event]\ (L \leftarrow L_1, \ldots, L_k)\ when\ (L_{k+1}, \ldots, L_m) \tag{3}$$

Note the word *event* is optional and it defines if the update command should persist or if it is only a one-time command.

To cancel persistent update commands, we use:

$$cancel\ (L \leftarrow L_1, \ldots, L_k)\ when\ (L_{k+1}, \ldots, L_m) \tag{4}$$

To deal with rule deletion, there is the *retraction* update command:

$$retract\ (L \leftarrow L_1, \ldots, L_k)\ when\ (L_{k+1}, \ldots, L_m) \tag{5}$$

meaning that, subject to precondition $L_{k+1}, \ldots, L_m$, the rule $L \leftarrow L_1, \ldots, L_k$ is retracted.

The main difference between *cancel* and *retract* is that the first is used to cancel persistent *always* commands and the other is used to cancel *assert* commands.

Knowledge can be queried at any knowledge state KS_q with:

$$\textbf{holds}\ B_1, \ldots, B_k, not\, C_1, \ldots, not\, C_m\ \textbf{at state}\ q\textbf{?} \tag{6}$$

and is true if and only if the conjunction of its literals holds at the state KS_q. In this equation *q* stands for an identifier of the knowledge state (it can be defined as an integer being *0* the identifier for the initial knowledge state); *not* stands for the default negation and the predicate *holds* verifies if the literals belong to the stable model of the knowledge base KS_q.

The language LUPS has a *declarative and procedural semantics* [2] so that the update commands not only have a definite declarative meaning but also can be readily implemented. The procedural semantics for LUPS is obtained by the translation of the LUPS program into a *normal logic program,* written in a *meta-language*. The translation of LUPS into XSB-Prolog is available at `http://centria.di.fct.unl.pt/~jja/updates/lups.p`

3 Legal Server

The legal server is a XSB-Prolog process able to deal with connections via a user defined TCP/IP port. The overall architecture is presented in figure 1.

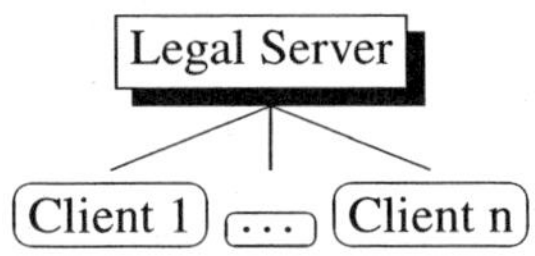

Figure 1: Architecture

There are two possible commands that clients may send to the legal server:

- Update
- Query

The clients send sequences of update rules and/or queries about properties and they receive the answers to their queries.

These commands will be described in detail in the next two sub-sections:

3.1 Update command

The update rules have the following syntax:

$$update(KB, Agent, LUPSList) \tag{7}$$

where KB means knowledge base and allowing the definition and the update of distinct knowledge bases; $Agent$ defines the name of the agent performing the action; and $LUPSList$ is a Prolog list of LUPS commands.

As an example, we may have:

$$update(law, crimeLaw, [(always\ (illegal \leftarrow abortion))]) \tag{8}$$

It is also possible to use predicate $update$ with only two arguments, KB and $LUPSList$, meaning we want to update or to query the KB as a top priority independent agent. This special top agent has also the possibility to define priorities among the different agents:

$$higherPriority(Agent1, Agent2). \tag{9}$$

The priority relations will have important consequences in the processing of the agents updates.

After receiving an update predicate, the legal server will create corresponding LUPS updates, evolving the KB received as a parameter to a new state. The translation between the client requests (rule 7) and the LUPS updates follows these rules:

1. For every request received from agent $Agent1$

   (a) For every LUPS command in LUPSList having a rule with head H create a corresponding command, substituting H by H_{Agent1}

   (b) For each distinct predicate H (head of some LUPS command) introduced by the request, create the new rule:

$$always\ (H \leftarrow H_{Agent1}, not - H_{A1}, \ldots, not - H_{An}) \tag{10}$$

   where $A1, \ldots, An$ are agents with higher priority than $Agent1$ and not and $-$ stand for the default and explicit negation, respectively.

The general idea of the first part of the translation is to index every conclusion (head of the rules) to the corresponding agent. The second part of the translation relates the agents beliefs with its more priority agents: an agent belief is only accepted if it is not contradictory with a belief of another more priority agent.

As a simple example, rule 8 would produce the following LUPS rules:

$$always\ (illegal_{crimeLaw} \leftarrow abortion) \tag{11}$$

$$always\ (illegal \leftarrow illegal_{crimeLaw}) \tag{12}$$

If, for instance, Constitutional Law is an agent of a higher priority, then we would have the following rule (instead of rule 12):

$$always\ (illegal \leftarrow illegal_{crimeLaw}, not - illegal_{constitutionalLaw}) \tag{13}$$

3.2 Query command

The query commands have the following syntax:

$$query(KB, Agent, \textbf{holds}\ B_1, \ldots, B_k, not\, C_1, \ldots, not\, C_m\ \textbf{at state}\ q\textbf{?}) \tag{14}$$

where KB means knowledge base and allowing the query of distinct knowledge bases; $Agent$ defines the name of the agent performing the action.

As in the previous section, it is possible to omit the second parameter and to query the KB from the special top agent. As an example, we may have:

$$query(law, \textbf{holds}\ illegal\ \textbf{at state}\ now^{3}\textbf{?}) \tag{15}$$

4 Examples

In the next two sub-sections two kind of examples will be presented:

- Evolution of laws
- Laws produced by distinct agents/entities

[3] *now* stands for the integer identifier of the actual knowledge state. Users are allowed to use identifier *now* and, even, to define arithmetic operations with it: *now - 1* standing for the previous state.

4.1 Evolution of laws

Suppose there is a law stating that in order to have a specific degree it is necessary to be enrolled in that degree and to verify certain conditions:

$$update(law1, [assert\ (degree(X) \leftarrow enrolled(X), cond1(X))]). \tag{16}$$

Now, suppose John enrolls himself in that degree:

$$update(law1, [assert\ (enrolled(john))]). \tag{17}$$

But, after that, there is an update in the law and the needed conditions change:

$$\begin{aligned} update(law1, [retract\ (degree(X) \leftarrow enrolled(X), cond1(X)),\\ assert\ (degree(X) \leftarrow enrolled(X), cond2(X))]). \end{aligned} \tag{18}$$

After this change John verifies $cond1$ and Mary enrolls herself in the degree:

$$update(law1, [assert\ (cond1(john)), assert\ (enrolled(mary))]). \tag{19}$$

Finally, Mary satisfies $cond2$:

$$update(law1, [assert\ (cond2(mary))]). \tag{20}$$

If we query the KB about who has a degree and in which states:

$$query(law1, \mathbf{holds}\ degree(X)\ \mathbf{at\ state}\ S\mathbf{?}]). \tag{21}$$

We will obtain the behavior:

$$X = mary, S = 5.$$

Only Mary has a degree and only at state 5 (we are assuming initial state to be equal to 0).

Note that, if we change update 17 to:

$$update(law1, [assert\ (enrolled(john)), assert\ (cond1(john))]). \tag{22}$$

We would get:

$$\begin{aligned} X &= john, S = 2;\\ X &= mary, S = 5. \end{aligned}$$

This answer reflects the fact that rule defining how to obtain a degree has changed. However, law updates are usually not retroactive: if John had a degree at state 2, then he shouldn't have lost his degree afterwards!

This requisite leads to a new schema for the representation of law changes[4]:

$$update(law2, [assert\ (degree(X) \leftarrow en(X), cond1(X))]). \tag{23}$$
$$update(law2, [assert\ (en(john))]). \tag{24}$$
$$\begin{aligned} update(law2, [retract\ (degree(X) \leftarrow en(X), cond1(X))\ when\ (not\ en(X)),\\ assert\ (degree(X) \leftarrow en(X), cond2(X))\ when\ (not\ en(X))]). \end{aligned} \tag{25}$$
$$update(law2, [assert\ (cond1(john)), assert\ (en(mary))]). \tag{26}$$
$$update(law2, [assert\ (cond2(mary))]). \tag{27}$$

[4]Due to formatting problems we will use en instead of the predicate $enrolled$

Rule 25 captures the notion that the law changes only to those that are not yet enrolled in the degree.

As intended, we'll have:

$$X = john, S = 4;$$
$$X = john, S = 5;$$
$$X = mary, S = 5.$$

4.2 Laws from distinct entities

In this example we will try to show that LUPS and DLP are also able to model prioritised rules without many changes.

Suppose there are three sources of knowledge defining what is needed to obtain a master's degree (conditions necessary and sufficient):

- S1: To write a thesis;
- S2: To obtain a certain amount of course credits;
- S3: To write a thesis and to obtain a certain amount of course credits (100 in this example).

We'll have the following corresponding commands:

$$update(law3, s1, [assert\ (master(X) \leftarrow thesis(X)), \quad assert\ (-master(X) \leftarrow -thesis(X))]). \tag{28}$$

$$update(law3, s2, [assert\ (master(X) \leftarrow credits(X, N), N > 100), \quad assert\ (-master(X) \leftarrow credits(X, N), N <= 100)]). \tag{29}$$

$$update(law3, s3, [assert\ (master(X) \leftarrow credits(X, N), N > 100, thesis(X)), \quad assert\ (-master(X) \leftarrow (credits(X, N), N <= 100; -thesis(X))]). \tag{30}$$

Suppose agents are related by the following relation $s1 < s2 < s3$:

$$higherPriority(s3, s2). \tag{31}$$
$$higherPriority(s2, s1). \tag{32}$$

With these constraints, the following update facts:

$$update(law3, [assert\ (thesis(john))]). \tag{33}$$
$$update(law3, [assert\ (credits(mary, 120))]). \tag{34}$$
$$update(law3, [assert\ (credits(john, 110))]). \tag{35}$$

And the following queries:

$$query(law3, \textbf{holds}\ master_{s1}(X)\ \textbf{at state}\ S?]). \tag{36}$$
$$query(law3, \textbf{holds}\ master_{s2}(X)\ \textbf{at state}\ S?]). \tag{37}$$
$$query(law3, \textbf{holds}\ master_{s3}(X)\ \textbf{at state}\ S?]). \tag{38}$$
$$query(law3, \textbf{holds}\ master(X)\ \textbf{at state}\ S?]). \tag{39}$$

We'll have:

$$master_{s1}(john), S = 4;$$
$$master_{s1}(john), S = 5;$$
$$master_{s1}(john), S = 6;$$
$$master_{s2}(mary), S = 5;$$
$$master_{s2}(mary), S = 6;$$
$$master_{s3}(john), S = 6;$$
$$master(john), S = 6;$$

These results, as intended, state that according with $S1$ John has a master's degree after terminating his thesis (state 4); accordingly with $S2$ this is accomplished only at state 6 for John (and 5 for Mary); and accordingly with $S3$ only John has a master's degree and only at state 6. As $S3$ is the most priority agent, its "opinion" is the accepted by the legal server.

5 Conclusions and Future Work

The use of dynamic logic programming and its associated language, LUPS, to model some characteristics of legal reasoning was proposed. Specifically, the problem of laws that change over time and the problem of laws produced by different sources with different reliabilities/priorities was dealt with.

Dynamic logic programming revealed to be a powerful methodology to handle these kind of requisites and the obtained solutions were quite satisfactory and easy to model. A legal server able to receive law updates and requests was also implemented. This server is able to handle requests from different agents and about different knowledge bases.

As future work, we intend to use an extension of DLP, MDLP – Multidimensional Dynamic Logic Programming, from J. Leite et al. [6] to allow a more generic approach and the integration of several dimensions, such as time and priorities, and to compare it with other existent approaches, such as Prakken and Sartor's work.

Another possible direction is to use the new language, EVOLP, proposed by Alferes et. al [1], to simplify LUPS.

We also intend to change the communication protocol to a standard agent communication protocol, such as FIPA ACL [12]. In this way, our legal agent may be able to interact with a larger community of computational agents.

Acknowledgements

We would like to thank the JURIX referees for their helpful comments on the first version of this paper.

References

[1] J. Alferes, A. Brogi, J. Leite, and L. Pereira. Evolving logic programs. In S. Flesca, S. Greco, N. Leone, and G. Ianni, editors, *JELIA'02 – Proceedings of the 8th European Conference on Logics and Artificial Intelligence*, pages 50–61. Springer-Verlag LNCS 2424, 2002.

[2] J. J. Alferes, J. Leite, L. M. Pereira, H. Przymusinska, and T. Przymuzinski. Dynamic logic programming. In *Proc. of KR'98*, 1998.

[3] J. J. Alferes, L. M. Pereira, H. Przymusinska, T. C. Przymusinski, and P. Quaresma. Preliminary exploration on actions as updates. In M. C. Meo and M. Vilares-Ferro, editors, *Procs. of the 1999 Joint Conference on Declarative Programming (AGP'99)*, pages 259–271, L'Aquila, Italy, September 1999.

[4] J. J. Alferes, L. M. Pereira, H. Przymusinska, T. C. Przymusinski, and P. Quaresma. An exercise with dynamic logic programming. In L. Garcia and M. C. Meo, editors, *Procs. of the 2000 APPIA-GULP-PRODE Joint Conference on Declarative Programming (AGP'2000)*, La Habana, Cuba, December 2000.

[5] R. Kowalski and M. Sergot. A logic-based calculus of events. *New Generation Computing*, 24:67–95, 1986.

[6] J. Leite, J. Alferes, L. Pereira, H. Przymusinska, and T. Przymusinski. A language for multi-dimensional updates. In J. Dix, J. Leite, and K. Satoh, editors, *Computational logic in multiagent systems: Proceedings of the 3rd international workshop CLIMA'02*, number 93, pages 19–34. Roskilde University, Denmark, 2002.

[7] Rafael Marin and Giovanni Sartor. Time and norms: a formalisation in the event calculus. In *ICAIL'99 – Internatinal Conference on Artificial Intelligence and Law*. ACM, 1999.

[8] H. Prakken and G. Sartor. Argument-based extended logic programming with defeasible priorities. *Journal of Applied Non-Classical Logics*, 1-2:22–75, 1997.

[9] H. Prakken and G. Sartor. The role of logic in computational models of legal argument – a critical survey. In A. Kakas and F. Sadri, editors, *Computational Logic: Logic Programming and Beyond. Essays in Honour of Robert A. Kowalski, Part II, LNCS 2048*, pages 342–380. Springer, 2003.

[10] H. Prakken and G. Sartor. The three faces of defeasibility in the law. *Ratio Juris*, 17(1), 2004.

[11] A. Provetti. The law of contracts in the event calculus. In *GULP'92 – 9th Italian Conference on Logic Programming*, 1992.

[12] fipa.org www. *FIPA ACL - Agent Communication Language*. FIPA - Foundation for Intelligent Physical Agents, 2001.

Reasoning With Legal Cases as Theory Construction: Some Experimental Results

Alison Chorley Trevor Bench-Capon
Department of Computer Science, The University of Liverpool
Liverpool, UK
{T.J.M.Bench-Capon, A.Chorley}@csc.liv.ac.uk

Abstract. In this paper we report some experiments designed to clarify some issues and to test some of the assumptions in the model of reasoning with legal cases advanced by Bench-Capon and Sartor. We identify the questions to be explored, briefly describe a tool developed to support these experiments and report the results of a series of experiments based on Aleven's analysis of US Trade Secrets cases. We then consider what light the experiments have thrown on our questions, and propose some directions for future work.

1 Introduction

In [3] a model of reasoning with legal cases was proposed in which reasoning with cases is seen as a three stage process:

1. constructing theories to explain past cases in terms of the factors they exhibit;
2. evaluating the competing theories in terms of their coherence, explanatory power, simplicity, etc.
3. applying the chosen theory to a new case.

In [6] and [7] we described a tool designed to support the construction of theories, and some preliminary experiments made using it. In this paper we report on the progress of this work, which embraces some extensions to the tool and some further experiments designed to cast light on a series of specific questions. Section 2 will introduce the questions we address. Section 3 will describe the current version of the tool. Section 4 will describe the experimental set up, and Sections 5 and 6 give the results of the experiments, together with some discussion. Section 7 summarises our conclusions and gives pointers to future work.

2 Questions Addressed

While [3] lays out a general approach to modelling reasoning with legal cases, it leaves a number of points of detail open. This paper is intended to cast light on how these issues might be resolved.

Three issues concern theory construction. First there is the question of how past cases are used in constructing theories, and how the rules of the theory are extracted from these cases. We would hope that there is some systematic approach to theory construction which can be applied, perhaps even automatically. In [6] we describe three approaches, which we call the *safe* approach, the *simple* approach and the *value driven* approach. We have again used these three approaches to construct different theories. Our first question is therefore:

Alison Chorley and Trevor Bench-Capon, 'Reasoning With Legal Cases as Theory Construction: Some Experimental Results' in D. Bourcier (ed.), *Legal Knowledge and Information Systems. Jurix 2003: The Sixteenth Annual Conference*. Amsterdam: IOS Press, 2003, pp. 173-182.

Q1: How should we select cases and extract rules for inclusion in the theory?

Within the general approach it is possible to include or exclude factors that appear in the cases and the domain analysis generally. This gives rise to the second question:

Q2: Should we be inclusive or exclusive with regard to factors?

In [3] preferences between factors determine preferences between values, which can then in turn determine preferences between other factors relating to those values. If this is so, we should expect to be able to include additional factors without major revisions to the theory. Thus we may pose a third question:

Q3: Is there evidence to suggest that values can be used to determine the relative importance of factors?

A key role of the theory is to explain preferences between rules in terms of a comparison between the sets of values promoted by the factors contained in the rules. The fourth question therefore is:

Q4: How should sets of values be compared?

A related question concerns what should be done when a case contains two factors relating to the same value, but favouring different sides. In such cases we must prefer a factor rather than a value. Our fifth question is

Q5: Is it possible to use a general principle to pre-order factors within a value?

In [3] it is assumed that factors promote values to an equal degree: if a rule contains a factor then following that rule is held to promote the value associated with the factor. It is not impossible, however, that different factors will promote values to different degrees, and that this possibility needs to be considered. This leads to the sixth question:

Q6: Is there evidence to suggest that factors promote values to different degrees?

Again, [3] does not allow for accumulation of factors: if following a rule promotes a value, then it is not relevant whether this is the result of the presence of one factor or several. Perhaps, however, a value is promoted to a greater extent if several factors are present. The seventh question is thus:

Q7: Is there evidence to suggest that values and/or factors have a cumulative effect?

We see these questions as central to the effective modelling of reasoning with cases in law in the manner of [3]. Obviously the experiments on a single domain with a limited number of cases described here cannot produce definitive answers to them: our hope, however, is that the experiments may help to move the debate forward, and indicate which lines may be worth pursuing.

3 The Theory Construction Tool

The theory construction tool is a program, written in JAVA, which provides a graphical user interface to support theory construction. The program requires two input files, one recording the cases available for theory construction and their associated factors, and the other associating these factors with their values. Output comes in two forms: one is a file containing the elements that make up a theory as in [3], and the other an executable Prolog program consistent with the theory. The tool supports all the theory constructors specified in [3], and the necessary file management and editing functions. Some more detail and a screen shot is provided in [6]. Since [6] we have given additional options for the way in which the code can be generated. This will be further discussed in section 4. We have also extended the tool to handle dimensions in the manner described in [3].

4 Experiment Design

The domain chosen for our experiments was US Trade Secrets Law as modelled in HYPO [2], CATO [1] and IBP [4]. The domain was chosen because it is well known and much discussed, and because a complete domain analysis together with a reasonable number of cases is available.

First values were associated with the factors identified in [1]. The attribution of values was largely informed by a consideration of the relationship between factors and abstract factors in [1]. The rationale for this is discussed in [6], where a complete list of the factors and their associated values is given. Next we extracted from [2], [1] and [4] a number of cases which we divided in two groups. The first group of 14 cases were to be available for constructing a program: for building the theory and refining the resulting program. The remaining 9 cases were then available to provide an independent test of the worth of the program produced. We would therefore be able to see both whether it is possible to construct a theory to explain a set of cases, and whether the resulting theory has predictive worth. The cases used and their associated factors are shown in Table 1. The factor numbers are as in [1]: the values are as in [6]: CA - that explicit confidentiality agreements should be made and enforced; RE – that a person with a secret should take reasonable efforts to protect it; LM – that a person should be able to develop a product using legitimate means; QM – that a person should not use morally (or legally) dubious means to obtain a secret; and MW – that litigation should only take place if the secret was of some material worth.

To address Q1 we constructed theories according to three different principles. For *Theory 1* we used the cases to generate rules and preferences in the manner of [9]. Each case generates three rules: conjunction of pro-p factors favours p; conjunction of pro-d factors favours d; and a preference between these two rules dependent on the actual outcome. *Theory 2* was supposed to reflect the sort of thinking embodied in rule induction style approaches. Here we chose a minimal set of factors such that at least one pro-plaintiff factor occurs in every case decided for the plaintiff, and at least one pro-defendant factor occurs in every case decided for the defendant. Where both pro-plaintiff and pro-defendant factors were present in a case, a rule preference was included to give the desired outcome. *Theory 3* was based on first determining an order for the values and then selecting cases to ground a theory expressing this ordering. A more extended discussion these three methods can be found in [6].

The programs generated from the theory were then executed on the remaining cases in Group 1. Not all cases were solved correctly: to cater as far as possible for such cases the program was refined. Essentially problems came from one of two sources. Although the theory orders values, and so determines the relative importance of factors relating to different val-

Table 1: Cases Used, Their Factors, Values and Outcomes

	Pro-P factors	Pro-D factors	Pro-P Values	Pro-D Values	Outcome
Group 1					
Arco		10 16 20		RE LM	D
Boeing	4 6 12 14 21	1 10	CA RE QM	RE	P
Bryce	4 6 18 21	1	CA RE MW	RE	P
CollegeWat	15 26	1	LM QM	RE	P
Den-Tal-Ez	4 6 21 26	1	CA RE QM	RE	P
Ecologix	21	1 19 23	CA	CA RE	D
Emery	18 21	10	CA MW	RE	P
Ferranti	2	17 19 20 27	QM	RE LM	D
Robinson	18 26	1 10 19	QM MW	RE	D
Sandlin		1 10 16 19 27		RE LM	D
Sheets	18	19 27	MW	RE	D
Space Aero	8 15 18	1 19	MW LM	RE	P
Televation	6 12 15 18 21	10 16	CA RE LM MW	RE LM	P
Yokana	7	10 16 27	QM	RE LM	D
Group 2					
FMC	4 6 7 12	10 11	CA RE QM	RE LM	P
KG	6 14 15 18 21	16 25	RE QM LM MW CA	LM	P
Mason	6 15 21	1 16	CA RE LM	RE LM	P
MineralDep	18	1 16 25	MW	RE LM	P
NationalRej	7 15 18	10 16 19 27	QM LM MW	RE LM	D
Reinforced	4 6 8 15 21	1	CA RE MW LM	RE	P
Scientology	4 6 12	10 11 20	CA RE	RE LM	D
Technicon	6 12 14 21	10 16 25	RE QM CA	RE LM	P
Trandes	4 6 12	1 10	CA RE	RE	P

ues, when we have factors relating to the *same* value but favouring *different* outcomes, either can be preferred while remaining consistent with the theory. Since the program is generated following an arbitrary selection of the order of such factors, if the choice is wrong we may need to modify the order of these factors within values. Secondly – for theory 1 especially - it is typically the case that there are preferences between values not included in the theory, because they do not emerge from the broadest construal of the rules. Where a case turns on such a preference, it may be necessary to refine the theory by explicitly including this preference. The particular refinements required are described in the next section.

Once the programs had been refined so as to deal, as far as possible, with the cases in the first group, they were tried on the second group of cases, to test the extent to which the theory explaining the "existing" cases, generalised to the "new" cases, with the view that the theory could be considered better according as to how well it generalised to the unseen cases.

To address Q2 we generated two versions of each of the programs. In one version (*selective*) only factors explicitly included during the construction of the theory were used: this is one natural interpretation of [3]. In the other version (*complete*) we included all the factors identified in [1], while still enforcing the value preferences from the theory. The idea here is that since the factors were used in the analysis of [1] they should be presumed to be relevant, and hence included in the theory. Q3 can be answered positively in so far as this extension does not require reordering the values.

Q4 has been the subject of some discussion in [e.g. 8]. Our initial version simply ranked factors and their combinations in order as determined by values. Effectively this method weights a set of values according to its most highly weighted value, unless a particular set of values has been treated explicitly. Where a case contains the same value as the most highly rated for both the pro-plaintiff and pro-defendant sets, the outcome is determined by preferring factors. Much of the refinement process may be seen as tuning this ordering of factors with common values. A second possibility, following [8] is to discount values found in both the pro-plaintiff and pro-defendant sets, giving the set a weight based on its most weighty value not in the other set. This "cancellation" process is produced by incorporating the absence of factors into the Prolog rules generated. A third possibility is to consider all the values in a set by assigning all its members a weight relative to the importance of the value to which they relate. There are two possibilities here, according to whether we count only the values represented, or increase the weight according to how many factors representing the values are present (that is, we use "bags" of values rather than sets). To explore this possibility we must assign weights to values. To examine Q5 we used two principles to pre-order values. In order to explore Q6, we had to go further, assigning differential weights to factors with the same values. Q7 is addressed by whether the use of sets or bags gives better results.

5 Experimental Results: Boolean Values

The initial experiments were set up as described in [6]. For the Theory 1, 4 cases were used, 2 plaintiff cases, 2 defendant cases (We found that using more cases to construct the initial theory typically led to less refinement, but had no effect on ultimate performance). For Theory 2 there were only 2 cases with a conflict to resolve so those are the only cases used to build the theory. For Theory 3 we ranked the values as CA>LM, LM>RE, RE>MW and RE>QM and selected 4 cases which could be used to express these preferences.

Once the theory has been constructed the Prolog code associated with it can be generated in several different ways.

The *original* method of code generation just sorts the rules present in the theory according to the value order and rewrites the rules as Prolog clauses.

The *cancellation* method creates rules of the form *f1 and not f2 and not f3... and not fn* where f2..fn are factors which relate to the same value as f1 but favour the opposite side.

For Q5 we used two approaches to pre-ordering values, one based on the principle that exceptions should carry more weight, the other using information found in the CATO factor hierarchy. The *exception* method creates more rule preferences by ordering the factors within each value. This is done by counting the factors that relate to each outcome. The factors promoting the less common outcome are taken to be exceptions and these are preferred to the other factors. The *exception and cancellation* method uses the exception method to sort the rules and the cancellation method to create the Prolog code. The *CATO* method also sorts the factors within each value. The factor hierarchy from [1] contains thin and thick arcs and these are used to represent whether the factor is strong or weak. The strong factors within each value are preferred to the weak factors. The *CATO cancellation* method sorts the rules using the CATO arc method and creates the Prolog code using the cancellation method. For all of the above methods the first rule to match each case fires and gives the case an outcome.

There were no refinements to be made to the selective versions of Theory 2 and Theory 3. For the selective version of Theory 1 all the methods for code generation needed the additional preference LM > RE and the *original* and *CATO* methods also required CA > RE. For Theory 1 with all factors, the *original*, *cancellation* and *CATO* methods for code generation could all be refined to improve the results for the main cases. The refinements for the *original* method are to set LM>RE, CA>LM (to handle Space Aero) and F23>F21 (to handle Ecologix); the refinement for the *cancellation* method is to set LM>RE and the refinement for the *CATO* method is to enforce F23>F21.

For Theory 2 with all factors the *original*, *CATO* and *CATO can*cellation methods for code generation can be refined to improve the results for the Group 1 cases. The refinement for the *original* method is to make F6>F10; the refinements for the *CATO* method is set F6>F1 and RE>QM; and the refinement for the *CATO cancellation* method to ensure F6>F10.

For the complete Theory 3 the *original* and *CATO* methods for code generation can be refined to improve the results for the main cases. The refinement for both of the these methods is to make F23>F21.

The number of errors for each method of code generation before and after refinement is shown in table 2. The results are split into the errors for the Group 1 cases and the errors for the Group 2 cases. Where there are two values in a cell the first value is the number of errors and the second is the number of undecided cases. The case will be undecided when there is not enough information in the theory to decide the outcome of a case. For Theories 1 and 3 the undecided cases are FMC, Scientology and Trandes, for Theory 2 the undecided cases are FMC, Mineral Deposits and Trandes.

Table 2: Misclassified Cases and Abstentions

		Theory 1				Theory 2				Theory 3			
		Selective		Complete		Selective		Complete		Selective		Complete	
	Cases	Before	After	Before	After	Before	After	Before	After	Before	After	Before	After
Original	Grp 1	3	1	3	0	0	0	4	1	1	1	1	0
	Grp 2	6/0	3/0	6	2	1/3	1/3	5	4	2/3	2/3	3	3
Cancel	Grp 1	1	0	1	0	0	0	1	1	0	0	0	0
	Grp 2	1/3	1/3	2	3	0/3	0/3	3	3	1/3	1/3	2	2
Except	Grp 1	3	1	0	0	0	0	1	1	1	1	0	0
	Grp 2	6/0	3/0	2	2	2/3	2/3	4	4	2/3	2/3	3	3
Except/ cancel	Grp 1	1	0	0	0	0	0	1	1	0	0	0	0
	Grp 2	1/3	1/3	3	3	0/3	0/3	3	3	1/3	1/3	2	2
CATO	Grp 1	3	1	1	0	0	0	3	1	1	1	1	0
	Grp 2	6/0	3/0	3	3	1/3	1/3	4	4	2/3	2/3	3	3
CATO/ cancel	Grp 1	1	0	0	0	0	0	2	1	0	0	0	0
	Grp 2	1/3	1/3	2	2	0/3	0/3	2	3	1/3	1/3	2	2

From a consideration of the results for the Group 1 cases, we can see that it is possible to develop a theory which will cover all the cases using the approach of either Theory 1 or Theory 3. Theory 2, however, cannot be refined to deal with Emery as it begins by ascribing undue importance to the value RE. We see this as an example of the over fitting that can occur using this sort of method. Thus as regards Q1, we feel that the approach of Theory 2 is inferior because of this danger. As regards Q2 we conclude that it is preferable to use the complete set of factors: Theory 1 cannot handle Ecologix on the original selection of factors, and there are many errors on the restricted set of factors for the Group 2 cases. Theory 2 does no worse on the full set of factors, and Theory 3 improves. With regard to Q3, it does seem that the use of the value order derived from the limited set of factors can be generalized to the full set of factors. The refinements required additional value preferences, clarifying the partial order, rather than overturning any existing preferences. Thus we conclude that using either the method of Theory 1 or Theory 3, and a full set of factors, it is possible to construct a theory in the manner of [3] which will explain a given body of cases.

The worth of the theory as an explanation of unconsidered cases is shown by looking at the results for Group 2. Here the results are a little disappointing, in that we are never able to achieve better than 7 out of the 9 cases correct. Note, however, that Theory 2 performs worse than the other two, again indicating the problem of over fitting.

The cases that give problems differ for Theory 1 and Theory 3. Theory 1 tends to fail always on Mineral Deposits and Scientology without cancellation, and FMC and Technicon when cancellation is used. Theory 3 fails on Mineral Deposits and Scientology and also, without cancellation, National Rejectors. Mineral Deposits is something of a special case: its outcome cannot be explained on the basis of the factors used in CATO, but relies on some special circumstances [5][1]. Again for Q1 there does not seem much to choose between the approach of Theory 1 and Theory 3. With regard to Q2, we may note that if we consider abstentions and mistakes together, we always obtain better performance by using all the factors. With regard to Q3, we feel that the use of values to determine the significance of unconsidered factors is vindicated, since whilst we may need to extend the partial order, we never need to change it. Note also that the unrefined theory never generalised more successfully than the refined theory.

For Q4, the results from Theory 1 and Theory 3 for the versions with all factors seem to give conflicting results, in that Theory 1 generally works better without cancellation, and Theory 3 with cancellation. This can be explained by reference to the particular cases. Theory 1 encounters problems using cancellation when F12 and F10 co-occur (that is when the secret was disclosed to outsiders, but under restrictions). That such disclosures were subject to restrictions seems to be a strong point in favour of the claimant, but this strength is lost if the factors cancel each other out. Given that Theory 1 places stress on the value related to these factors, this results in the misclassification of such cases. Theory 3 benefits from cancellation since the two factors related to the value it typically stresses are not the strongest factors in National Rejectors, which is misclassified without cancellation: thus its ability to ignore them through cancellation is helpful. There is not really sufficient data here to come to any firm conclusions: however, we would suggest that cancellation is quite possibly undesirable, since the *combination* of F12 and F10 appears to improve the plaintiff's case, and the weakness of the pro-plaintiff factor F15 in National Rejectors might be better handled in some other way rather than hoping that there will be a cancelling factor also present. We feel that the approach of the next section provides a more promising line of attack.

For Q5, we should expect to find less refinement needed in the two approaches using pre-ordering on values. This is indeed the case: only once is refinement needed when we pre-order the factors within a value, whereas refinement is always required when we do not. The use of exceptions to pre-order looks promising, but the dataset is too small to say that it will always obviate the need for refinement. The pre-ordering does not, however, carry any gains for the ultimate performance: it merely simplifies theory construction.

6 Experimental Results: Numeric Values

In order to explore Q6 and Q7, we must again modify the code generation, and the execution of the Prolog program. Instead of relying on the order of the execution of the rules to enforce priorities, we attach numerical weights to each factor, and consider every factor present in order to determine the relative strength of the plaintiff's and defendant's cases. The size of the numbers produced may be an indicator of confidence in the predicted decision, but we lay no stress on this here.

The numeric method assigns weights to each value and hence to each factor within the value. The weight is positive for a plaintiff factor and negative for a defendant factor. The weight for each value is decided by the value preferences, a value which is preferred being given a larger weight than the value to which it is preferred. Three approaches are used:

- The first approach just counts *the values* present in each case. If the value is associated with a plaintiff factor then the weight is positive, otherwise the weight is negative. This will allow for the cumulative effect of values: several lesser values may together outweigh

[1]This could, of course, be explained by including an additional factor to represent these special circumstances, but it is probably dubious practice to include a factor applicable to a single case.

a stronger one. This addresses Q4 in that it allows all the members of a set to be considered, rather than just the strongest member. Note that this effectively incorporates the cancellation method above, since if factors favouring both sides are present the positive and negative values will cancel out.

- For the second approach *all the factors* present in the case are counted. Again the weights for the plaintiff factors are positive and negative for the defendant factors. In this approach several factors for the same value will have a cumulative effect, addressing Q7.
- The third approach gives a basic weight to the value which is then modified by the factor depending how much the factor promotes the value. For a strong factor the weight is multiplied by 10, for a weak factor the weight is divided by 10 and for a normal factor the weight is unchanged. This is to allow for different degrees to which a factor promotes a value, addressing Q6. Two methods of identifying strong and weak factors were used. In one case we used the "KO" (i.e knockout) and weak factors of [4] and in the other we gave strong weight to the factors we identified as "exceptions", as above.

The results for just counting the value weights and counting all the factors is shown in Table 3 and the results for using differential values in Table 4. Misclassifications in both tables are shown in bold.

If we compare the theories using all factors, we can see that for Theory 1, the cumulative value approach is superior to any of the approaches previously tried, failing only on the problematic Mineral Deposits. For Theory 3, there are two errors, as with the best previously seen. On this basis we may feel that Q4 is answered by the suggestion that all the values in the set should be considered. With regard to Q7, however, there seems no gain in allowing factors to have a cumulative effect: Theory 1 has an additional error, and Theory 3 also does not improve.

Turning to Q7, we can see that using the weights from [4] we have a problem with Space Aero. This is because of the presence of two opposing KO factors. Except for this problem, using these differential values seems to improve the situation, especially when compared to cumulative factors. This is to be expected perhaps: without differentiation, accumulating weak factors can give them too much importance. This is also indicated by the comparatively poorer performance of the exception method which does not identify weak factors, with consequent misclassification of National Rejectors. (It also fails to pick out F20, Information Known to Competitors, as a strong factor and so misclassifies Scientology, which relied on this factor).

We tentatively conclude therefore that values should be considered cumulative, and that if factors are to be accumulated they should be given different weights, which should identify both strong and weak factors.

7 Summary of Results

With regard to our seven questions we have come to the following tentative conclusions. These conclusions are tentative because our dataset is not large enough to allow tests for statistical significance. On the other hand, the small set of cases allow for detailed consideration of aberrant cases, which gives insight into the problem. We do, therefore, believe our results to be indicative.

Q1: We feel that the approach of Theory 2 is not suited as it overfits the data. The approaches of Theory 1 and Theory 3 both have some good and some bad aspects.

Table 3: Cumulative Values and Cumulative Factors

	Value Results						Factor Results					
Theories	t1s	t1c	t2s	t2c	t3s	t3c	t1s	t1c	t2s	t2c	t3s	t3c
Arco	-0.3	-1	-1.5	-2.2	-0.7	-1	-0.3	-1.7	-1.5	-3.7	-0.7	-1.7
Boeing	0.4	0.8	0.3	**-0.3**	1.5	1.6	0.1	1.5	0.3	0.7	1.5	3.1
Bryce	0.5	0.8	0.3	0.4	1.6	1.6	0.5	1.5	0.3	0.7	1.6	3.1
CollegeWat	0.5	0.5	1.5	0.9	0.8	0.5	0.5	0.5	1.5	0.9	0.8	0.5
Den-Tal-Ez	0.5	0.8	0.3	0.4	1.6	1.6	0.5	1.5	0.3	0.7	1.6	3.1
Ecologix	**0.4**	-0.3	-0.4	-0.7	**1.2**	-0.3	**0.1**	-0.6	-0.4	-1.4	**1.2**	-0.6
Emery	0.5	0.5	0.3	**-0.3**	1.6	1.3	0.5	0.5	0.3	**-0.3**	1.6	1.3
Ferranti	-0.3	-0.9	-2.2	-2.1	-0.3	-0.9	-0.6	-1.9	-2.9	-4.3	-0.3	-1.9
Robinson	-0.1	-0.1	-0.7	-0.5	-0.1	-0.1	-0.7	-0.7	-0.7	-1.9	-0.1	-0.7
Sandlin	-0.3	-1	-0.7	-2.2	-1	-1	-1.2	-1.9	-1.4	-4.3	-1	-1.9
Sheets	-0.2	-0.2	-0.7	-0.6	-0.2	-0.2	-0.5	-0.5	-1.4	-1.3	-0.2	-0.5
Space aero	0.5	0.5	0.8	0.9	0.5	0.5	0.2	0.3	0.8	0.3	0.5	0.3
Televation	1.2	0.8	1.8	0.4	1.6	1.6	1.2	1.1	1.8	1.1	1.6	1.9
Yokana	-0.3	-0.9	-0.7	-2.1	-0.7	-0.9	-0.6	-1.2	-0.7	-2.8	-0.7	-1.2
FMC	**-0.3**	0.1	0	**-1.1**	0	0.9	**-0.3**	0.4	0	**-0.4**	0	1.2
KG	1.5	1.2	1.8	1.2	1.6	2	1.5	0.5	1.8	**-0.3**	1.6	1.3
Mason	1.1	0.7	1.8	0.3	1.5	1.5	1.1	0.7	1.8	0.3	1.5	1.5
MineralDep	**-0.2**	**-0.9**	0	**-2.1**	**-0.6**	**-0.9**	**-0.2**	**-1.6**	0	**-3.6**	**-0.6**	**-1.6**
NationalRej	**0.5**	-0.1	**0.8**	-0.5	-0.2	-0.1	-0.1	-0.7	**0.1**	-1.9	-0.2	-0.7
Reinforced	1.1	1.5	1.8	1.9	2.2	2.3	1.1	2.2	1.8	2.2	2.2	3.8
Scientology	-0.3	0	-1.5	-1.2	0	**0.8**	-0.3	-0.4	-1.5	-2	0	**0.4**
Technicon	0.4	0.1	0.3	**-1.1**	0.8	0.9	0.4	**-0.3**	0.3	**-1.9**	0.8	0.5
Trandes	**-0.3**	0.7	0	0.3	0	1.5	**-0.6**	0.7	0	0.3	0	1.5

Table 4: Differential Factor Weights

	Weights from Brüninghaus and Ashley						Weights from Exceptions					
	t1s	t1c	t2s	t2c	t3s	t3c	t1s	t1c	t2s	t2c	t3s	t3c
Arco	-0.03	-7.1	-15	-15.22	-0.07	-7.1	-0.3	-1.7	-1.5	-3.7	-0.7	-1.7
Boeing	0.64	2.04	0.3	1.96	1.5	3.64	0.1	6.9	0.3	13.3	1.5	8.5
Bryce	0.77	1.77	0.3	1.33	1.6	3.37	0.5	4.2	0.3	7	1.6	5.8
CollegeWat	1.67	1.67	1.5	2.43	1.7	1.67	6.8	6.8	15	14.4	7.1	6.8
Den-Tal-Ez	1.67	2.67	0.3	2.23	2.5	4.27	0.5	4.2	0.3	7	1.6	5.8
Ecologix	-2.33	-3.03	-6.7	-7.07	-1.5	-3.03	**0.1**	-6.9	-0.4	-4.1	**1.2**	-14.1
Emery	0.77	0.77	0.3	0.33	1.6	1.57	0.5	0.5	0.3	**-0.3**	1.6	1.3
Ferranti	-6	-13.6	-29	-30.4	-3	-13.6	-0.6	-1.9	-2.9	-4.3	-0.3	-1.9
Robinson	-1.96	-1.96	-7	-6.04	-1.9	-1.96	-0.7	-0.7	-0.7	-1.9	-0.1	-0.7
Sandlin	-6.06	-6.13	-14	-14.29	-3.07	-6.13	-1.2	-1.9	-1.4	-4.3	-1	-1.9
Sheets	-5.9	-5.9	-14	-13.9	-2.9	-5.9	-0.5	-0.5	-1.4	-1.3	-0.2	-0.5
Space aero	**-2.23**	**-1.23**	**-5.5**	**-4.47**	**-2.2**	**-1.23**	6.5	6.6	14.3	13.8	6.8	6.6
Televation	1.47	2	1.8	3.08	2.23	2.8	7.5	12.8	15.3	27.2	7.9	13.6
Yokana	-3.03	-3	-7	-7.12	-0.07	-3	-0.6	-1.2	-0.7	-2.8	-0.7	-1.2
FMC	**-0.03**	0.67	0	0.23	0	1.47	**-0.3**	5.8	0	12.2	0	6.6
KG	1.5	1.13	1.8	1.05	2.23	1.93	7.8	9.5	15.3	19.5	7.9	10.3
Mason	1.37	1.6	1.8	2.28	2.13	2.4	7.4	9.7	15.3	20.1	7.8	10.5
MineralDep	0.07	**-0.7**	0	**-1.62**	0.03	**-0.7**	**-0.2**	**-1.6**	0	**-3.6**	**-0.6**	**-1.6**
NationalRej	-5.23	-5.2	-12.5	-12.52	-2.27	-5.2	**6.2**	**5.6**	**13.6**	**11.6**	**6.1**	**5.6**
Reinforced	1.37	3.37	1.8	3.73	2.2	4.97	7.4	11.2	15.3	22	8.5	12.8
Scientology	-0.03	-6.43	-15	-14.87	0	-5.63	-0.3	**5**	-1.5	**10.6**	0	**5.8**
Technicon	0.67	0.6	0.3	0.08	1.43	1.4	0.4	5.1	0.3	10.7	0.8	5.9
Trandes	**-0.06**	1.24	0	1.56	0	2.04	**-0.6**	6.1	0	12.9	0	6.9

Q2: Should we include all factors? We feel that this is preferable: the relevance of our factors has already been established by the analysis of [1], and further selection does ignore relevant factors. Note, however, that considering only the factors appearing in a selection of cases does succeed in establishing a value order.

Q3: No especial problems were encountered in using all factors according to the ordering of values established in a selected few cases: this is consistent with the assumption of [3] that the importance of a factor is determined by the value it promotes.

Q4: We feel that there is evidence to suggest that all values in a set should be considered when comparing sets.

Q5: We feel that pre-ordering factors within a value saves a considerable amount of refinement, simplifying theory construction. Exceptions can help as a general principle, but perform less well that the expert judgement of [4].

Q6: We feel that there is evidence, also suggested by [4], that factors promote values to differing degrees. This becomes important if it is wished to ascribe a cumulative effect to factors

Q7: While, as in Q4, we feel it is important to give values a cumulative effect, the case for giving factors a cumulative effect seems less persuasive.

For future work we intend to attempt to confirm the tentative conclusions given above by a trial on a larger data set, either in this domain or some other, which will enable some measure of significance to be attached to the findings. Additionally, we have already extended the theory construction tool to handle dimensions as described in [3]. We intend to perform some experiments to explore the benefits of operating at this level. In particular we feel that this may give some insight into identifying strong and weak factors.

References

[1] Aleven, V. (1997). *Teaching Case Based Argumentation Through an Example and Models.* PhD Thesis. The University of Pittsburgh.

[2] Ashley. K.D., (1990). Modelling Legal Argument. Bradford Books, MIT Press, Cambridge, Mass.

[3] Trevor Bench-Capon and Giovanni Sartor, A model of legal reasoning with cases incorporating theories and values. *Artificial Intelligence*. In Press.

[4] Stefanie Brüninghaus and Kevin D. Ashley. Predicting Outcomes of Case-based Legal Arguments. Proceedings of the Ninth International Conference on AI and Law: ACM Press, New York, 2003, pp233-42.

[5] Stefanie Brüninghaus. Private Communication. September 2003.

[6] Alison Chorley and Trevor Bench-Capon, Developing Legal Knowledge Based Systems Through Theory Construction. Technical Report ULCS-03-013, Department of Computer Science, The University of Liverpool, 2003. http://www.csc.liv.ac.uk/research/techreports/tr2003/ulcs-03-013.pdf

[7] Alison Chorley and Trevor Bench-Capon, Developing Legal Knowledge Based Systems Through Theory Construction. Proceedings of the Ninth International Conference on AI and Law: ACM Press, New York, 2002, pp85-6.

[8] Prakken, H., (2000). An exercise in formalising teleological case based reasoning. In J. Breuker, R. Leenes and R. Winkels (eds*), Legal Knowledge and Information Systems: Jurix 2000.* IOS Press, Amsterdam, pp 49-57.

[9] Prakken, H. & G. Sartor. 1998. Modelling Reasoning with Precedents in a Formal Dialogue Game. *Artificial Intelligence and Law* 6: 231-287.

Previous Publications by JURIX

Conference Proceedings

- *Legal knowledge and information systems: The Fifteenth Annual Conference*
  JURIX 2002 (London)
  Bench-Capon, T., Daskalopulu, A., Winkels, R. (eds.)
  ISBN 1 58603 299 2(IOS Press)
  ISBN 4 274 90564 0 C3055 (Ohmsha)
- *Legal knowledge and information systems: The Fourteenth Annual Conference*
  JURIX 2001 (Amsterdam)
  Verheij, B., Lodder, A.R., Loui, R.P., Muntjewerff, A.J. (eds.)
  ISBN 1 58603 201 1(IOS Press)
  ISBN 4 274 90488 1 C3000 (Ohmsha)
- *Legal knowledge and information systems: The Thirteenth Annual Conference*
  JURIX 2000 (Twente)
  Breuker, J.A., Leenes, R., Winkels, R. (eds.)
  ISBN 1 58603 144 9 (IOS Press)
  ISBN 4 274 90416 4 C3000 (Ohmsha)
- *Legal knowledge based systems: The Twelfth Conference*
  JURIX 1999 (Leuven)
  Herik, H. Jaap van den, Marie-Francine Moens, Jon Bing, Bea van Buggenhout, John Zeleznikow, Carolus Grütters (eds.)
  ISBN 90 71478 64 5
- *Legal knowledge based systems: The Eleventh Conference*
  JURIX 1998 (Groningen)
  Hage, J.C., T.J.M. Bench-Capon, A.W. Koers, C.N.J. de Vey Mestdagh, C.A.F.M. Grütters (eds.)
  ISBN 90 71478 58 0
- *Legal knowledge based systems: The Tenth Conference*
  JURIX 1997 (Amsterdam)
  Oskamp A., R.V. De Mulder, C. van Noortwijk, C.A.F.M. Grütters, K. Ashley, T. Gordon (eds.)
  ISBN 90 71478 54 8
- *Legal knowledge based systems: Foundations of Legal Knowledge Systems*
  JURIX 1996 (9th conference Tilburg)
  Kralingen R.W., H.J. van den Herik, J.E.J. Prins, M. Sergot, J. Zeleznikow (eds.)
  ISBN 90 361 9657 4
- *Legal knowledge based systems: Telecommunications and AI & and Law*
  JURIX 1995 (8th conference Maastricht)
  Hage J.C., T.J.M. Bench-Capon, M.J. Cohen, H.J. van den Herik (eds.)
  ISBN 90 5458 252 9

- *Legal knowledge based systems: The relation with Legal Theory*
  JURIX 1994 (7th conference Amsterdam)
  Prakken H., A.J. Muntjewerff, A. Soeteman (eds.)
  ISBN 90 5458 190 5
- *Legal knowledge based systems: Intelligent Tools for Drafting Legislation, Computer-Supported Comparison of Law*
  JURIX 1993 (6th conference Enschede)
  Svensson J.S., J.G.J. Wassink, B. van Buggenhout (eds.)
  ISBN 90 5458 089 5
- *Legal knowledge based systems: Information Technology and Law*
  JURIX 1992 (5th conference The Hague)
  Grütters C.A.F.M., J.A. Breuker, H.J. van den Herik, A.H.J. Schmidt, C.N.J de Vey Mestdagh (eds.)
  ISBN 90 5458 0341 3
- *Legal knowledge based systems: Model-based legal reasoning*
  JURIX 1991 (4th conference Rotterdam)
  Breuker J.A., R.V. de Mulder, J.C. Hage (eds.)
  ISBN 90 6040 989 2
- *Legal knowledge based systems: Aims for research and development*
  JURIX 1990 (3rd conference Leiden)
  Noortwijk C. van, A.H.J. Schmidt, R.G.F. Winkels (eds.)
  ISBN 90 6040 948 5
- *Legal knowledge based systems: An overview of criteria for validation and practical use (Exploring the quality of applications resulting from research programs in the Netherlands)*
  JURIX 1989 (2nd conference Utrecht)
  Kracht D., C.N.J. de Vey Mestdagh, J.S. Svensson (eds.)
  ISBN 90 6040 917 5
- *RI-paradigmata: Toekomst van Nederlands onderzoek in de rechtsinformatica (Paradigms in legal informatics: Exploring the future of Dutch research programmes in legal informatics)*
  JURIX 1988 (1st conference Amsterdam)
  (In Dutch with summaries in English)
  Berg P. van den, C.A.F.M. Grütters, O.W.M. Kamstra, T. van Willigenburg (eds.)
  ISBN 90 6040 886 1

Reports

- *Informatietechnologie en Recht*
  (Rapport van de tijdelijke adviescommissie Informatietechnologie en Recht met betrekking tot de opzet van onderzoek op het gebied van informatietechnologie en recht)
  1991 (In Dutch)
  Franken H., J.C. Arnbak, J.M.A. Berkvens, B.K. Brussaard, A.W. Koers,
  I.Th.M. Snellen, A.H.J. Schmidt (red.)
  ISBN 90 6040 966 3
- *Information Technology and the Law*
  1991 (English version)
  Franken H., J.C. Arnbak, J.M.A. Berkvens, B.K. Brussaard, A.W. Koers,
  I.Th.M. Snellen, A.H.J. Schmidt (eds.)
  ISBN 90 6040 987 6

Contact Information on JURIX

Those interested in the activities of JURIX may contact

Radboud Winkels	President of JURIX
Address:	Universiteit van Amsterdam Faculty of Law P.O. Box 1030 NL-1000 BA Amsterdam The Netherlands
Phone:	+31 20 525 3485
Fax:	+31 20 525 3495
E-mail:	winkels@lri.jur.uva.nl
Jurix Website:	http://www.jurix.nl

Author Index

Andrade, F.C.P. 149
Ashley, K.D. 153
Bellucci, E. 21
Bench-Capon, T. 173
Boer, A. 91
Borges, F. 11
Borges, R. 11
Bourcier, D. 11
Brüninghaus, S. 153
Chorley, A. 173
Delgado, J. 111
Delgado, J.J.I. 101
Dongilli, P. 131
Drachsler, M. 147
Dulong de Rosnay, M. 121
Engers, T.M. van 71,91,143
Galitsky, B. 141
Gallego, I. 111
Gamper, J. 131
García, R. 111
Gordon, T.F. 81
Governatori, G. 151
Graça, N. 163
Gray, P.N. 51
Gray, X. 51
Heel, E. van 71
Hoekstra, R. 1,91
Holmström-Hintikka, G. 31
Jordaans, A. 1
Leenes, R. 1
Liebwald, D. 147
Llorente, S. 111
Maat, E. de 143
Muntjewerff, A.J. 1
Quaresma, P. 163
Renaux, P. 61
Rotolo, A. 151
Schweighofer, E. 147
Smith, C. 145
Tuzet, G. 41
Winkels, R. 91
Zeleznikow, J. 21